MEMORY IN OUR BONES

EXPLORING THE MYSTERIES OF MIND, BODY, AND SPIRIT

H. Elizabeth Burke, M.A.

EarthSong Foundation Press
Tiburon, CA
2008

Copyright © 2008 by H. Elizabeth Burke

All rights reserved. No part of this book may be reproduced or transmitted in any form or by any means, electronic or mechanical including photocopying. Recording or by any information storage and retrieval system without written permission from the author, except for the inclusion of brief quotations in a review.

First edition
EarthSong Foundation Press

Printed in the United States of America

Library of Congress Control Number: 2008903926

Cataloging-in-Publication Data
Burke, H. Elizabeth.
Memory in Our Bones: Exploring the Mysteries of Mind, Body, and Spirit / by H. Elizabeth Burke

    p. cm.

    Bibliography: p.

    ISBN: 978-0-615-20450-5

    1. Mind and body. 2. Energy psychology. 3. Reincarnation. 4. Spiritual healing. 5. Huna 6. Buddhism—Psychology. 7. Meditation—Taoism. I. Title.

BF 367

153.3'2—dc22

LOVE IS THE KEY:

IT IS THE BLINDING LIGHT OF ILLUMINATION.

THERE IS NOTHING TRUER IN NATURE,

NOTHING MORE HEALING AND NOTHING MORE

ENCOMPASSING THAN THIS.

Marika
Channeled by Elizabeth Burke, 1988

DEDICATION

To my husband, Christopher, and my mother, Ann and to the Energy, who brought this work to life.

May all sentient beings be free from suffering and from the causes of suffering, and may all sentient beings find peace, happiness, and healing.

ACKNOWLEDGMENTS

I wish to thank all my teachers and friends, who, unknowingly over the past twenty-five years, have aided in the unfolding of this work. I bow in deep gratitude to my husband, my mother, my clients, to the monks of the H'sien Taoist Monastery and to the energy that pervades my being and flows through me.

From the bottom of my heart, my deepest thanks go out to my husband, Christopher, who has supported me, listened to me brainstorm, and lent his loving and generous support to me as I brought this book into being. Aloha nui and mahalo nui loa. I wish to bless and thank my father and mother, Rellie and Ann, who brought me into this life and set me on my path. Special thanks go out to my mother for her endless support.

I wish to express my deep gratitude to Dr. Peggy Ann Wright, Marylee McInnis, and Pam Towry-Church, for their emotional and intellectual support and guidance. Our dialogues throughout the preparation and writing of this book were invaluable. They nurtured the writer in me, and for this I will always be grateful.

A deep bow to my friend and publicist Joe Marich, whose continued humor, advice, and insights helped me when things got rough. I am grateful for his efforts and unwavering good sense.

I also wish to thank Leza Lowitz, Alexandra Kennedy, and Dr. Larry Dossey for their kind words of endorsement and support.

Finally, I wish to thank Richard Allen, Joseph Crane, Roswitha Mueller, Leza Lowitz, Susan Victor, Dr. Donatella Rossi, Yvonne Vergez, Mary Kay Martin, Dr. Martin Albert and good friend Jeff Clark for their editing ideas, creative suggestions and criticism as this book evolved. A wholehearted thanks you to my copyeditor, Patricia Yates, for her superb copyediting and perseverance. My thanks also go out to: Meagan Shapiro for her drawings, Dale Nutley for his graphics help with the illustrations, to Pat Rasch, and Diana Hume for their typesetting advice and Rachael Gurske, for her artful eye, as I endeavored to create the cover for this book.

CONTENTS

PART ONE: BODY ... 9

AUTHOR'S NOTE ... 11
Exercises: Breathing Meditation for Centering ... 19
   Grounding Meditation ... 20
   Protection Meditation ... 22
Drawings
   Electromagnetic and Gravitational Field Triangles
   and the Aura ... 23

PRELUDE ... 25
Lightening Strikes—Transformations of Body & Mind

CHAPTER ONE ... 35
**Building a Case for Cellular and Systemic Memory:
A Scientific View**

CHAPTER TWO ... 49
**The Biology of Trauma & Spiritual Challenges of
Embodied Trauma**

INTERLUDE ... 63
Healing Origins: Resolving Physical Symptoms

PART TWO: SPIRIT ... 77

CHAPTER THREE ... 79
Survival of Consciousness and Healing

CHAPTER FOUR ... 95
Reincarnation and Rebirth

CHAPTER FIVE — 105
"Source"—A Timeless Seamless Reality
Understanding Essence
Exercise: Connecting To Your Aumakua — 114

PART THREE: HEART — 117

CHAPTER SIX — 119
Open Heart—Open Mind Reflections on Healing
Exercise: Another Connecting and Grounding Exercises — 137

CHAPTER SEVEN — 139
*Working With the Wisdom Self, Huna, Energy
and the Chakras*
Drawings
  Placement of the Chakras — 151
  Spiral Connections — 156
Exercise: Infinity Breath Meditation — 160

INTERLUDE — 161
*Healing the Origins of Relationship Patterns:
A Journey Across Time*

PART FOUR: MIND — 173

CHAPTER EIGHT — 175
*What Is Mind? What Is Memory?—Understanding
Embodied Memory and Imagery's Role*

CHAPTER NINE — 193
The Power of Beliefs—Their Grip on Our Reality
Exercise: Working with Imagery — 202

CHAPTER TEN — 205
The Heart Essence of Transforming Embodiment

PART FIVE: THE PROCESS — 225

CHAPTER ELEVEN *Creating an Environment for Transformative Change and Developing the Intuition*	227
CHAPTER TWELVE *Finding Our Story—Looking For Embodied Memory*	235
CHAPTER THIRTEEN *Finding Origins—Working With Embodied Memory*	245
CHAPTER FOURTEEN *Making, Embodying and Sustaining Change*	263
PART SIX: TIME AND ENERGY	271
INTERLUDE *Working Dimensionally: Understanding the Weave of Parallel Time, Past Lives and Karmic Connections*	273
CHAPTER FIFTEEN *Ethics and Energy Psychology*	289
PART SEVEN: THE OPPORTUNITY	295
CHAPTER SIXTEEN *Where We Go From Here*	297
ADDENDUM *Notes to Practitioners*	301
Glossary	317
Bibliography	323
Resources	331
Permissions, Credits & About the Type	333
Index	335
Endnotes	334
About the Author and Contact Information	358

Part One: The Body

AUTHOR'S NOTE

> Past life phenomena are extremely relevant, and...our knowledge of them can help us resolve conflicts and live better lives in the present.
>
> Stanislav Grof [1]

What I have experienced myself, and observed in clients since 1984 is that traumatic experience, powerful emotions, affinities, behaviors, and beliefs, continue beyond physical death. These experiences remain unconscious and lie dormant within our minds and are preserved within our bodies, and can resurface when triggered by people, places, objects and emotions that are similar to those we have felt in the past. Memories survive until they are resolved and can have a profound effect on our minds, bodies, and emotions.

Lynn's Story

In 1991 I witnessed for the first time in someone other than myself the extraordinary grip past life memory has upon our physical body. Lynn, a massage therapist in her late 30s, came to see me because she had been experiencing an irregular heartbeat for about a year. She had investigated her heart's unusual beat while studying massage, but she always fell short of understanding why her heart plagued her so. Then, one day the symptoms intensified, and she was rushed to the hospital as her heart raced out of control. After exhaustive testing, Lynn was diagnosed with a congenital heart defect that she had had since birth. Now, years later, in a class I was teaching, Lynn would discover the cause of her heart's irregular and rapid beat.

As I lead her class in a simple visualization into their hearts, Lynn swept beyond the heart of her 30s, 20s, and childhood. Almost instantly, she felt cold stone under her back and saw a canopy of rain forest overhead. In that moment, images, memories and emotions poured into her consciousness, as she remembered and relived the original wound to her heart that corresponded to her present-day symptoms. This new knowledge helped her begin to release the trauma held deep in her heart. She sat in awe as understanding dawned of how she had been impacted and affected by these ancient memories that were held in her heart from another time and place. Miraculously she said that within a period of six months she was symptom free. I realized then that others could experience what I had and heal their most perplexing and traumatic physical problems by exploring the origins of their symptoms. My life took a dramatic turn as I realized the possible applications of what I had now seen in another person. This book and the years of research it represents are a culmination of that wintry night fifteen years ago.

Since that time I have witnessed clients' remarkable recoveries as they have released memories from their childhood, from pre-natal experiences and from past lives. In this book you will meet Sara, who faced and released memories of fear and trauma, enabling her to live happily with a man she loved, and Alia, who found the reason for her chronic stomach and digestive ailments in another life where she had died of cancer. You will hear the stories of people who have faced physical, emotional and relationship problems and by understanding and unraveling the imprinted memories and emotions held within their cells and body they have found peace. I will share their stories and give you the tools to journey within to find healing and release for yourself.

The exploration of past lives in therapy is not new nor is the idea that people can heal their present symptoms by reviewing their past lives. Transpersonal psychologist and researcher Dr. Stanislav Grof notes, "In the process of experiencing episodes from past lives, people often heal emotional and physical symptoms that they suffer from in their present lives."[2]

What I bring to this area of therapy and research that is new is that these memories are embodied. They are alive within us. Memory is etched into our very cells, bones, muscles, organs, and strands of DNA. Our body and consciousness hold these imprinted memories in place until we are emotionally and mentally ready to review and release them. By tracing these imprints back to their origins, our problems and symptoms can be changed at a core level. Transformation, healing and purification of these embodied and systemic memories is what Transforming Embodiment ® offers us. It is a core healing of body, beliefs, and emotions. Clients, when engaging in the practices of Transforming Embodiment, have repeatedly reported that they feel this healing and transformation within their very cells.

I am aware that psychology offers many other possible explanations for what I have seen and what I will be sharing with you. Traditional clinical psychology maintains that past life and transpersonal experiences can be best understood as fantasies, delusions, dreams, archetypal patterns or even as dissociative identity disorders. This is the more traditional view, but Stanislav Grof, one of the leading figures in transpersonal psychology and an expert in the field, says the following,

> Whether or not experiences of this kind [childhood, birth and incarnational memories] reflect 'objective reality,' their therapeutic value is unquestionable. A therapist who is unwilling to support them because of intellectual skepticism is giving up a therapeutic tool of extraordinary power.[3]

Like Grof, I believe that if we are experiencing "memories" from infancy, from before birth, or from another lifetimes, then, they are important and we must honor them. I have found that it is almost irrelevant to think of these experiences as fact or fiction; if they are present, they are real to us.

Personally, I believe that consciousness survives and that we have lived before, because I have experienced other life memories personally and witnessed them clinically. It is not my intention, however, to convince anyone that rebirth, reincarnation or the survival of consciousness do, in fact, take place. Experience alone can bring us to these transpersonal understandings.

My sole wish is to pose these questions: what if past lives do exist, and how might this information and understanding change our current views of healing? How would our perceptions of illness and disease change if the roots of our suffering were not merely perceived as physical or emotional? What emotional and spiritual lessons or gifts could some once-dreaded experience hold for us? And finally, how can these experiences help us to understand our lives and ourselves in the present?

In this book I will try to answer these kinds of questions and share a new way of perceiving memory and mind-body healing. I will show you how memory is embodied and I will present scientific and spiritual evidence that supports this idea. I will also introduce you to the process of Transforming Embodiment ® or TE ®, a set of practices that I developed in the early 1990s, that arose out of my classes to become the core of the therapy I now do with people.

The practices themselves are simple and direct and are a combination of questions, meditations, deep inquiry, and purification practices. Transforming Embodiment is an interactive mind-body integrative therapy that uses inner imagery, intuition, shamanic principles, energy and psychic techniques, and chakra psychology to discover the origins or causes of physical symptoms, recurring patterns, and painful emotional states.

When applied, this therapy can help untangle challenges in relationships, deep emotions, painful memories, fears and physical and psychosomatic symptoms. Basically, when taken to its barest bones, Transforming Embodiment works to transform and resolve our fears, limiting beliefs, and pain. By working in this way with our fears, anxieties and painful emotional and physical symptoms, this therapy can open up new pathways to deep and lasting healing.

In Transforming Embodiment, working with embodied or systemic memory is seen as a very direct way for us to remember, release, and reorganize our responses to current life triggers. By discovering and re-experiencing our past and past life events, we can finally connect the dots and see what causes have created our current confusions and problems. Causal relationships, when brought into the light, give us a unique opportunity to resolve and ultimately heal our most perplexing present-day problems. As a result of integrating these experiences, deep release and healing can occur for each of us.

These practices enable you to discover the cause-effect relationships that exist between your past and present that are operating in your life now. Through intuitive insights and by working directly with your body and consciousness, you can understand these casual relationships and finally lay them to rest. This book, its exercises and meditations, can help you see these interconnections between your past and present and teach you how to resolve, re-integrate, and release the shock, traumatic experiences, and emotional wounds you have carried with you.

These meditations will help you observe your mind and evoked events, and teach you how to be detached from situations while simultaneously experiencing them. The ability to observe enables you to view and remember even the most traumatic events from your past without further harm to your being. Observant engagement enables you to both process your experiences and make change to them.

My hope is to awaken and reconnect you to your inner wisdom and self, and to guide and empower you through deep inquiry, to the origins of why you experience life as you do. Because Transforming Embodiment works with spontaneous imagery and memory that have been held within our minds and bodies there is a brilliant aliveness to these practices. Healing is a process that is vibrant with energy, imagery, sensation, and intuition. This is because spirit guides this process and connects us to our inner wisdom self. Intuition paired with discernment, is what guides us. Our inner wisdom self is accessible and ready to help us at a moment's notice. We need only ask for this help and connect to our hearts. The book will teach you how to begin this journey, and it will share my personal and clinical experiences, observations, anecdotal evidence, and research into how survival of consciousness can affect us all.

The following spiritual and healing traditions have helped shape the practices of Transforming Embodiment. Huna[4], because of its deep relationship to belief systems and its psychological construct of the three aspects of the self, is especially important, because it demonstrates how we can relate to and work with the different aspects of the body, mind and spirit directly. Buddhist knowledge about reincarnation and rebirth are deeply significant because these profound teachings give us a foundation for how consciousness may survive and examples of tulkus[5] who have. With this knowledge, the idea that memories and experiences from other lives can be carried into the present, and that the residual energies from these distant karmas can impact us every day through our mindstream, is more feasible.

Taoist and Buddhist meditation practices and mindful attention can help us connect to, explore our deepest self, and lead us into states of stillness and quiescence. Meditation is a very direct way in which we can begin to understand the nature of our minds, and it gives us the resources for cultivating acceptance, compassion and equanimity, as well as curiosity and openness to our present experience.

Taoist energy practices and Western psychic techniques are also a part of Transforming Embodiment's foundations. Our chakras also give us a time-tested ancient template for understanding ourselves. They are a rich ground for energetic and psychological inquiry, and when paired with increased intuitive sensitivity, worlds can open up from deep within these energy centers of our being. We are energy as well as flesh and bone, and the psychological and emotional details held within our chakras and body are indispensable as we endeavor to understand ourselves and find meaning for the complexity that we embody.

All of these pieces when woven together become Transforming Embodiment. Through my personal experiences and transformations and as a channel-embodying Source, I have gained a unique perspective and certain skills that I will share here, so you may learn how to heal yourself.

When I first began this book in 1995, I was unaware of much of what I did with clients. The process came naturally to me and was an extension of my teaching and channeled work. Many of the ideas I describe in the following chapters though they were implied I did not recognize them until I began to explore what I naturally did with people. Through a continuing and deep exploration of this work that I've practiced for so many years, I have become conscious of the process itself—its nuances and complexity have been revealed to me. Years of study, meditation, reading, and life experiences, both in this timeline and in others, have contributed to the creation of this process, as have my teachers, clients and friends, whom I have learned from, taught and brainstormed with. I wish again to express my appreciation to them all. I hope this book will allow you to explore a bit further and perhaps learn something new about healing, memory, and causality.

Please remember to use what works for you. As a teacher I invite you to question deeply and to test out what I am sharing with you. Be discerning and discriminating because blind faith can be a trap. I encourage you to question, to be skeptical, and to examine your experience and what I am saying carefully. See if what I am sharing resonates and fits before blindly accepting it. This combination of cultivating intellectual incisiveness with intuitional insight provides a working safeguard for all of us, so use all your faculties, your intuition, and your mind.

Working with energy and your intuition is not mysterious nor is it solely the arena of psychics and intuitives. I have taught intuitive classes for fifteen years and rarely have I found a person who cannot tune into their intuition, once they have learned how to quiet their thinking mind. Valerie Hunt, elder statesperson within energy medicine, says that wherever there are molecules there are emotions and wherever there are emotions, there is energy. The emotions within us and within others create vibrations, and we can tune into these vibrations.

We have a rich landscape of information and energy under the surface, just waiting to be tapped. Your body, mind, organs, and cells are alive with this energy and each of you can tune into it. Stillness and silence are key factors in establishing a connection to the energy that flows within us. Each of you has a different way of cultivating and experiencing this energy. Some of you may feel it, others may sense it, dream about it, or literally see it, but there is no doubt that when you apply light focus, with a mind that is curious and free of doubt, information and truth from deep within you will be revealed.

Our potential for healing lies within each of us, not outside but deep within us in our cells, bones, organs, and chakras. Our "past" has more of an impact upon us than we may realize. We embody our past and the totality of our experience, our emotions, and memories float within our being and are available for us to explore and heal. Changing our reality is in our hands and in our hearts. With these things in mind, let us begin.

Please do the preliminary practices as outlined. Each exercise builds on the previous one and it is important to take them one at a time and to master each before moving on. This caution is based on sixteen years of clinical practice and teaching and nearly twenty years of working personally with energy, transpersonal states, and phenomena.

I also ask each of you to be gentle with yourselves, to go slowly, and listen deeply to the song of your heart and body-mind. Always connect to your higher knowledge, your wisdom self, and inner knowing. Cultivate this relationship and let your intuition as well as your intellect guide you.

This work can take you into areas that will confound and confuse you at first, so it is imperative to be grounded and centered before undertaking these exercises. Deep emotions may arise but, like clouds in the sky, you must watch them as they float by—do not attach to them just let them go. Do this with mindfulness and equanimity, as you probe deeper into your mind and body, and may you all find healing, happiness and greater peace.

The names of all my clients, students, and the names of participants in clients' stories have been changed in examples, case studies, and interviews to protect individual privacy.

Breathing Meditation for Centering

Take a deep breath and as you exhale, let go of any physical tension from your body. Take a second deep breath and this time as you exhale let go of any emotional tension or cares from your day. Just allow yourself to come fully into the moment. Now I want you to focus your attention on your breathing. Notice where it begins, does it start in your chest, belly, or both? Just stay with your breath for a few cycles, gently breathing in and out, not changing anything, just experiencing it as fully as you can. Now I want you to initiate your breath from your chest. You can put your hand on your chest to help feel the breath as it rises and falls. Stay with that for a few minutes. Notice how you are feeling as you breathe in this way. Relax and take another deep breath, and release the focus on your upper body. What was it like to breathe in this way? How do you feel? Just notice the quality of your mind and emotions after breathing in this way. Now I want you to initiate your breath from your belly, feel your belly rise and fall as your breath flows in and out of your body. Breathe into your belly for a few minutes and notice how it feels to breathe in this way. Notice any feelings that may arise as you focus on the breath. Then, as before, let go of breathing in this way and let the breath naturally rise from the belly into the chest. If you want you can put a hand on your belly and the other on your chest. Just let yourself relax and breathe, nothing to do—just breathing and being breathed for a

> *few minutes. Again, notice how this feels, notice your thoughts, emotions and feelings. Also, notice if your focus upon your breathing changed the quality of your mind.*

Breath is the simplest way to bring us back to our center. It is always with us. By breathing with awareness the energy within you and around you can settle. So, we use this centering technique before undertaking any inner exploration as a way to stabilize our emotions, reactions, and mind. You may read this exercise onto a tape and listen to it in the morning or evening. This exercise is best done in tandem with the grounding and protection meditations. Do the centering practice, along with the grounding and protection, each day for at least two to four weeks before delving into any of your body's memories and symptoms.

Do the centering meditation first, then move on to do the grounding and protection exercises below. There is a rhythm to these meditations I have inserted pauses to give you a sense of pacing.

Grounding Meditation

> *Take a deep breath and as you exhale, release any physical tension from your body. (Pause). Take another deep breath and let go of any emotional or mental tensions from your body or mind. Let go of any cares and concerns from your day and allow yourself to come fully into the moment. (Pause). Take a third deep breath and this time as you exhale I want you to see a golden ray of light above you. Feel and see this light come into your being through the top of your head. See and feel or imagine this warm golden light moving gently down your body, through your head, passing over your face and down your neck. (Pause). See*

and feel it washing over your shoulders, moving into your upper back and chest, down your arms and into your belly. (Pause). See and sense this golden light bathing your internal organs as it continues flowing into your low back and pelvis, out your fingers and spine. Now see this light branch into two streams as it moves into both of your legs and down through your thighs, knees, calves, and ankles until it finally comes to rest at your feet. (Pause). Let the light pool at your feet. (Pause). Imagine and sense this golden light moving gently into the earth now. See it going into the earth like water—easily and effortlessly. Feel it move as deeply into the earth as is comfortable for you until it finally comes to rest. (Pause). Allow yourself to feel the support and energy of the earth, and when you are ready, I want you to imagine dipping your hand into the earth's energy, like you would dip your hand into a basin of water. Bring this essence of the earth back up through all the layers of the earth, and place this energy at the base of your spine. (Pause). You may feel a sense of weight stability or connection when you place this earth essence into your energy body. So, take a few minutes and notice how you feel, and imagine the earth is your foundation. It can nurture and help you stay connected even in the most stressful times.

This grounding exercise may give you the feeling of sitting on a secure and firm rock ledge or bench. It is from the earth that you are able to receive nurturance, stability, and a deep abiding sense of presence in the moment. This may be because the vibration of the earth's energy is slower and denser than our own. This practice along with the protection exercise below is best if practiced on a daily basis. Anytime you journey within you need to do these visualizations.

Protection Meditation

> *Take a few deep breaths and imagine or visualize that there is an oval bubble around your entire body. The edge of this oval bubble represents the edge of your aura and is at a distance of about one arms length around you in all directions. It is to your left, to your right above you, below you, behind you, and in front of you. With this in mind, visualize or trace a band or ribbon of golden light along the edge of this oval bubble and ask that this energy field be free from any influences be they known or unknown to you as well. This request is directed to your aumakua or wise inner guide.*

Golden light neutralizes negative energy or feelings before they enter your field of energy. It also allows energy to ebb and flow unlike white light that seals you off from your world. Protection, like grounding and centering, is necessary to do before doing deep inner work. These three meditations or visualizations are the preliminary practices we use. This protection meditation is used to create a safe space and protective environment that is free from any or all interference be it known or unknown to you, which creates a field of clarity and protection around you. Know that your aura can fluctuate in size depending on how you feel and that the arms length distance is an only a guideline, so you may from time to time need to adjust this visualization practice.

Author's Note

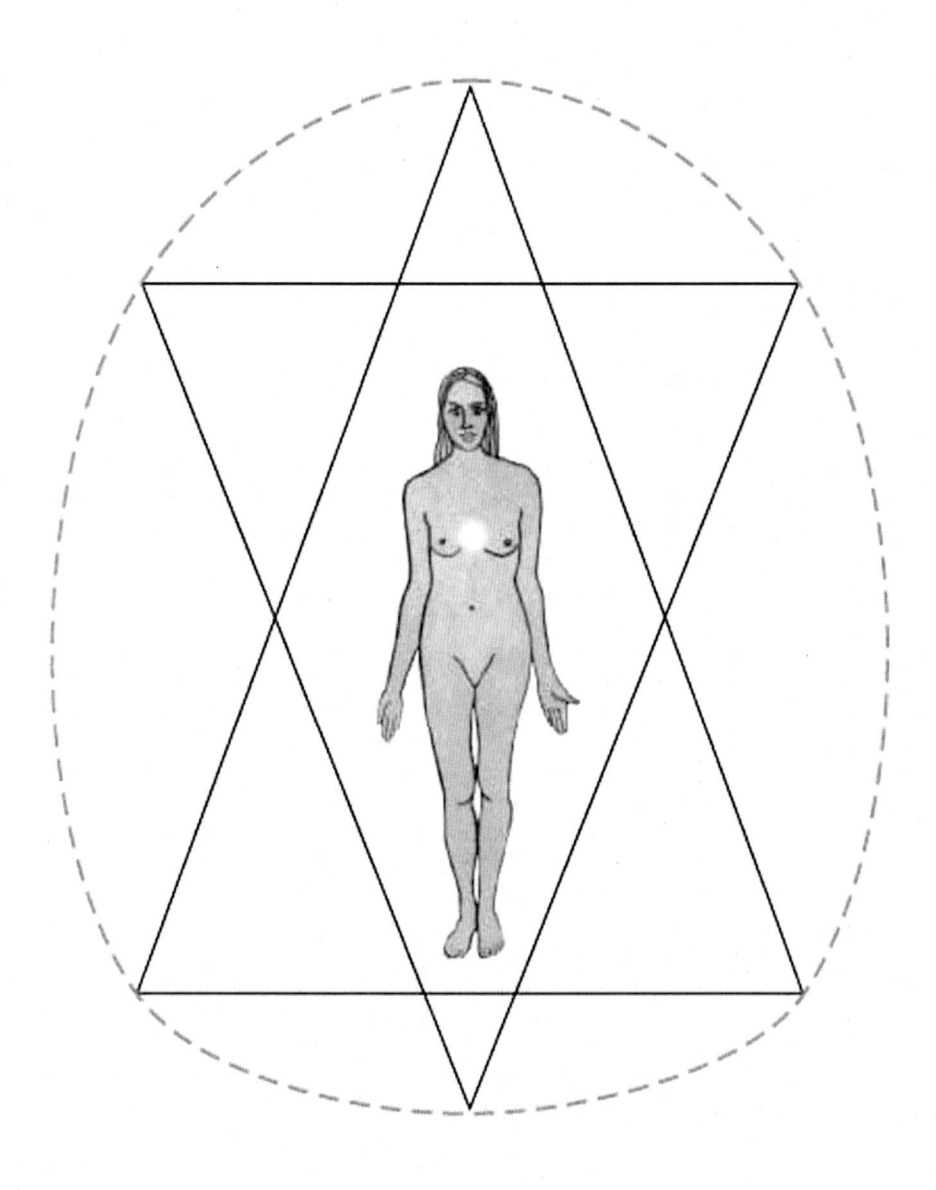

PRELUDE

LIGHTENING STRIKES
TRANSFORMATIONS OF BODY AND MIND

> Frequently it appears that an illness or crisis with one's health is the key that turns on nonlocal ways of knowing …freeing the mind to behave nonlocally in time & space.
>
> Larry Dossey[6]

I began my life as a singer. Why is this important if I am writing a book on consciousness and healing, you might ask? My answer, because singing formed me and defined me as a healer. For thirteen years, I studied singing with a marvelous bel canto teacher. She demanded much of me, since I was her last student, but what was essential, beyond the voice, was her command and plea, "Leave everything at the door once you walk into my studio." Little did I know how important this was or what a form of meditation vocalize would become for me or how it would open up the gates, channels and the chakras of my body to heal, but it did.

Singing was a part of me, like my arm, it was who I was. As a child, my mother would play something on the piano or the stereo and I could pick it out on the piano or sing it with no trouble. I had a good ear and I always sang, but I never wanted to be a performer. Singing was something else for me, it was more about sound, vibration, and the cosmos than repertoire or performance. It was vast and overwhelming when the voice sang through me, but so pure, just essence and energy, no ego involvement, just vibration running through me, singing me. This experience would be my foundation when years later the voice of Marika and the channel would course through me just like melody and song.

Under my teacher's tutelage, singing opened me up to my essence, built my confidence, and taught me more than I would ever know. I had always been a sensitive, knowing things and feeling things that were intangible to the eye, so singing made sense and made the world I lived in—a world of vibrations and feelings and some kind of inner knowing—make sense too. It also shaped and sharpened my perception of energy.

I will always be grateful for my voice lessons and the life lessons I learned at the foot of my teacher. Like apprentices of old, I owe her so much, for she taught about life and spirit, as well as how to sing from vowel to vowel, creating a legato line that was forgotten by modern singers. Much later I would learn that all the hours of vocalize, scales, arpeggios, turns, triads and octave leaps had been balancing my chakras and energy body and preparing and opening these centers and channels.

Awakenings

Twenty-three years ago, I survived a three year-long *kundalini* awakening and shamanic initiation[7]. This psychic opening and rewiring of my nervous system and psyche would forever change me. It was this singular event that would lead to the creation of Transforming Embodiment ®. It would also change, in the most personal and intimate way, my understanding of time, space, and consciousness, as well as my relationships and what it meant to be human. But I am getting ahead of myself.

It all started when I got pneumonia, which lasted for months because I couldn't take antibiotics (due to allergies). After that, it was like a cascade as my body went through one illness after another. I was sick for twenty-six weeks that year as one system after another broke down, leaving me extremely weak and in the end, unable to eat or walk. Muscle spasms and bone pain so intense that it felt as if my spine was on fire, raked over my body. Physical and emotional pain was my only reality during this time and they tormented me relentlessly. They were constant companions while everyone else in my life faded into the background and disappeared.

Overwhelmed by the pain of my body and the pain of the world around me, my heart broke open—and I withdrew. I moved into a dreamlike state of consciousness. I still don't know how much time elapsed between the onset of the spinal and endocrine problems and when I re-emerged. I realize now that this extreme set of circumstances was an initiation, leading to a deep psychic awakening, but at the time, I questioned my sanity and thought I might die. I was scared, overwhelmed, and utterly alone.

My senses were so acute during this time that any food that had been cut, plucked, or harvested with any violence screamed, and I psychically felt that pain. Meat was out of the question and finally all I could consume was rice and water. Everything in my life had receded—my friends, family, work—leaving only pain, but, whose pain was I feeling? Was it my own? Was it larger than that? Who was the "I" experiencing the pain? And what boundaries were being stripped away, that I could feel the pain of the world so acutely? As my sensitivity increased my psychic and empathic impressions kept expanding. My sense of self lost all individual definition as I merged with something much larger than myself. It was all very confusing and overwhelming.

One day, unable to move from my bed, a book in the bookcase next to my bed came to my attention. It was *Gradual Awakening* by Stephen Levine. This book, with its visualizations and meditation instructions, showed me how to explore the pain that ravaged my body. I practiced these meditations realizing that I was not my pain but that the pain I felt was a confluence of constrictions and entangled energies, muscles, thoughts and feelings. As I unwound these muscles and energies and the emotions that accompanied them, the pain in my body gave way. I became lighter and was set free. With the help of a nutritionist and wonderful body worker, I slowly began to walk and eat again. These experiences awakened my inner knowing, which helped me gauge, for example, what foods I could eat. I now had access to a quiet inner voice within me.

As I reflected back on my life, having survived this passage, I realized how incredibly similar it was to my birth and the early months of my life. You see, I was born nearly twelve weeks early and was very tiny (only 3.5 pounds) and the doctors discovered soon after my birth that I could not eat without vomiting. Being so tiny, I was immediately put into a incubator.[8] My mother couldn't touch me and the only contact I had was when the nurses changed me and fed me through a needle in my back. Doctors told my mother and father I would probably be blind, deaf and dumb, if I survived. This was especially hard for my mother and father who had lost another baby a few years before. Everyone who knew me, family, friends, doctors, and nurses were afraid and deeply concerned. For a month, fear and prayers spun around me as I lay in this glass encased world.

Finally, on Easter, having lost a third of my body weight, I took a turn for the worse and nearly died. The next morning I had emergency exploratory surgery to see why I could not eat. During this surgery, the surgeons found that the pyloric sphintcer muscle at the base of my stomach was closed off; they gently teased it open and saved my life. Once before I had felt isolated and been near death. The emotional weight of that time resonated deeply with my present circumstances.

In the months that followed my intuition grew. It guided my hands when I did massage, and when friends talked about things that were troubling them, insights arose. This sense of knowing and connection I now felt was stronger than ever before. My mind was quiet and still—I reveled in this state and as time passed, things seemed normal. My body and spirit were strong again; but this normalcy was changed in an instant one day when I walked into the bakery where I worked.

Remembering

Early one morning in the fall of 1984, I walked into work as usual. As I turned the corner to hang up my bag, I saw a young man with his back to me. My body instantaneously reacted and before I realized I had taken a step—or even a breath—I had wound my way back through the bakery to the outside courtyard. My body had literally propelled me backwards through the bakery and out the open doors in a matter of seconds. I realized—I knew this man—my body knew him—even though I had never seen him before in my life.

Over the next few days, the past opened to me like a flower, and the details of where and how I had known Stefan and what our relationship had been was steadily revealed to me. Circumstances threw us together and we became lovers, as unexpectedly in the present, as we had in the past. It was the most unconditional experience and love I had ever felt, I knew him, I had loved him in the past and I loved him now, even though he would soon expatriate to Europe and I would never see him again.[9]

A few months later, I met Alex: I didn't trust him, but I knew I had to be with him to complete something that was unfinished. One night at work, as I looked down the coffee bar he walked by, his profile suddenly changed into an Etruscan soldier with a high helmet and proud aquiline nose[10]. In the blink of an eye, he flipped back and was the man I knew in the present. Shaken to my core, I asked my manager if I could take a break, but even as I sat at the end of the bar, this soldier's face and my uneasy feeling would not go away. Like a movie, the story of where and how I knew him unfolded and over the next few days, more of our history was revealed to me, as if in installments. I learned that Alex had killed me and all the young women and girls in a temple, women who were under my care in ancient Sumeria. I learned how my own arrogance in the past had been my downfall. These long forgotten parts of my Self flowed in me, giving me new-found strength and humility. There was no need to be with Alex anymore.

Two years after Stefan moved to Europe, I dreamt I was standing in an office. The first thing I saw was a clock on the wall that read noon and a man standing at his desk looking out a window with his back to me. As he turned around, I realized I knew him; he looked a bit older, but it was Stefan. He smiled, walked over to me, embraced me and said, "I know who you are now." With tears in our eyes, we simultaneously asked each other if we were happy, and both answered, yes. We embraced again, looked into each other's eyes and said, perhaps next time. I awoke in California close to tears and glanced at the clock by my bed. It read a few minutes after 4:00 am, exactly the eight-hour time difference between us. I was stunned.

I knew I had been in Stefan's office and this had been no ordinary dream.

Later in 1984, through a friend, I met Colin, and we began to sit together[11]. After so many mind bending experiences, meditation was a godsend. I had studied Buddhism, but only practiced meditation sporadically, until I started sitting with Colin and practicing in the small Taoist monastery where he was a priest. Sitting with experienced monks imbued the meditation space with peace and deep quiescence, which was deeply restorative for me. I found deep tranquility practicing the ancient Taoist meditation of *Tso Wong*[12].

Tso Wong translates as "sitting and forgetting"[13] and is a yin-practice that is deeply connected to the earth. In this practice, we focus on our breath, our minds merge with our breath, and our thoughts naturally settle. As time passes, all else falls away, leaving deep stillness and the spacious emptiness of the Void. This stillness is linked to the natural world and reminds me of the first snowfall of the season. There is a richness to this stillness, where activity slows down, and everything becomes quiet, and the energy all around us pauses, and expands. The practice of Tso Wong, especially with accomplished sitters, helped me to stabilize my mind, to settle my emotions and to experience serenity, emptiness, and timelessness, that I had not known before.

As winter approached, all the members of the monastery dispersed when our building was sold. Colin went to the northwest and Chris[14], and I moved north for school, then south, after marrying in July of 1986. In September, Colin came to live with us and we began to do intensive sitting meditation practice.

In November of 1986 it became clear that an energy wanted to speak through me. This was scary at first and I grappled with the idea that someone wanted to use me as a channel[15], but in the end I realized it wasn't that different from singing, when I got out of my own way and let the voice sing me.

Transformations

During this time, my body would heat up intensely and my legs would shake uncontrollably. Heat and fire would spontaneously surge, moving me like a whip, as immense energy rushed up my spine and flew out the top of my head. Sometimes my whole body would convulse, as though I had been plugged into a light socket, and I would fall to the ground and flop on the floor, like a fish out of water. During these times I would have to throw the excess energy off my hands. It was just too much to hold. Colin felt this energy, and Chris saw it as ribbons of light streaming out my fingertips.

Energy flowed through me like electric current and anyone who saw me might think I was having seizures, as I was overtaken by this profound energy that would bring me to my knees. Even today, the energy whips through my body, sending it into a gentle convulsion. At this time, the current in my body was so strong, I could even start cars with dead batteries, which was pretty unnerving.

To withstand this, all I could do was ground myself. Again and again, I sent the energy into the earth. The earth, not the heavenly realms, became my foundation, and the more I released and fell into the stillness of the earth, the more energy I could hold. Resistance was not an option and I never even considered it. I knew in my heart that this energy would not harm me as it coursed through every nerve, muscle, and bone in my body and awakened my cells. The force of these energies melted away ancient blocks and energy burnt new pathways through my mind, body, and chakras. No aspect of my self was left untouched, as my physical and energy body were rewired and upgraded. I truly believe that the only thing that saved me from being overwhelmed by these deep changes was my meditation practice, and the understanding that all energy is inherently neutral.

On January 5, 1987 as Chris, Colin, and I were sitting in meditation I felt a profound stillness engulf me, I fell into trance and a voice spoke through me. This voice was slow at first and seemed to flow from out of the void. It was distinctly different from my own. The syntax was ancient. Later we would learn that this voice was the voice of Marika[16], who was aligned with my personal energy and was the essence and culmination of all the higher Selves I had ever been or ever would be. Marika would tell us that she was a warrior priestess, and as she spoke with such love, kindness and directness, the energy of Source[17] flowed through me.

Over the next few weeks, we learned more about this channel, which included two very distinct energies or counsels. One is Taoist in character, with remarkable humor, energy knowledge, and a love of the natural world, while the other is more Buddhist. This latter aspect is full of wisdom and deep compassion. It has the ability to cut through illusions, and see into one's innermost self. Together they embody humor, insight, joy, wisdom, and compassion.

I trance-channeled Marika for about five years. I never remembered what I said; sessions were taped, and when I transcribed them I learned what was said. It was very healing for Chris and I, and Colin too, that first year as we cleared past lives and old karmas. Chris held the space[18] and asked questions when I was channeling and soon we surpassed Colin's experience. He counseled me to let Marika teach us directly and she did just that. She taught, advised, cajoled, and laughed at and with us. She sang to us of spirit and the earth and the marriage of these two dragons. Out of the void, she spoke to us and answered our questions and those of others around us. It was like having at my fingertips, an enormous library full of knowledge beyond my own knowing. The accuracy of the information that came through surprised us all. Information that seemed implausible made sense to people who asked probing questions about the mysteries in their lives. A vast range of understanding and knowingness literally poured into my being as I surrendered to the energy of the channel.

Even when I was sick, I could channel. Illness vanished as this powerful *chi* flowed through my body. Quiescence and energy occupied the same space and everything else fell away. Then in 1992, the energies of the channel asked me to embody their very essence. Other mediums I knew were horrified—wondering how I would do this—but I knew that Marika and the energy would not harm me. As I learned to embody the energy, a broader and enhanced communication developed.

This expanded connection allowed clients and students to be touched by the energy of the channel directly through the words that were spoken and the energy that could be felt. The environment was rich with this energy and I taught from this place, which included Marika and what I began to call Source, which was described as the beginning point from which everything emerged. It was vast and pervasive and included the energies I had become so intimate with, Marika, and the counsels of Buddhist and Taoist energies. Questions still sparked the process but now, not only were words spoken, but images, feelings, and complete stories emerged when people posed questions to me about their lives.

I learned the foundations of Transforming Embodiment in my very being, through a firing process[19] that continues to teach and transform my clients, my students and me as spirit leaps into our lives with insight, brilliance, and unconditional acceptance. This is how I came to do the work I am sharing with you. May it help each of you in some small way.

1

BUILDING A CASE FOR CELLULAR AND SYSTEMIC MEMORY: A SCIENTIFIC VIEW

Science has recently discovered three startling new possibilities regarding how we think, feel, love, heal and find meaning in our life. This research suggests that the heart thinks, cells remember, and that both of these processes are related to an as yet mysterious, extremely powerful, but very subtle energy with properties unlike any other known force.

Dr. Paul Pearsall [20]

The Systemic and Cellular Nature of Memory

The research of Drs. Candace Pert, former chief of brain chemistry at the National Institute of Mental Health, and Paul Pearsall suggest that memory is both cellular and systemic. What they propose is that the cells in our body store information and energy, and that these cells as 'info-energy,' travel throughout the system via the neuropeptides, neuroreceptors, the circulatory, immune and endocrine systems.

Over twenty years ago, Dr. Herbert Weiner anticipated the role cellular memories would play in healing. He believed that disease was a breakdown in the communication with and between cells. Advances in neuroscience, immunology, and psychoneuroimmunology may now be substantiating Dr. Weiner's hypothesis. Dr. Candace Pert's work sheds light on how cellular communication occurs within the body.

According to Pert's research, the body's communication system contains two chemical substances, neuropeptides, and neuroreceptors. These neuropeptides fit into these receptors thus activating communication between the brain and body and within the body itself. Neuropeptides are produced by nerve cells in the brain, and these chains of amino acids serve as neurotransmitters that communicate and connect the entire nervous system. "Pert's groundbreaking work gives credence to the idea that there is a complex, body-wide systemic memory including our cellular structure."[21]

What we see from this discovery is that neuropeptides and neuroreceptors circulate throughout the body, linking and unlinking in an active and intricate system of communication. Information and energy are exchanged within this far-flung network that links the body and mind. This new scientific understanding also leads to the possibility that cells communicate and that some form of memory is stored within them. "Assumptions that the brain thinks independently of the body and heart,...and that our cells cannot remember are not in keeping with either the newest scientific knowledge from cellular biology or the oldest wisdom of ancient traditional medicines."[22]

Dr. Paul Pearsall's research is fundamental because he is seeing these cellular or systemic memories be transferred from donor to patient in transplant recipients. Pearsall notes in his book *The Heart's Code* that many heart transplant patients feel some kind of spiritual imprint from their donors. Before writing an article on one heart transplant recipient's experience, Charles Siebert, a medical writer for New York Times Magazine, attended a party with over one hundred heart transplant recipients. He found that almost every recipient reported "'spiritual memories' or feelings of the energy of their donor."[23]

Pearsall believes that there may be many possible sources of cellular memories[24]. The heart, Pearsall believes, plays a major role in the interchange of information, energy, and communication within the body and between the body and mind.

Julie Motz, a pioneer in energy healing who works within surgical settings, agrees that memory is systemic and cellular. In her book *Hands of Life*, she shares a cell biologist's belief that "all the functions of the body—including sensation, emotion and memory—exist in the individual cells."[25] She also notes "Memory precedes the formation of the nervous system and must therefore exist on a cellular level."[26]

Cellular and Systemic Memory and Neuropeptides: The Science of Dr. Candace Pert

Science is beginning to support and affirm the links between the body and mind challenging the old Descartian way, which we have lived by for centuries. Neuroscience and psychoneuroimmunology are at the forefront of this inquiry. Recent scientific discoveries are finding that neuropeptides are linked not only to the brain but also to the body and possibly to each emotion we feel. Neuroscience is giving new credence to the concept that the body-mind is one system. Dr. Candace Pert has been a leader in this field for decades, and her findings are relevant and illuminating.

What Dr. Pert's work reveals, with the discovery of the opiate receptor and the creation of a methodology for finding neuropeptides[27], is that the brain, mind, and body are connected by a complex communication network via neuropeptides and ligands. With her discoveries the ground by which science understood the brain body relationship was forever changed. The body went from being a mechanistic object to a lively communication and information network that is interconnected to the entire somatic system that is very likely intelligent. Her work is also notable because she proposes that this communication is both cellular and systemic.

Dr. Pert, through her in-depth and groundbreaking experiments, learned that nerve cells act on nerve cells over great distances, crossing the brain/body barrier that science once firmly believed was in place, via neuropeptides that fit into specific receptors that exist throughout the body as well as being within the brain.

Surely what we were seeing was the basis for some kind of complex communication within the brain. And since the brain peptides and their receptors were showing up throughout the far-flung systems of the body, perhaps this was an indication that communication was taking place not just within the brain, but between the brain and the rest of the body.[28]

As Pert's work progressed she found she could no longer make a strong distinction between the brain and body. She determined that they were one system, which she refers to as 'bodymind.' Her discovery gives us a possible scientific basis for what metaphysics and alternative medicine had surmised for years.

Pert's research established that neuropeptides and neuroreceptors that were once thought to be solely within the brain were found within the whole system, including the immune and endocrine systems. Pert discerned that neuropeptides both modulated and mediated the communication within the entire organism while receptors sorted out this information exchange within the body.

How this is done, very simply, is that receptors sit on the outside of cells along the entire cell membrane, like little keyholes, waiting for specific neuropeptides which are like keys to fit into these tiny key holes. This is how communication between the brain and body takes place. Neuropeptides freely float within the system until they find the specific receptor to link with and a dialogue then begins. The receptors receive the messages of the neuropeptides and ligands, and transmit information from the cell surface to deep within the cell. These receptors[29] act like the eyes and ears for the cells. This communication is bi-directional meaning that is happens from brain to body and body to brain. Neuropeptides send messages all over the brain and body. Neuropeptides, long chains of amino acids, talk, while receptors, twisted up proteins consisting of long sequences of amino acids, listen or hear.

The brain and body are connected by this network and these neurochemicals may be the substrate of emotions and may provide the physiological basis for emotions, Pert reasons. Her research regards the limbic system as the possible seat of emotions within the brain, since this system is flooded with neuropeptides. She maintains that neuropeptides are the molecules of emotion, and that body wisdom is present throughout the mind and body.

> "Peptides existed in all parts of the brain, not only in the hypothalamus...peptides also appeared in the cortex... and in the limbic system." "By understanding the distribution of these chemicals throughout the nervous system we got the first clues that led us to theorize about peptides being the molecules of emotion."[30]

Pert's research also found that hormones were not produced solely by glands as presumed before and that hormones were not stored in one place in the body. Insulin it was discovered was not only a hormone but a neuropeptide as well. Insulin was made and stored in the brain and within the pancreas, and neuropeptides were found in both the pancreas and brain. Hormones were another source of neuropeptides and the immune system also produced neuropeptides.

Conceptually the nervous, hormonal, and immune systems were the same. Peptides that were found in the brain were also found in the immune nervous and endocrine systems. While the links between the brain and other body systems had been demonstrated by Dr. Pert's and her colleague's research, the immune system had been thought of as a separate system. This was no longer the case when Ed Blalock's research, from the University in Texas, pointed out that these systems were interconnected. Pert research affirmed Blalock's discovery that the immune system communicates not only with the endocrine system but with the nervous system and brain as well. It was also determined that the same receptors in the brain were in the immune system as well.

This connection between hormones and neuropeptides is significant because in Eastern traditions and yoga the glandular or endocrine system is linked to the chakra system. So, we can postulate that there may be a link between hormones, neuropeptides, and the subtle energy centers within the body. This also may pertain directly to memory.

> We know that the immune system, like the central nervous system, has memory and the capacity to learn. Thus, it could be said that intelligence is located not only in the brain but in the cells that are distributed throughout the body, and that the traditional separation of mental processes, including emotions, from the body is no longer valid. If the mind is defined by brain-cell communication, as it has been in contemporary science, then this model of the mind can now be seen as extending naturally to the entire body. Since neuropeptides and their receptors are in the body as well, we may conclude that the *mind* is in the body, in the same sense that the mind is in the brain, with all that that implies.[31]

If the immune system and the nervous system have memory then it follows that the hormonal or endocrine system would have memory as well.

Memory and Neuropeptides

> Using neuropeptides as the cue, our bodymind retrieves or represses emotions and behaviors. Dr. Eric Kandell and his associates at Columbia University College of Physicians and Surgeons have proved that biochemical change wrought at the receptor level is the molecular basis for memory. These recent discoveries are important in appreciating how memories are stored not only in the brain, but in a *psychosomatic network* extending into the body, particularly in the ubiquitous receptors between nerves and bundles of cell bodies called ganglia, which are distributed not just in and near the spinal cord, but all the way out along pathways to internal organs and the very surface of the skin. The decision about what becomes a thought rising to consciousness and what remains an undigested thought pattern buried at a deeper level in the body is mediated by the receptors. I'd say that the

fact that memory is encoded or stored at the receptor level means that memory processes are emotion-driven and unconscious (but, like other receptor-mediated processes, can sometimes be made conscious).[32]

What this means is that the cells within our bodies possess a form of memory, and this memory is driven by our emotional responses and behaviors. Further, the spine and nervous system are connected to the internal organs in the body and to the surface of the skin, so memory may be found in our organs and within the body's systems. The spine and the chakras or energy centers of the body are closely aligned by their proximity, so memories may also extend into the subtle body or chakras as well. Pert's analysis suggests that memory is encoded in our cells and receptors. The mechanism of communication that occurs between neuropeptides to receptors delivers, as it were, memories, emotions, and behaviors to the cells and organs within our system.

Emotions would then be stored along with memories since the memory process is driven by emotions according to Pert. These memories and emotions would be unconscious but accessible. "I believe that repressed emotions are stored in the body—the unconscious mind—via the release of neuropeptide ligands, and that memories are held in their receptors."[33] This leads to the understanding that memory is embodied and systemic. Pert's findings support what I have personally experienced and clinically seen. Memories flow throughout the body and are encoded in our cells, organs and energy centers.

The info-energy that Pearsall describes is a form of memory and these memories are not only a part of our cells but are a part of our consciousness. I believe these memories are enduring and unfading, so the question arises, where does the information, emotion, or energy, created by events or circumstances go, since it cannot be extinguished, when we die. If what Pearsall and Pert have found is true then a hypothesis that info-energy as a form of memory, and a form of the subtle mind could be carried forward within consciousness beyond the physical death of the body is plausible. If these memories are carried within our consciousness and mindstream, as Buddhist scholars believe, then these imprints of former memories and affinities may be present when consciousness re-embodies or re-emerges.

Indestructible Nature of Memory and Emotions

Understandings from physics suggest that energy cannot be destroyed, so the info-energy of the neuropeptides and receptors, as a form of energy and possible memory is also indestructible. Emotions are laden with tremendous energy, the question as to where when we die does this information and energy, in the form of emotions, and memories or affinities go, since it is inextinguishable? My research and experience have shown me that the info-energy, as memory is carried forward or continued in consciousness, beyond the physical death of the body.

In an article for *Advances* Dr. Pert takes this a step further "I think it is possible now to conceive of mind and consciousness as an emanation of emotional information processing, and as such, mind and consciousness would appear to be independent of brain and body."[34] This is a remarkable statement from a neuroscientist, that the mind and consciousness are independent of the body is an idea and area that until now has been off limits to modern science. Spiritual traditions and practices such as those within the Buddhist tradition have delved into the matter of mind and consciousness but not until recently has science entered into this dialogue. At a symposium on Survival and Consciousness Pert addresses the question, can the mind survive the death of the physical brain?

> I think it is important to realize that information is stored in the brain, and it is conceivable to me that this information could transform itself into some other realm. The DNA molecules surely have the information that makes the brain and body, and the bodymind seems to share the information molecules that enliven the organism. Where does the information go after the destruction of the molecules (the mass) that compose it? Matter can neither be created nor destroyed, and perhaps biological information flow cannot just disappear at death...Who can rationally say 'impossible'?[35]

This scientist's speculation while it may seem outrageous is supported by my findings that memories as imprints reappear in consciousness when that consciousness re-embodies. Matter and mind cannot be destroyed nor can the emotions, memories, or imprints held within them.

Dr. Candace Pert's Work and the Survival of Consciousness

How is Candace Pert's work relevant to the survival of consciousness hypothesis? What Dr. Pert's work does and why it is substantive is that she links the body and the mind scientifically, giving greater credibility than ever before, to the idea that the mind and body are interconnected. She also gives us an understanding of how previously separate systems are now linked and are an interactive communication network. She also notes that this communication occurs at a cellular level and that emotions are a part of this complex communication or information network. The origin of emotions may be found in our body's cells and our emotions would interact on the cellular level as well as with the endocrine, nervous and immune systems. If the body and mind can scientifically be shown to be linked, and our emotions are in the body and cells as well as the brain, and mind, and our cells carry a form of memory, then memory too could be free flowing within the system and in the cells.

Dr. Pert's research gives us the foundation for cellular memory and shows us that emotions reside in the body. Her work dovetails into Dr. Pearsall's research, which deals with systemic memory. He believes that a nonlocal energy which he calls L energy pervades the system and that this energy is stored in the heart. L energy Pearsall maintains flows through the body like the neuropeptides, freely communicating within the system. He feels it is this L energy that carries memories, and that this may be how transplant patients "receive" a donor's memories.

Dr. Paul Pearsall's Research and Theories

Pearsall believes that information is carried in the energy of the heart, and that this energy circulates within the body to the cells via the cardiovascular system. He explains that this energy is indestructible and that "whatever memories of a life experience anyone has ever had may be able to become our individual memories."[36] This could be one possible explanation of how memories are transferred from donors to transplant patients.

Pearsall spoke with Dr. Candace Pert about his theories about cellular memories and shared with her some of his stories from transplant patients. These stories Pert said were not surprising. "She pointed out that, since the cells in the heart are loaded with molecules that necessarily contain at least the same form of memory, these memories could well come along with the heart and join the new body and brain."[37] This is an amazing statement and may provide a backdrop for what I have seen both personally and clinically. Pearsall continues,

> Transplanted hearts come with their own info-energetic cellular memories. The subtle effects on personality and consciousness reported by certain heart transplant recipients are beginning to provide new clues about the nature of the heart's code. Wherever there is energy, there's information.[38]

Memories cross the barriers of time and death as info-energy that is everlasting. This energy has the capacity of being propelled forward, after the death of the physical body, through the vehicle of consciousness as spiritual traditions have maintained.

Another study done in 1993 under the direction of the United States Army Intelligence and Security Command reported that donated white blood cells showed excitement in the laboratory when the individuals who donated the cells watched violent (emotionally laden) TV. The donors were up to 50 mile away from the lab and the cells. This cell excitement lasted for up to two days, so the cells were affected long after donation. It was noted that the cells appeared to be remembering or independently experiencing their donor emotions. This would fall under the category of a nonlocal event Pearsall points out "The donated cells remained energetically and nonlocally connected with their donor and seemed to 'remember' where they came from."[39]

Transplant Patients Encounters with Donor Memories

Pearsall's research bravely suggests that donor's "memories" are transferred to organ transplant recipients. I would extrapolate that if an organ's "memories" can survive a donor's physical death, and be passed on in the form of the likes and dislikes to a recipient of that organ, why is it implausible to think that a person's consciousness could be reborn in another body? Why couldn't consciousness, as a nonlocal phenomenon, cross the barriers of time and space and reemerge after death? The concepts of reincarnation and rebirth certainly support this idea. What I have seen and experienced in my clinical practice is that consciousness, at least in the form of memories and affinities, does survive death, and that there are consequences that affect us physically, psychologically and emotionally.

Dr. Paul Pearsall psychoneuroimmunologist and researcher, found when he studied transplant patients that donor's memories and affinities were transferred along with the transplanted organs. His own life-saving immune system transplant prompted his study of different types of organ transplants. The stories are often amazing and breathtaking. One story was about a young doctor Glenda who lost her husband in a car accident. She told Dr. Pearsall that she and her husband had argued about something silly before the accident that took her husband's life, and she was never able to say, I'm sorry to her husband.[40]

Years later she was gifted with a brief meeting with the young man who received her husband's heart. After a long wait in the hospital chapel Dr. Pearsall suggested that he and Glenda should leave saying that perhaps the recipient had changed his mind. Glenda asked that they wait a few minutes longer, and as reluctant as she was to believe it, she said she felt her husband's presence in the hospital "I felt him come in about thirty minutes ago."[41]

Moments later the young man and his mother arrived. The young man apologized for being late and said they had been unable to find the chapel for the last half hour. Glenda who was usually shy talked briefly with the young man and his mother, and then unexpectedly she asked if she could put her hand on he young man chest. Both were a bit embarrassed. The young man looked at his mother, perhaps for reassurance and then put his hand to his chest. He nodded his head, and unbuttoned his shirt. Glenda reached out and gently put her hand on the young man's chest. Tears rolled down her checks as she closed her eyes and said, "I love you David. Everything is copacetic."[42] She moved her hand away from his chest and hugged the young man. They sat down holding hands in silence. The mother of the young man took Dr. Pearsall aside at this point and spoke in a heavy Spanish accent,

> My son uses that word 'copacetic' all the time now. He never used it before he got his new heart, but after the surgery, it was the first thing he said to me when he could talk. I didn't know what it means. He said everything was copacetic. It is not a word I know in Spanish. Glenda overheard us, her eyes widened, she turned toward us and said, 'That word was our signal that everything was OK. Every time we argued and made up, we would both say that everything was 'copacetic.'[43]

The young man then shared story after story about the changes he had experienced since the transplant surgery. His mother also shared that before the surgery her son was vegetarian and very health minded, now she said he loved fatty foods and meat, and while he formerly loved heavy metal music, since the surgery he had loved 50s rock-and-roll. He also noted that he had recurring dreams of bright lights coming straight at him.

> Glenda responded almost matter-of-factly that her husband loved meat, was a junk food addict, had played in a Motown/rock-and-roll band while in medical school, and that she too dreams of the lights of that fateful night.[44]

Stories like this of cardio-sensitives, as Pearsall calls them, are not uncommon. He collected 140 transplant stories and delved into the research of other doctors who have studied the impact that heart transplants have on personality. Dr. Bunzel who practices surgery at University Hospital in Vienna reports that fifteen percent of his test group felt their personality had changed after the transplants. Six percent were willing to believe these changes were due to the transplantation. Pearsall gathered similar statistics.

Pearsall writes that the denial that some patients feel about donor's hearts and the possibility of affinities from donors may be the brains' way of defending itself and maintaining its own integrity. When a flood of information, emotions, and energy, from a transplanted heart blend with the recipient, Drs. Pearsall and Bunzel found that patients experienced a high degree of denial. This denial may be a way for the ego to remain intact, and for the personality to maintain cohesion. Personality changes do seem to occur nonetheless.

Dr. Pearsall's cases include a forty-one year old male that received the heart of a nineteen-year-old woman who was hit by a train. He shared with Dr. Pearsall that he feels nineteen again and he is sure he received a young man's heart because of the incredible energy he feels coursing through his body. His wife confides that her husband is like a kid again, completely changed, and that he talks about power and energy all the time. She notes he has dreams of driving a huge truck, or that he is the engineer of a large train.[45]

Another of Dr. Pearsall cases tells the story of a thirty-six-year woman, who received a heart lung transplant. She recounts that she dreamt about a pretty young girl, bursting with joy and happiness, and remarks that she has experienced a new happiness that she has never felt before since her transplant. The donor in this case was a twenty-one year old woman who was struck by a car as she ran across the street to show her fiancé a picture of her wedding dress.[46] There are more stories like these that Pearsall shares of how a part of a donor's consciousness appears to be carried forward, and how transplant recipients, food affinities, language choices, sexual desire, energy levels and temperaments all seem to change, sometimes very dramatically.

Reconnecting Science and Spirituality

Since 1987, scientists from various disciplines have been privately meeting with His Holiness the Dalai Lama to explore the connections between science, spirituality, and Buddhism. These Mind and Life Conferences provide an environment where communication between the disciplines is fostered. This open and spirited dialogue spurs on new research and rebuilds a bridge between science and spirit.

Physicians and scientists are questioning and even challenging the old Descartian way, which we have lived by for centuries. Leaps in neuroscience have lead to completely new ways of viewing the brain, the body, and consciousness. Not in centuries have we seen such a spirit of inquiry.

As a deep shift in consciousness takes place, the paradigm we have known is changing.

More and more, we understand that the capacities of the mind are limitless and we are only at the threshold of exploring this new and remarkable frontier. Elders in the field of body-mind healing, like Valerie Hunt Ed.D., who has studied energy, behavior, the brain and emotions for decades believes that by clearing past life experiences and events, the tissue is cleared of the pattern it holds, and that this may be cleared for generations that follow us.

She feels that multiple personality disorders are the memories of multiple past lives coming into conscious awareness and that current life events and memories can trigger other life experiences. Memory stays in the tissue as well as in the brain she has found, and in order to totally heal we must touch this cellular level she explains. Past life memories fit into the field of consciousness model and she concludes that past life memories are not a belief. They are known all the way to the core of one's being and this body knowing is the key.

These inventive and progressive scientists and researchers give me great hope that one day the integration of spiritual, psychological, emotional and traumatic events from past and other lifetimes will become a part of integrative medicine. I have seen again and again how memories are held within our bones, energy centers, and cells and how these memories deeply shape our lives. Therapies like Transforming Embodiment give each of us a new means to find our way through these sometimes complex and intense memories and emotions. But the gifts are great because as we reach into the core of our being to find the truth within us we heal ourselves at the deepest level possible—changing our lives and reality forever as a result.

2

THE BIOLOGY OF TRAUMA AND THE SPIRITUAL CHALLENGES OF EMBODIED TRAUMA

Some things must be dealt with at the roots. Trauma is one of these things.

Peter Levine [47]

In 1914 Freud defined trauma "as a breach in the protective barrier against stimuli leading to feelings of overwhelming helplessness."[48] The importance of this observation is critical for those wishing to understand trauma. Overwhelming feelings and helplessness are the key features when identifying trauma. It is also crucial to comprehend that trauma for an adult is significantly different than what we may have experienced as children. What we as adults view as non-threatening can be overwhelming to the child in us. As adults undertaking to heal early trauma we must not discount our feelings that we had as children or teens.

Dr. Peter Levine, author of *Waking the Tiger*, like myself, has found that quite ordinary events, those that may be perceived as benign, can be traumatic. As an example, at the age of three Anne, a client of mine, was excluded when her older sister and brother were taken for ice cream by her grandparents. This seeming simple event set the stage for feelings of exclusion and isolation that threaded through Anne's life and relationships. In our work together, she linked this event, which was very traumatic for her, to her difficulty in forming significant relationships, and she also connected these feelings of isolation to a lifetime as a holocaust survivor. This early experience, whether a reflection of an earlier time or not, proved to be extremely challenging in Anne's life and relationships.

Trauma also includes rage and terror, says expert Peter Levine, who also notes that the body at a cellular level perceives surgery as a mortal wound and that hospitalization presents a mortal danger. I would expand this list and include war, abandonment, betrayal, hunger, neglect, and loss to the list of traumas we may endure. All these would be possible mortal threats, since they impinge upon our ability to survive.

I have found that many events from childhood and adolescence are traumatic even if they are not rage or terror based. Many traumatic patterns are survival based. What I have repeatedly witnessed is that acute feelings of helplessness fall from the mind into the body, when the emotions and feelings surrounding events are just too much for a person to handle. When overwhelming feelings and emotions takes over, we must step away from the stimulus producing the emotion. If unresolved, these intense feelings will descend into the body and become unconscious, causing complications both emotionally and physically. Symptoms and psychological and emotional problems can develop if the residual energy, memory, and feelings are not released. The energy will quietly wait until we are capable of addressing the trauma.

Many people in the body-mind field feel as I do, noting that unresolved trauma stays in the body. In 1997 Dr. Candace Pert when speaking at a Wellness Conference along with Dr. Brian Seaward, Elaine Sullivan and David Lee concluded that trauma is stored in the body when the brain gets overloaded. The brain literally bounces the info-energy back into the body via peptideurgic nerves that go from the brain to the skin. Trauma, Pert says is stress from information overload. "We have seen how strong emotions that are not processed thoroughly are stored at the cellular level."[49] Julie Motz, author of *Hands of Life*, shares Bonne Bainbridge Cohen, a pioneer in body and movement education and the founder of the School for Body-Mind Centering, thoughts, "a protective mechanism keeps neuronal circuits in the brain from being overloaded with traumatic information until the brain is ready to handle it."[50]

These ideas fit into those of Dr. Mona Lisa Schultz who agrees and says that if a memory is stressful it leaves the brain and goes into the body. Peter Levine also adds that a threat not dealt with successfully stays in the body.

Valerie Hunt, researcher in the dynamics of field energy and the mind, believes that trauma stays in the tissues and the brain and that when trauma is finally released, so is the memory. She believes as I do that we must move through all the layers: tissues, emotions, beliefs, and spirit to release trauma and the memories associated with it. Hunt feels that only energy is released, while I believe it is a combination of energy, emotion, and memory that is erased from the mind and body.

Fight, Flight, and Freezing: Our Biological Imperatives

When thinking about shock or trauma we generally assume that there are two options open to us: fight or flight. Each may be well known to you, and you may even have a response that you favor. Levine has found from his observations with animals that there is a third possibility: freezing.

He has found that in the animal kingdom when a leopard, for instance makes a kill of a gazelle he will often drag his prey to a secluded area and leave it there while he returns to hunt. Levine found that animals could survive this ordeal by freezing or playing dead. In so doing they save their own lives, because while appearing dead they are not, they are frozen, immobile and in a state resembling death. From this state of immobility or freezing if left alone they will reawaken and literally shake their trauma off. By shaking, they mobilize their inner resources and energy again and are able to run away. The gazelle regains control of its body by trembling and shaking. From his biological research and observation Levine concludes that there are three options instead of the familiar two, and he has found that this unfreezing process is essential in order to break and heal the cycle of trauma. This, he feels, is the key to undoing and recovering from traumatic events.

Biology and the Phases of Traumatic Response

What Peter Levine has discovered is that the core of traumatic reaction is made up of four elements: hyperarousal, constriction, disassociation, and freezing and helplessness. Hyperarousal is the nervous system's first response to a threat, stress, or conflict. It is at this point that we may feel our heart rate increase and our breathing may become faster. Muscle tension, racing thoughts and tension prevail. This process of hyperarousal cannot be controlled, as it is an instinctual response. During hyperarousal the body is marshaling its resources so it can fight or flee. Interestingly, the body does not discriminate between real or imaged threats when in this state of hyperarousal.

Constriction is the next phase and it is the body's way of focusing perceptual awareness, so our full attention is on the threat. Muscles contract and the blood within the body is made available to the muscles so we can take defensive action. This focuses our attention, and these two states, hyperarousal, and constriction allow us to do amazing things. We have all heard stories on the news of firefighters who lift girders or beams to free a victim or a comrade or of the mother who lifts a car off a trapped child. These are examples of hyperarousal and constriction being mobilized in a positive way. However if the energy of these first two phases is not mobilized then disassociation and freezing occur next.

Disassociation is the body and mind's way of protecting us from continued escalating arousal. It also protects us from pain and death. In the case of the gazelle spoken of earlier this disassociation would ease the pain that the animal would feel as prey. Levine writes of an attack upon David Livingston by a lion while on safari, and shares these facts from Livingston's journal:

> Growling horribly close to my ear, he shook me as a terrier does a rat. The shock produced a stupor... It caused a sort of dreaminess in which there was neither sense of pain nor feeling of terror, though quite conscious of all that was happening.[51]

As we can see, a person in a traumatic state is disoriented, and there may be an out of body feeling of detachment, accompanied by a spacey or dreamlike state.

At this point, if there is not a successful escape, the next phase of freezing and helplessness takes over. Freezing and helplessness operate in tandem. The body cannot move and there is a rising feeling of powerlessness. The excessive overflowing energy that is unresolved closes down the nervous system. This creates immobility, which increases the fear and terror, and from here the cycle begins again, which leads to a state of hypervigilance.

There is also another biological aspect, called orienting that is present when we are imperiled. This response is based on our primitive need to identify the source of our distress. An easy way to connect with this idea is to think of a time when you were in an unfamiliar place, like a new home or a friend's house, and as you were falling asleep you hear a noise. Our first instinct is to identify where that noise is coming from. Our mind rapidly scans our environment to see if the noise was inside or outside the house, for instance. When we orient or discover the source of the noise our body and mind relax. If we are unable to identify the noise our body will freeze just like an animal in the wild. It will continue to try and identify the sound that we heard.

To summarize, the traumatic cycle includes: arousal, unsuccessful escape, fear, helplessness, and immobility. The recovery cycle includes immobility, arousal, running or successful escape and empowerment.

Ideal and Dysfunctional Responses

In the ideal scenario, when we are faced with a traumatic situation or event the nervous system searches for images that relate to the situation we are confronted by. In this way we are able to determine the appropriate level of response or reaction. As the nervous system searches it also selects actions that are most suited for the threat at hand. The active response of moving out of the threatening situation would naturally be next and would complete the ideal response when endangered. [52]

The dysfunctional or maladaptive response is one that never completes. The nervous system is constantly searching but fails to be able to orient in reference to the threat. The nervous system is unable to find the necessary information, so it is incapable of making an appropriate response. Strong emotions and panic emerge as one continues to search for images that will alleviate the situation. When this fails to happen the cycle continues and trauma escalates. Deeper feelings of anxiety flood the system as one is compelled to find an image to alleviate the threat or trauma. At this point the nervous system may choose any image or memory and this selection is usually indiscriminate. These images are often associated with other highly emotional states which fuel the "traumatic vortex," according to Levine.

The biological or instinctual outweighs the rational and if we are incapable of fighting or fleeing then the freezing response, which is our body's last option, will take over. When we can't release the bound up energy that accompanies an adrenaline rush by trembling, like the gazelle who awakens from its near death state having been dragged off and left for dead, the energy amplifies and is bound up within the nervous system, Levine asserts. Freezing constricts the energy that would have been discharged by either fight or flight and keeps it held within the system. If we are unable to unfreeze and shake off the trauma,[53] or complete it by getting away, immobility will set in.

The inability to release the energy that is a part of the nervous system's natural biological reaction to threat will embed the trauma into our psyche. The traumatic event will become fixated at this juncture, and from this point on we may unknowingly recreate similar traumatic situations in order to release the bound up energy held within us.

Our Three Options

So when faced with a threat, we can fight, flee, or freeze. Think back to a situation that you have experienced in your life where you felt the rush of adrenaline take over. Maybe a memory of a near miss while driving comes to mind or of a child who was in your care running out into the street. Now think of your response, what did your body automatically do? Did you run into the street after the child or swerve out of the way of the other vehicle? If so these are common reactions and would illustrate how we move through a threatening situation. "If, in contrast, the bodymind succeeds in locating the source of its distress, the primitive need is satisfied. A natural, successful defensive response will then arise to complete the experience."[54] Freezing might take the form of that split second of hesitation that sometimes occurs when faced with something that frightens or scares us. If we move on and allow ourselves to face the challenge of the situation before us, we escape the traumatic vortex that Levine speaks of.

In our daily lives we experience these near misses and are often successful in completing or surmounting these challenges. However, there are events in our lives where we are unable to complete this cycle and it is these events that can continue to plague us. When trauma is acute and we foresee no options we often freeze and in so doing the emotions, thoughts and experience of that moment are frozen in time and remain within us. I believe this is how trauma is embedded into our being. I have also noticed that shock is often a precursor of trauma and that shock hits the body like a water balloon, energetically splattering over our energy body and spilling into our chakras and aura. If we have the opportunity to clear shock in the moment we are often well served. [55]

Understanding Trauma

The following illustrates how an individual can cope with trauma at different times in very different ways. When my client, Peren, was in her teens her boyfriend tried to rape her at a party. She fought and successfully got away from him and returned to her other friends by the pool. While she was shaken and very afraid for many years, she felt that she recovered because she fought and got away. Levine might say this was a successful biological response to a threat. The components of threat, an adrenaline rush, and a successful escape occurred.

However, eleven years later she was assaulted again by someone she knew. This time she froze; she was unable to move or do anything. This truly astonished her. During this assault, she relived the earlier attempted rape, but this time she was helpless. This caused her much anguish and pain and her response completely puzzled her. Earlier in life, she had fought and gotten away but why now, she asked, did she freeze? As we worked with these memories we found that she felt that she would be killed or harmed even more if she struggled. This confused her because she had struggled earlier in her life and had been able to get away.

Gently we went a bit deeper, so she could discover why she had frozen. As she held that question in her mind's eye, many other lifetimes surfaced and the theme of helplessness, violence and rape were common themes. She found personal memories and memories from the collective mind of woman. She felt many emotions as she worked with these memories and wept deeply. With these tears came a sense of relief as understanding dawned, and she grasped that she had not been weak. Freezing had been an act of survival as well as a natural traumatic response. Realizing this, acceptance surfaced, and her sense of self-betrayal melted away. As she grappled with and let go of these emotions, and the ancient histories she had held, her body changed noticeably. The rigidity in her back and shoulders and hips receded. She felt now that she had regained a lost portion of her self and her strength.

I would add that at the time of the attempted rape she never told anyone about it. She felt at fault and was silenced. Her boyfriend made humiliating remarks to his friends about her; she was not allowed to feel the empowerment that came with the successful escape. Only feelings of betrayal, embarrassment, and depression survived, so while she was able to get away she was never able to shake off the trauma fully. This may be why the reenactment of the original transpired. "We are inextricably drawn into situations that replicate the original trauma in both obvious and unobvious ways."[56] This revisiting occurs so we can have another chance to release the pent up emotions and energy within the body, so the traumatic incident can be released once and for all.

Symptom Formation

I have observed that symptoms form from the body's responses to both stress and trauma, and traumatic symptoms and memories are not limited to traumatic events from this lifetime alone. When immobility takes over we either freeze or collapse, and freezing in fear creates traumatic symptoms. If immobility is maintained or feelings are left incomplete, symptoms form, and our reactions to life threatening situations remain symptomatic until they are completed.

Levine's work outlines and details how the nervous system's and the body's instinctive reactions take place both in functional and dysfunctional ways. What he has seen in animals has worked for patients, who have found great relief when they are allowed to go back to the moment of immobility and unfreeze their response by trembling or shaking the trauma off.

When a person is confronted with a threat or feels that they are in danger, the system is overpowered with brain chemicals and information. The mind and body reach a point of overload and shut down, suppressing the trauma, which then merges or drops into the body. When this energy persists within the body-mind symptoms manifest. "The nervous system compensates for being in a state of self-perpetuating arousal by setting off a chain of adaptations that eventually bind and organize the energy into symptoms."[57] Symptoms may take months to develop, but unless the trauma is completed chronic symptoms will be produced. Levine notes that traumatic symptoms are ever present and they can come and go for decades. As a traumatized person re-experiences trauma, suppression increases, and symptoms will worsen. The longer these symptoms persist the more complex they become. Whole constellations of beliefs, memories, and events, either actual or imagined, can coalesce to create intricate woven pathologies.

Reenactment

Intense energy builds up during a traumatic experience. If we are unable to release this energy through fight, flight, or freezing, the impaired energy with no place to discharge, will seek a means of release. The body-mind will recreate similar situations until the energy is freed. There is a deep need to release this embedded energy from our system; re-enactment is the body's way of trying to get us to let go of this bound energy.

"Freud coined the phase 'repetitive compulsion' to describe the behaviors, relationships, emotions and dreams that seemed to replay early trauma."[58] He observed that people put themselves into situations that were similar in order to resolve or find solutions for the original trauma. The body, in its quest for homeostasis and balance, will repeatedly bring events into our lives until we release the body sensations, feelings, and energy surrounding a traumatic event.

The reenactment of scenarios that are akin to original trauma occurs widely in both memories from childhood and memories of other lifetimes. The biological foundation for the creation and reenactment of symptoms is not limited by time or space, it would seem. The physiological roots of trauma and the successive reenactment of like situations can travel via one's consciousness from one lifetime to the next, just as karma is brought forward from one lifetime to another. This is one of the spiritual challenges of trauma, for if we are able to disperse the energy and the associated beliefs and feelings, we are gifted with not having to revisit the trauma.

Undoing Trauma

Body sensations show us where we hold trauma. Better than the mind and memory, our body holds the keys to discovering and recovering from traumatic experiences. "The body is the unconscious mind. Repressed trauma caused by overwhelming emotion can be stored in a body part, thereafter affecting our ability to feel that part or even move it."[59] In Transforming Embodiment we work directly with the part of the body that is holding the repressed trauma. This gives us the ability to vision, and feel the sensations surrounding the trauma from within the mind and body. We work with both these aspects to trace and uncover traumatic experiences.

We are empowered when we can access our inner awareness and our body's sensations relating to the events that challenge us in our lives. Levine concurs and states, "The healing of trauma is a natural process that can be accessed through an inner awareness of the body."[60] Levine also believes that when our natural biological instincts are allowed to guide us trauma can be healed. This understanding that the roots of trauma are linked to our instinctual responses is profound because it gives us a new way to move out of trauma. It outlines how our nervous systems react and respond and shares with us a fundamentally different approach to working with trauma, not solely with the mind but also with the body.

The key, he feels, is to unite, integrate, and transform the polarities of expansion and contraction within us and to discharge the held energy of fear so we may heal. He explains that the entire nervous system changes when moving from a traumatic state to a peaceful one.

Chapter Two

"When we successfully renegotiate trauma, a fundamental shift occurs in our beings."[61] I have seen this as clients release memories, images, feelings, and beliefs that challenge them. Peace washes over them like a gentle rain. Relief shines from their eyes where panic and anxiety once were. Our body's experience is truly a gift and as we work directly with how our experiences are embodied, we find healing.

Remembering Trauma

Where Levine's work differs from conventional thought is that he feels that the reliving of a trauma reinforces the traumatic vortex. He believes that the searching for a memory can re-traumatize and solidify frozen immobility. His work has also led him to understand that the felt sense is more important than beliefs, interpretations, or explanations. And he feels that it is unnecessary to dredge up old memories and to relive emotional pain in order to heal. Remembering severe trauma, he notes, can re-traumatize individuals.

This may be the case with severe trauma, in which he specializes, but I have not found this to be true with the clients I have seen. I have discovered that if we understand the circumstances surrounding traumatic events and death experiences, as well as the beliefs, ideas, emotions and felt sense of an event we can safely release symptoms. With severe trauma we need to be delicate in our approach. Memories of traumas that originate in other lifetimes carry with them deep emotions, phobias and fears, but my clients have learned through their own experience that by revisiting these moments they can release forever the symptoms that have often plagued them.

Memories naturally arise as we experience the body's sensory awareness of events. With skill we can learn to traverse and maneuver through this maze. Our feelings and emotions, when we have cultivated a mind that is spacious and non-judging are less likely to be overwhelming. The shamans of Hawai'i understand that our world arises from our beliefs and so the understanding of beliefs can provide us with powerful insights, and they can allow us to break the cycle of repetition. Perhaps we can use these tools with those of Levine to understand and release ourselves from the grip of trauma, so our inner wisdom which is innate in us can lead us to deep and lasting healing.

Trauma, Death and Transformation

The spiritual challenge of trauma is that traumatic events continue when our consciousness leaves our body. The intense energy from these experiences is only dissipated when we review, relive in some cases, and release the energy constellations that accompany the trauma. I would add that if the trauma were a deathblow, then as the Buddhists maintain, the shock of that traumatic event would be propelled forward as consciousness leaves the body. This information, with all the feelings, overwhelming shock and distress, would be the person's last thoughts and as such they would imprint and create circumstances that would be mirrored in the next incarnation. To me, this is the ultimate frontier and spiritual challenge of trauma. Trauma continues in all of us when consciousness holds the imprint in our cells, bones, tissues, and mindstream. If we can release trauma in this lifetime we will not have it resurface in our next life. I believe that if we truly want to heal the core of our being we must understand the origins of our symptoms and release them. There is great power and empowerment in this understanding. We are given the tools to transform our lives if we can review moments of death and trauma, and our very embodiment is the key that unlocks our ancient past.

Ian Stevenson, author of *Twenty Cases Suggestive of Reincarnation*, has studied and collected cases of children with birthmarks from previous death wounds for a quarter of a century that would confirm the idea that information can be translated from one body to another or from one incarnation to another. It seems plausible that not only does consciousness continue but the shocks and traumas continue as well. If what Levine has found were true, that symptoms continue until they are resolved, why, if consciousness continues, would these symptoms not continue as well? "When we are traumatized, an echo of this feeling of being frozen remains with us."[62] So, when we are frozen in trauma and immobility the memory and feeling and sensations are suspended in the body-mind and within consciousness. The emotions and feelings and fear remain intact awaiting a stimulus that is reminiscent of the original trauma or wound, so the embodied trauma can ultimately be released.

With the many clients I have seen, the power of trauma stays within consciousness and re-embodies, sometimes repeatedly, until the trauma is completed. This is similar to what Levine has seen in his work with trauma victims. The unwinding of trauma from the core and cells within us may prove to be the new frontier to work with in psychology and healing. As we delve into the body connecting literally at a systemic and cellular level to the roots of our biology we may find our ultimate healing.

INTERLUDE

HEALING ORIGINS: RESOLVING PHYSICAL SYMPTOMS

> These sensations [the felt sense or internal body sensations] serve as a portal through which we find the symptoms, or reflections of trauma. In directing our attention to these internal body sensations rather than attacking the trauma head-on we can unbind and free the energies that have been held in check.
>
> Peter Levine [63]

The first two interludes in this book present two different ways to use Transforming Embodiment. Each focuses on resolving emotions and memories from the past and on healing origins. These cases represent snapshots and do not capture the complex interwoven structure of issues and beliefs each client explored, experienced, and reorganized. They describe only one part of the puzzle, reflecting upon a single thread within the fabric of each person's story. Knowing this, I hope the reader will understand that the simplicity seen in these cases is deceptive, and may not display the complexity or the interwoven nature of the process itself.

Both Lynn and Sara had mastered certain techniques, described in the preface, and each did these preliminary practices before we started our sessions.

Lynn's experience took place during a 12-week course that focused on the physical body. In this class, Lynn learned to merge with the different organs in her body to gain information about the memories, emotions, or experiences held within her various organ systems. She learned to connect and follow the deep imagery within her body to explore her physical symptoms and emotional difficulties. Body sensations served as another doorway into the memories held within her cells, bones, and tissues.

In searching for the origins of current problems, Lynn experienced past life memories quite spontaneously. These memories held the key for Lynn and by transforming these memories deep healing and release took place as the original root cause of her fears, relationship issues and even her physical symptoms were understood and finally laid to rest.

Family History

Lynn's father had a number of heart attacks throughout his life without knowing it. Being a Christian Scientist, he had not sought medical help until deep into his illness. By the time he saw a doctor his heart was only working at 30% of it's full capacity. The doctors said it was too late. They were able to monitor some of his symptoms through medication, but Lynn's father died within a year. Knowing of her father's history Lynn was worried when her heart began to bother her, but she felt that her diet and exercise program would help her stay healthy.

However, as a massage student in 1990 Lynn suddenly began experiencing an erratic heartbeat." My heart would just race and scare me to death, and at other times it would just jump—like it was going to come out of my chest. It was extremely alarming."

Lynn's Symptoms and Medical Diagnosis

I never noticed the symptoms until I started doing massage. My symptoms became especially intense while I was studying cranial sacral work. We were learning how to initiate massage work from our hearts, and were discovering how to let our hearts and intuitions

Interlude

direct our hands. This technique required that our hearts be relaxed and open, so the energy from our hearts could flow into and out of our hands. My heart just went crazy when I tried to do this work. It fluttered and jumped all over the place. I told my teachers about my feelings and they congratulated me. They said my heart was waking up. I had my doubts.[64] I felt there was another reason beyond the holistic explanations my teachers gave me. I sensed that something else might have been causing my symptoms.

As my massage training continued, my symptoms worsened, and were so acute that I was rushed to the hospital at one point. The doctors in the ER hooked me up to an EKG and discovered that I had an irregular heartbeat. At that time, they sent me home with a mobile heart monitor to track what was happening to my heart and suggested that I see a cardiologist. After a series of tests, mitral valve prolaspe was ruled out. I went back to my doctor and was diagnosed instead with an irregular heartbeat that was caused by a thickening of the mitral valve in my heart. This defect, I was told, had been present since I was born, and according to my doctor it may have been due to a magnesium deficiency during my mother's pregnancy. The doctor told me that this thickening caused a slight regurgitation in my heart and this was what I felt when my heart beat irregularly. He explained that this extra beat was providing additional blood flow to my system. He also assured me that this condition was not life threatening and he recommended that I begin taking magnesium supplements. After my visit to the ER and a cardiologist I understood the physical nature of my symptoms, but I still felt something was missing.

I continued to work with my cranial sacral teacher to find out why I was experiencing these symptoms. I learned to appreciate the rhythm and the exceptional beat of my heart, but I knew I did not have the whole story. What was the symptom trying to tell me?

During a massage my instructor was giving me, the image of a sword in a stone came into his mind. He told me he felt that the sword was my anger and that the stone would not be healed until the sword was removed. We worked together with this Arthurian imagery but I continued to have this nagging feeling that there was something more. When he had referred to the stone, something resonated deep within me, but I couldn't tap into the meaning or the experience associated with the stone at that time.

Our First Contact

I saw Lynn a few times before she joined the second course in a year-long training I was teaching. During those sessions we did a review and I taught her the preliminary practices[65] she would need and I examined her chakras. We noted which chakras might interest her during the upcoming classes. Lynn said very little about her heart symptoms and seemed more concerned about her throat chakra. I mentioned that there were issues in her heart chakra that might need to be addressed but we went no further at that time. We practiced some of the meditation and visualization techniques and met for class a few days later. Visualization practices are used to help create a space or environment that is conducive to inner exploration and healing, and so students can begin to experience their *body of experience* [66] and inner world.

> When you and I first started working together I was still quite aware of my irregular beat. I would notice it and it would always cause me a little bit of fear, even though I knew what it was physically. I knew what it was called and how to manage it but still there was this deep-seated fear that I had not been able to access. This fear became more intense when I moved to New Mexico and moved in with my boyfriend. His voice was a voice that I recognized but I couldn't tap the memory. I knew the voice, I just didn't know from where. It's funny, because the first time he spoke to me, I lost my balance. I was standing on solid ground and almost fell into the street. My body was remembering something but I couldn't consciously get what it was. It wasn't until class with you that the stone image and my feelings about my boyfriend became clear to me.

Instructions to Lynn's Class:

Take a deep breath and let go of any unnecessary

tensions from your body, take a second deep breath and on the exhale let go of any mental or emotional concerns from your day. Take a third deep breath and this time as you exhale I want you to do your grounding and protection meditations. Finally bring your attention back to your chest and take a few deep breaths and gently connect with your own inner wisdom. You may feel this energy as a warmth or see it as a radiating light, ask this aspect to be with you and guide you tonight.

Journeying Into the Heart

We are going to be working in the area of the heart tonight. I want you to begin by 'going into'[67] the area of your heart, enter into your physical heart, feel and hear your heart's beat. If you need to, you can put your hand on your chest to help you connect with your heart. I want you to notice your heart chakra but focus on the energy of your physical heart. As you connect to your heart investigate your heart's nature. This is a bit different than our earlier work. Now I want you to see, feel and sense the organ itself as it beats and pumps blood through your cardiovascular system. Notice if there are any areas of tension or holding. (Pause). Is there anything that draws your attention, (pause) any dark areas, (pause) spots, (pause) heat, or cold (pause)? Notice any images or memories as well, just scan your heart, and see what you find. (Long Pause). Now, I want you to investigate the thing that drew your attention the most. Follow whatever arises, and see where your experience takes you. If your mind wanders just refocus on the question, what is my heart holding, and what does it wish to share with me at this moment? Keep breathing regularly let the images and feeling just float into your attention, and if things get intense, bring your attention back to your breath. Know that you can watch your experiences like a movie or participate in them. Just gather any information about your heart you can. (Long Pause). Now I want you to take a few deep breaths and this time I want you to see your heart of ten years ago, twenty years ago and so on moving back in ten year intervals. Explore what your heart was experiencing and feeling at different times in your life. Ask and receive any messages and see if there are any old patterns of holding, old beliefs or emotions that need to be understood or released. Ask your inner self and heart if any healing needs to occur. Just listen to your heart and communicate with your heart.

Lynn Shares Her Experience

The night of the class I remember noticing my heart jumping and beating wildly as I walked up your steps and into your house. It went ba boom ba boom ba boom very loudly. I thought, what is this? As I asked that question, I sensed I was going to be touching the illusive fear I had been feeling for years and learn more about it. As I sat down I felt a deep calm radiating from you. I experienced again your comfort and ease with deep emotions and fearful experiences that I had felt during our review and this made me feel safe and I was able to relax a bit.

As you led the exercise that night I swept through the ages of my heart very quickly and almost immediately felt the cold of a stone under my back. It was the most eerie feeling; I felt myself literally lying on a stone slab, but I knew with one part of my mind that I was sitting on your couch. The sensation of the stone, though, was overwhelming. I felt the coldness of it on my back and I was no longer in class.

I looked up and saw a canopy of trees above me. I knew I was in the rainforest somewhere in South America. Simultaneously, voices outside of me, from what seemed like the ethereal plane, told me I was a gift to the gods and that this was a great honor. I realized that I was nearly thirteen years old and very close to beginning menses. All of this happened in a flash. Knowing was instantaneous. I felt the cold of the stone underneath my body again and I knew I was awaiting sacrifice. I realized this ritual had to be performed before I started menstruating. Suddenly I knew I would never grow up, have a lover or a family. I felt I was being cut off at the brink of really understanding things. I felt I was being completely silenced and anger flared in me. I did not feel any of this was an honor. All around me I saw the faces of my people, people I had known all my life and I was very afraid.

I was experiencing this lifetime so clearly that I opened my eyes to reassure myself that I really wasn't there, but I couldn't see your living room, the other students or you. All I could see was the faces of my people standing around my body in a circle. Your tranquility was still a tactile experience for me, though. If it weren't for your calming presence, openness and acceptance, I don't think I could have gone through what happened next.

Suddenly I felt a knife being plunged into my chest with great force. It tore through me. It was so extreme, even now, I can feel the knife being driven into my chest through my sternum. Next my ribs were separated and my chest opened. My heart lay exposed to the heavens. The physical sensations at this point were very difficult. It felt like a heart attack and even now when I hear people talk about open-heart surgery or see it on TV I know and completely understand each sensation.

During this I kept thinking this couldn't be happening. I remember seeing a silver bracelet on the man's arm who was holding the knife and as I looked into his face I knew that vacant expression. It was the same look that my boyfriend gets.

I had such a strong feeling that I would be saved, that somehow this man couldn't possibly do this. It was all kind of unreal, not the feelings, or the memory—

they were very real—but I kept thinking that someone was going to stop this. As it was happening I thought, they're not going to do this—not to me. This won't happen to me. I'm too special (she laughs). They've told me since birth I am special, they won't—they can't—let this happen. Something's going to change, something or someone is going to intervene—even if it isn't him. I really thought divine grace or something would stop this but that didn't happen, not at all.

I was afraid to admit at the time that the man holding the knife and offering my heart to the gods was somehow my current boyfriend. It was hard to comprehend that they were one and the same but I felt sure this was true. Dan wears the same type of wide bracelet and the expression was all too familiar. Dan has this knack of no expression. It's a very peaceful kind of blankness and that's what I saw. That's how I knew it was him. I despised that face—there's just nothing there, no awareness, and no recognition, just blankness.

At the time I thought, oh no! No, (she groans) don't let it be him (she laughs now), not the man I adore, not the man I live with. But it was definitely him. There was that look on his face, as he cut my heart out of my chest and raised it over his head. He murmured a blessing or some kind of chant and bit into my heart. All was lost as he passed my heart around to the tribe.

Since I was a child I've always asked the question, why do I hold myself back? I know the answer to this question now, because a voice inside me said, 'Why, shoot! They might rip your heart out for it.' At that moment, I understood why I was afraid to connect, touch, write, and speak my truth.

It was only when I lifted out of my body that the experience stopped being physical. I started hearing the voices again telling me stories and my chest stopped hurting. I was fine then. I remember I kept rising higher and higher until I saw an aerial view of the rain forest and I thought, "this is the grace" as I spiraled up and out of the forest.

I used to get goose bumps as I remembered this, which is funny because for months I felt quite a chill when I remembered the cold slab underneath my body. I don't get goose bumps any more; I don't feel the chill or the irregular heartbeat. It's as quiet as can be now.

Changes and Healing Effects from the Experience

I immediately felt a change in my heart. I experienced the biggest exhale I have ever felt in my life. I totally relaxed. I'll never forget it. It was like a wind blew through me and at that point, my heart slowed down instantly. For the first time, I could feel a root grow from my heart, from the very center of my chest into the earth. I felt so connected.

The first two weeks after my experience in class my symptoms became almost constant. I thought what have I done? What have I opened up? I was very afraid. Fortunately I came to class and was able to work with my feelings each week. The timing was ideal for me because of the support I got during class. I would've run away screaming, (she laughs) if I didn't have your support and help. I'm sure I would have shut the experience out, would still have symptoms and I would not be with my boyfriend. (She laughs). During that first month, more of my experience filled in. I got new pieces of information, glimpses of that lifetime, and I was able to see the connections to my present with your help. As my understanding and awareness increased my symptoms lessened.

Over the next five months, my symptoms only occurred two or three times a month. I noticed my heart beating irregularly when a part of me was being asked to die in my relationship, when I was being asked to grow up and let go of my selfishness, control or ego and also when I saw that blank expression on Dan's face. I also recognized that when conflicts arose between Dan and me during those months that I was better able to communicate and negotiate when our desires were at odds, instead of acting like a spoiled child. As my fear subsided and I established a new way of being in my life, my heart became quieter and quieter and I remember reminding myself that I was fine, even the blank face didn't bother me anymore. (She laughs.)

I think I was really tested at first though. That always happens, when we decide to change, or choose a new path and grow. During that transition the new way of being is challenged. That's how we do our reality check, by being challenged. That's how we know something is true.

I was definitely tested over and over again, and every time I would think I'm all right, I'm okay now. My heart is in here (she touches her chest) it's safe. (She laughs.) I still have it, I'm older than 14, (long pause). I made it. (She laughs again.)

It's like I have been there and done that—I did that. (This is said with great conviction.) It's funny, I don't think I realized what I just said. I DIED there. I died there and I don't feel afraid, now. My heart doesn't jump any more—not a thing, Elizabeth, the symptoms are gone, and so is the fear.

Integration

I can "work from my heart" now. When I begin a massage I ground and open my awareness from my heart and I feel a grounding cord in my heart move down through all my chakras and into the earth. I had never been able to sense that before. I feel so much more connected, and I know that I'm here. To work from my heart, to stay in my heart, when I try something new and even when my boyfriend and I have differences, is what it's all about for me now. I no longer feel separate, distanced or cut off from people, afraid or needing to control everything to be safe. My heart is open now and I can be me. I can do whatever on a physical level, and my heart stays quiet.

I even think I'd like to go to South America and travel around the country and go into the rain forest. Plus, when I think about this my heart remains calm. That is so amazing to me. I no longer have the feeling that if I went to South America I would never return. Remember when I was sharing my experience in class, and I said I guess I won't be going there (to South America) anytime soon—that's not a good vacation destination for me? (She laughs.) You chuckled and said not unless you want to come away screaming, and you laughed. Your laughter just melted my fear. It was a bit disarming but so perfect. It let me relax and not take myself so seriously and it also let me know that I was here in this body and in one piece. My anxiety and all the emotional charge I was feeling just vanished.

Conclusions

Lynn learned that her past life experience was about emotional maturity and overcoming fears and her need to control. She said that in her current relationships with men she had always been taken care of and spoiled like a child. She understood why she had been comfortable with this and yet conflicted at the same time over this kind of treatment. She said that when she was in massage school she consciously recognized her anger at this inequality for the first time. Her lifetime in South America where she had been chosen, which made her feel special, and her experience of sacrifice and of being cut off from knowledge that awaited her as she entered womanhood, were keys to understanding her anger and behaviors in relationships. She felt that this was where her original conflicts had been laid out. As these memories resurfaced the patterns in her life began to make more sense to her. As the story took shape she understood how and why she responded and reacted in this lifetime and how much this former lifetime still impacted her. She understood how being taken care of related to her being chosen and singled out for sacrifice and how this was a double edged sword. She liked being cared for and the security of that but did not like the limitations. She felt that her immaturity stemmed from having been killed before reaching adulthood, and she knew her anger was associated with this death and not achieving the status of womanhood.

She realized too that this other lifetime had shaped her need to control her experiences and her world in the present. She also understood how her fears were linked to this control. Her fear of expression and feeling from her heart were suppressed in this other lifetime. Her own words, "why, shoot, they might rip my heart out for it" was the key to understanding this complex belief system. While she longed to express herself she also was afraid to do so because even if she was told that her sacrifice was an honor she never felt this to be true. Somehow she felt she was being punished, so how could she speak her truth if death loomed over her. But this she felt was the demand of spirit. She was being asked to be more authentic, and true to herself as well as more adult in her relationships. She truly understood how her fears and emotions had limited her work as a massage therapist, and how they had affected her relationships. As we worked together over the months Lynn accepted her death and knew with every fiber of her being that life was eternal. She was certain that her consciousness or spirit had moved on and her fear of dying, that she felt we all have, had shifted. She remembered how much of a relief it was to finally move into the ethereal realm after reliving her ritual sacrifice and she was no longer afraid of death.

Lynn's case reveals how complex and interwoven our lifetimes can be and how one can shape the other. The moment of death, especially when that death is traumatic, carries our emotions and beliefs from that moment forward. This created a set of problems for Lynn that included physical symptoms, problems within relationships, and a variety of emotional issues and fears, many of which remained unconscious until that night in class.

What I find most interesting and what struck me at the time was that another person other than myself could effectively change her physical symptoms by remembering an ancient past where she had been mortally wounded in the very organ that presented symptoms in this lifetime. Her experience was visual, auditory and deeply kinesthetic, like so many of my own experiences of this kind had been, and unlike other clients who watched their experience like an old movie, Lynn relived her experience in the same way I had. She, too, felt that she was reliving memories. Whether this is truly a case of survival or just a story that filled in the blanks and connected the dots in Lynn's life and mind doesn't matter. What really matters is that her very persistent and difficult symptoms were changed and that they had not recurred eight years later.

This is why I feel Transforming Embodiment may have possible applications in the field of healing and medicine. The practices of Transforming Embodiment could possibly explain many inexplicable phenomena, such as symptoms that appear out of nowhere, or symptoms that are not changed by usual treatment guidelines. Transforming Embodiment gives healers another option beyond the normal protocols used in traditional medical and psychological therapies.

Part Two: Spirit

3

SURVIVAL OF CONSCIOUSNESS AND HEALING

[Our essential oneness with the universe] is not sameness or unqualified identity, but an organic relationship, in which differentiation and uniqueness of function are as important as that ultimate or basic unity. Individuality and universality are not mutually exclusive values, but two sides of the same reality, compensating, fulfilling, and complementing each other, and becoming one in the experience of enlightenment. This experience does not dissolve the mind into an amorphous All, but rather brings the realization that the individual itself contains the totality focalized in its very core.

Lama Govinda [68]

What Survives?—The Nature of Mind and Nonlocality

There are a number of ways to view consciousness or mind. Traditionally, consciousness is seen as starting at birth and ending at death. In this view, the boundaries of the body are the boundaries of the individual. The mind, or consciousness, does not venture outside of the body except perhaps to dream. However, the view that the mind is nonlocal is taking on new significance. Physics and consciousness studies are coming closer to an understanding of consciousness and the mind.

> The recent discovery that all matter emits quanta of energy that is coherent, non-local, and carries usable information about the material object demonstrates that quantum physics pertains to all matter and not just particles. Further, these emissions can be modeled by the same mathematical formalism used in laser holography. Non-local information about the physical universe provides the missing link between objective science and subjective experience, including mystical experience.[69]

Dr. Larry Dossey, in *Recovering the Soul: A Scientific And Spiritual Search* notes that the work of the great physicists and mathematicians, including Schrödinger, Gödel, Einstein, Margenau, Bell and Bohm support the idea that the mind may be nonlocal.

My clinical and personal experiences have led me to believe that consciousness is nonlocal in nature and "capable of escaping the boundaries of the body," as noted by researcher Dr. Jennie Wade[70] and that it (consciousness) is free of the limits of time and space, as described by Dr. Paul Pearsall as well. Consciousness and mind, when trained to be open, fluid, and connected, have an innate ability to expand past the limits of our current understanding. Nonlocal principles support the idea that the mind and consciousness may be able to reach far beyond the confines of the brain and body to be everywhere in time at the same time, as well as being able to connect and merge with the universe around us. As we dip into this universal stream of consciousness that is nonlocal, we may find the ancient histories of our individual selves and an interconnection that exists between all inhabitants on this planet we call home.

Dossey writes that nonlocal experiences also carry a sense of wholeness or unity with them. Many of my own explorations and adventures in consciousness may be explained within the framework of nonlocality. The interconnectedness that I felt is not uncommon when the mind and heart are open and free of judgment and expectations. Clients repeatedly describe a sense of interconnectedness after working within the fluidity of time and space. Dossey continues about the nonlocal nature of mind saying,

> For if the mind is nonlocal, it must in some sense be independent of the strictly local brain and body. And if the mind is nonlocal, unconfined to the brains and bodies and thus not entirely dependent on the physical organism, the possibility for the survival of bodily death is opened. If the mind is nonlocal in space and time, our interaction with each other seems a foregone conclusion. Nonlocal minds are *merging* minds, since they are not 'things' that can be walled off and confined to moments in time or point positions in space.[71]

I propose that if the mind is nonlocal then consciousness as an aspect of mind has the potential of continuing beyond death. "Since energy and the information it carries cannot be destroyed; where does the information (energy) go after the destruction of the molecules and neuropeptides (mass) that contained it are destroyed."[72] This is a marvelous question. I believe one possible answer is that the information is stored within the subtle mind, or consciousness. Since consciousness and the energy it bears cannot be destroyed, then it must continue to exist. Further, I submit that when consciousness continues beyond death, it impacts us on all levels when the energy reemerges.

I have seen this again and again in myself and clients who have recovered traumatic memories from other lives and times. Our memories continue because of their intensity and often unresolved nature, and the images and stories that accompany them, manifest at spiritual, psychological, emotional and physical levels, depending on their nature. These energy patterns will re-embody within consciousness again and again in varying forms until the imprinted trauma, intense emotions or memories are released from our cells and the psychic layers of our consciousness and soma. These memories can be the foundations underlying emotional pain, physical symptoms, relationship, and psychological conflicts that we are challenged by. This may sound like science fiction but it is not. It is just taking us to the next step beyond the Descartian paradigm, the mechanistic, linear and hierarchical ways of viewing the world and universe we live in.

The richness of our experience is not bound to the body or the mind from the vantage point of nonlocality. Mind and consciousness interact with other minds and our consciousness is far more fluid and free flowing than we ever thought possible. The impact this concept imparts is monumental.

Universal Mind and Timelessness

Dossey asks the question, "What would Universal Mind 'look' like?" and cites professor Henry Margenau.[73] Margenau explains, "Its knowledge comprises not only the entire present but all past events as well. Much as our thought can survey and come to know all space the Universal Mind can travel back and forth in time at will."[74] This definition of Universal Mind is what the energies of the channel have defined as Source. Source is described as the beginning point where all experience arises from, and the body of experience, which I described earlier, may be an aspect of Universal Mind.

In the practices of Transforming Embodiment we experience a distinct sense of timelessness. Time appears to be fluid, not a constant linear phenomenon. Nonlocality may account for why the ability to access time and other lives becomes available during this process. In Transforming Embodiment, all time becomes contained in the present moment and within the spaciousness of the moment. As we slow down our thinking, time becomes limitless and space boundless. Both time and space are accessible within and from the present moment. All of life's experience arises out of the moment, which includes all time and all space. This spaciousness and timelessness that my clients and I have encountered may be the expression of Universal Mind and nonlocality. In nonlocal reality "...all of space begins to appear as a seamless garment, totally unitary, and...all of time appears undivided into past, present, and future."[75] The reality of Transforming Embodiment is a nonlocal one, since the divisions between past and present selves and experiences are undivided and seamless.

Chapter Three

Nonlocality and nonlocal ways of thinking, perceiving and experiencing are very different from local ways of viewing reality. Within nonlocality we are no longer contained or limited to only our physical and tangible body. From this expansive perception a natural interconnectedness arises. "Nonlocal reality's most prominent feature is a central unity to all things and events. In addition, time is seen in a nonordinary way. Past, present and future are illusions we project and are not fundamental."[76]

"Nonlocal influences also act instantaneously."[77] Nonlocality might explain how psychics and intuitives like myself are able to communicate with people in other cities and countries or even with the dead. Nonlocality may also explain how contact with other higher consciousnesses can occur. With intention, a quiet mind, and an open and expanded sense of consciousness, minds even at great distances can be contacted. This contact can occur in the blink of an eye, or in a single breath. An example of this might be when a mother "knows" that something has happened to her child or when a spouse "feels" that their partner is in trouble. These gut feelings or hunches may be examples of nonlocality at work in our daily lives. In this way, nonlocality could explain how information can be gained in paranormal ways.

Dossey cites physicist John Hagelin, a leader in unified field theory,

> [Hagelin] suggests that the experience of pure consciousness—the 'unbounded infinite expansion' that persons frequently describe—is actually a direct experience of the unified field.[44] In this state the qualities of wholeness, completeness, and unity of the unified field are directly apprehended by the psyche, and the sense of timelessness and infinity leaps into conscious awareness.[78]

In Buddhist thought, the mind is considered nonlocal. This understanding comes from centuries of meditation masters' insights and direct experience into the essential nature of mind. Sogyal Rinpoche, author of *The Tibetan Book of Living and Dying*, says, "Mind is revealed as the universal basis of experience—the creator of happiness and the creator of suffering, the creator of what we call life and what we call death."[79]

In Buddhism there are two aspects of mind that stand out, *Sem* and *Rigpa*. "Sem [ordinary mind] is the discursive, dualistic, thinking mind, which can only function in relation to a projected and falsely perceived external reference point."[80] This is the mind we know each day, the one that thinks, projects, feels, manipulates, experiences all emotional states and pulls us forever onward, with its continual chattering or planning.

> Then there is the very nature of mind, its innermost essence, which is absolutely and always untouched by change or death. It is hidden within our own mind, our sem, enveloped and obscured by the mental scurry of our thoughts and emotions. Just as clouds can be shifted by a strong gust of wind to reveal the shining sun and wide-open sky, so, under certain circumstances, some inspiration may uncover for us glimpses of this nature of mind.[81]

This hidden aspect is called Rigpa and Rinpoche describes it as "a primordial, pure, pristine awareness that is at once intelligent, cognizant, radiant, and always awake. It could be said to be the knowledge of knowledge itself."[82]

Dossey's term Universal Mind is likely to be Rigpa. Sogyal Rinpoche writes that "Saints and mystics throughout history have adorned their realizations with different names and given different faces and interpretations, but what they are all fundamentally experiencing is the essential nature of the mind."[83] Whether the name is God, Shiva, Allah, or Buddha nature, these are all fundamental experiences of the essential nature of mind.

The essential nature of mind or Buddha nature exists in all of us. It remains unseen because the ordinary mind occupies us so thoroughly. Sogyal Rinpoche explains, "For even though we have the same inner nature as Buddha, we have not recognized it because it is so enclosed and wrapped up in our individual ordinary minds."[84]

With our minds thus enraptured by the confines of our individual identity we may miss not only the mind's true nature—but the mind's nonlocal possibilities as well. Nonlocality may be difficult to grasp because, if the constraints of thinking locally are dissolved, the ego is then at risk and will defend itself to solidify its sense of identity. So while science may be finding hypotheses and theorems that suggest the mind is nonlocal, the ego may be fearful of accepting this as possible, because a drastic reordering of how we think of our world and ourselves would have to occur.

Nonlocality gives us a means for interpreting a wide range of transpersonal, intuitive, and parapsychological events and abilities. It also may explain how transplanted organs from donors to recipients may carry the memories and affinities from one personality to the next. From here it is not such a giant leap to conceive that consciousness can survive bodily death. We might ask: What is it that animates our memories and carries them forth from donor to recipient as Dr. Paul Pearsall describes, or possibly from one incarnation to the next as Dr. Ian Stevenson's meticulous work of twenty five years shows? How much broader and more sweeping is consciousness? Perhaps it is Rigpa or Universal Mind that is the key and nonlocality is the doorway.

Current Survival of Consciousness Models

There are a number of ways in which survival of consciousness is viewed. In Christianity the soul survives. This view is fairly materialistic and there is a lack of a story for the transition from life to death. The story is more concerned with a hereafter that is known as heaven or hell, and the soul survives in some ambiguous way to later be resurrected. In this view there is no belief in rebirth other than through resurrection.

In Buddhism there is the belief in rebirth and the *bardo,* which one traverses from death to the moment of rebirth. There is an enormous amount of information about what one might perceive within the bardo state. Our emotions and mental tendencies of attraction and revulsion all appear to be heightened within the bardo and drive our consciousness forward. This process is one that is evolutionary rather than materialistic. Consciousness survives as a mind stream that carries the tendencies and karma of the individual forward. In reincarnation, as seen in India, there is a complete survival of the personality after death. In essence there is a belief that the soul survives intact to be reborn again based on the karma from the previous lifetime.

In Christian Science there is the belief that the soul pervades all of life. This soul crosses a threshold at death and enters into another dimensional reality. This idea of crossing into another reality is also found in China, where they believe that the dead live in a parallel reality that is much like our own.

In shamanic traditions there is a basic belief that there are many levels and dimensions of reality. Within this view the duality or dichotomy of life and death is an artificial one. Shamans travel between these dimensions with ease since they understand the flexibility that exists between the worlds. The Hawai'ian shamans I worked with shared that the kahuna[85] tradition believes in reincarnation and rebirth. Time is perceived as occurring all at once and so the ability to travel within time is an ability shamans possess. The ability to travel between dimensions like the shamans of other traditions is a given.

A recent Gallop poll found that 67% of the people they polled believed in reincarnation or the survival of consciousness in some form. These individuals believed that after death some sort of journey into another phase of reality takes place and that a disembodied aspect of self, as well as the physical self in some cases, makes this journey.[86]

So, how can we know that rebirth takes place? What does research and experience tell us? Research and anecdotal evidence suggest that there may be several ways of knowing that the survival of consciousness occurs. The prediction of the rebirth of tulkus and the Dalai Lama, as announced in dream to elders within the spiritual community is one such way. This has gone on for centuries within Tibet. Other evidence may include birth marks and defects; spontaneous memories from children about previous lives; recognition of people from a previous lifetime; the display of traits of the previous personality; and in the cases of violent death, birth marks on the areas of fatal wounds. Some of these phenomena have existed for centuries, while others have been extensively researched for over twenty-five years. Dr. Ian Stevenson from the University of Virginia is one such researcher and probably the most well known within the psychological and scientific communities.

Chapter Three

Evidence to Support the Survival of Consciousness

Dr. Ian Stevenson in his research of children who remember past lives (1974) has documented many cases where birthmarks appear on the body in the locations where the previous person was fatally wounded. He describes how a mother marked the body of her dead child with suet around its ankle. Later when she gave birth to a new baby a scar was on the infant's ankle in the exact location of the suet marking.

Another case that is even more compelling comes out of Nigeria. Body marking of dead children is practiced in Nigeria so spirits won't come into a child's body. In this case, a father who had lost many children took the following precautions. He cut off the fingers and toes of his newly dead child and bound his legs together. The father then put the body parts in a bag and hung them by the door, to scare away any spirits. He later remarried and had three healthy children with his new wife over an eleven-year period. Many years later not knowing the meaning of the bag or its story, his new wife threw the bag out during a remodeling project. The next year they had a new baby, who was born without fingers and toes and had a scar where the legs of the dead child's limbs had been bound together.

Dr. Stevenson's studies are meticulously documented. His cases come from many continents, and he has followed some children for many years. During his research he has taken children to villages where they claim they have lived before. These villages are often far away from a child's current home, making it unlikely that the child had been there, but upon returning to these past life homes the children recognize people, places, and can describe the events of their deaths in many cases. Dr. Stevenson has medical documentation for at least sixty-two of his cases that support reincarnation. His studies, more than any others, support with strong evidence that consciousness may survive bodily death.

Tibetan culture firmly believes in rebirth. When tulkus or high lamas die they will often give instructions of where they will be found when they take a new birth. Footsteps may be imprinted in the ashes of a tulku that point in the direction of where the teacher may be reborn. Divination and clairvoyant powers may also be employed to find these remarkable teachers.

When searching for the previous incarnations of great teachers, like His Holiness the Dalai Lama, high lamas and monks use objects from the teacher's previous lifetime to test a child suspected of being a tulku [87] or reincarnated teacher. Prayer beads, eyeglasses, personal items and ritual objects used by the previous incarnation are set out with other similar objects and these remarkable children are asked to pick out what items were theirs in their past lifetime.[88]

The current Dalai Lama is the fourteenth incarnation of Chenrézig, the Tibetan deity of compassion. He is a living Buddha, who out of compassion returns to this world, again and again, with the conscious intent to relieve whatever suffering he finds and to share the wisdom and compassion of his boundless heart until all sentient beings are enlightened. Tulkus too, like the Dalai Lama, forego abiding in the heaven realms until all sentient being are enlightened. The Dalai Lama is quoted in *My Land and My People* as saying,

> Buddhas are reincarnated solely to help others, since they themselves have already achieved the highest of all levels...All such incarnate beings, as I already indicated can influence by their own wishes in each life the place and time when they will be reborn and after each birth they have a lingering memory of their previous life which enables others to identify them.[89]

I was very fortunate to have been in the presence of a child tulku, the reincarnation of Kalu Rinpoche. It was remarkable to see this child of four officiate over a long blessing ceremony and participate in an equally long spiritual empowerment and teaching. He sat still in a way children rarely do, and while he took great joy in the rubber tiger puppet I offered him, at the end of the blessing ceremony, he also seemed remarkably different from other children his age. There was a distinct presence within this child, whose demeanor far exceeded his years. It did not seem far-fetched that this youngster could be the elder Kalu Rinpoche reborn.

Vicki Mackenzie in her book *The Boy Lama*, shares the unique stories of many of Lama Yeshe's students, who encountered surprisingly similar behaviors and intimate knowledge that only Lama Yeshe

Chapter Three

could have known when they met the young tulku Lama Osel. These personal proofs are remarkable.

One former student, Suzanna, remembered the following: she had just heard that Lama was very ill and leaving for California. Distraught, she dropped everything at home in Italy and boarded a plane for Delhi. At the Delhi airport she met Lama Yeshe as he was making his way to his plane. He was being assisted by two of his students who were helping him walk. When she saw this she burst into tears. Lama was thin and weak but upon seeing her he smiled and took his arms off the shoulders that held him up and raised his arms over his head and "swung them back and forth, clicking his fingers as if doing a dance. 'Don't worry my daughter, I am all right,' he said."[90] This was the last time she would ever see Lama. When she heard that Lama Yeshe's reincarnation had been found and announced, she wasted no time and went to Holland to see Lama Osel, who was visiting a center with his mother. He was 17 months old.

When Suzanna met him, Osel took no notice of her, no recognition or hint of the close bond they had shared over the years. Disappointed, she said to a nearby monk, " 'Well, I guess I have been a bad student.' "[91] The monk proceeded to turn to Osel and said,

> You remember Suzanna, don't you?' Osel stood up, put his baby arms in the air and swung them back and forth and tried to click his fingers, as though dancing. No one present, except possibly Osel himself, could understand why such a simple gesture should make Suzanna once again burst into tears. This was all the proof she needed. Lama Yeshe had kept his word. He had not forsaken her.[92]

Other stories include how a skeptical monk and scholar devised his own test, as a way of obtaining personal proof that Lama Osel was truly Lama Yeshe reborn. He took a pair of Lama Yeshe's sunglasses and put them on a table with four or five other pairs. When Osel came into the room, he went over and played with the sunglasses a bit, and then took up the pair that formerly had belonged to Lama Yeshe and tapped this monk on the head with them, as if to drum the proof into him. Another story is of a Californian nun, who had done a three-year retreat under Lama Yeshe's supervision and was given the practice of Vajrayogini by Lama as a special meditation practice to use during her retreat. She too met Lama Osel in Holland and one day while baby-sitting Osel, he picked one of three deity cards off her bed, which she had just bought, and thrust it very firmly, face down, onto her heart. When this nun looked at the picture it was Vajrayogini. "It was such a specific thing to do—so direct. Osel knew what he was doing. It certainly convinced me! This was Lama giving me my deity again, she said."[93]

These stories demonstrate how Lama Osel, who as early as 17 months, was able to "remember" intimate moments with his former students from his former life.

Lama Zopa Rinpoche, Lama Yeshe's former heart disciple, has also noticed many similarities between Lama Osel and his former teacher Lama Yeshe. Mannerisms, and traits such as compassion and equanimity, have persisted. Lama Osel also displayed knowledge of spiritual practices at just two years old. When he went to India he wanted to bless people and did this spontaneously. "In my view Osel's behavior is rare, even among other incarnate lamas of his age he [Lama Zopa] said."[94] Lama Osel also recognizes places where Lama Yeshe stayed. When asked by Vicki Mackenzie if Lama Yeshe and Lama Osel were one and the same person,

> Lama Zopa closed his eyes and thought. Eventually he looked at me kindly and gave me his explanation: The beautiful rose plant that we see today is but a continuation of yesterday's plant. Similarly, Lama Osel's holy mind is a continuation of Lama Yeshe's holy mind. You see, the consciousness associated with the particular body which was named by the Abbott in Tibet, Lama Yeshe—that same mental continuum associated with a western body born in Spain now bears the merely imputed label, Osel. It is the same continuity. For the West to understand reincarnation it is necessary to begin to understand mind.[95]

Chapter Three

When Vicki Mackenzie asked Lama Osel in the relaxed atmosphere of his home in Kopan " 'Are you Lama Yeshe?'; Osel: 'No, I am Tenzin Osel.' Then he paused for some long seconds, thinking, formulating words. 'Before I am Lama Yeshe now Tenzin Osel, one monk.' "[96] He was only about three at the time of this conversation.

> The distinction between Lama Yeshe and Lama Osel is important. Osel is not Lama Yeshe—we will never see, hear, touch the figure who was Lama Yeshe, but we do have Lama Osel, who is the continuation of the mind of Lama Yeshe but with his own persona.[97]

There are more stories and I am sure that new ones have surfaced as this boy has grown. These stories and the remarkable abilities of these tulkus may be the clearest evidence we may find that the mind stream does continue and that reincarnation and rebirth do occur. These stories and the evidence collected by Ian Stevenson may well hold the keys. These new children being born within the last two decades, Lama Osel, Serkong Rinpoche, Ling Rinpoche, Trijang Rinpoche, Serkong Dorje Chang, Song Rinpoche and the reincarnations of His Holiness the Karmapa, Kalu Rinpoche, and Dilgo Khyentse Rinpoche may help us unravel this mystery. Tulkus who have returned in western bodies like Lama Osel, Tenzin Sherab, and Trinley Tulku may help translate their experiences as well as the dharma, so that the Western mind can comprehend and remember that Mind is a continuous stream that flows from beginningless time, indestructible.

Working with the Dead

Jessie became a client of mine after a difficult break up. The first year we worked together, we resolved many painful layers about intimate relationships as well as a series of traumatic memories from her childhood. As our work together seemed to be coming to a close, her mother suddenly died. For the next ten months we processed the grief and deep loss of Jessie's most cherished friend and confidant, her mother. Relationship issues and depression continued to surface during this time.

Then one day in April, Jessie mentioned that her right hand had been progressively getting numb. She described how the numbness had begun in her baby finger and spread to her ring finger then, half way up her middle finger. She noted that as time passed the numbness worsened, eventually including the palm of her hand and her wrist.

I asked if she would like to work somatically to investigate this numbness. Jessie agreed that it would be good to do this. I asked her to take a few deep breaths and relax, letting go of any cares or concerns from her day. As her breath became even and slow, I asked her to create a connection between herself and the earth to stabilize and ground her which she did with ease because she was familiar with the technique.

When she was ready, I asked her to merge with her right hand, to become her hand, and focus her consciousness and attention solely on it, to let her consciousness flow into her hand and to be it. As she did this she told me calmly that she saw her mother's hand. She said it was covering her own, as if her hand were being held or grasped. We sat with this a moment and Jessie let the emotions of this realization sink in. Hearing from Jessie's spirit that it would be appropriate to release this image, I asked her if she could remove her mother's hand from her own. Jessie proceeded to gently pry her mother's fingers and palm from her own hand. Deep sadness welled up, and Jessie began to sob. She felt herself letting go of her mother yet again and somehow she felt her mother was letting go too. As Jessie released the emotions and imagery, she began to regain the sensation in her hand and little finger for the first time in months. She asked for a large paper clip that was sitting on my desk. Puzzled, I gave it to her. She tried to open it and to her surprise she did it with ease. Jessie explained that she had been unable to do this simple task for months using her right hand.

To complete the process, I had Jessie shift her attention to her right arm and invited her to notice the quality of the energy as she followed her arm up to the shoulder and base of her skull. Nothing stood out, so I directed Jessie to scan[98] her skeletal system on her right side. Upon surveying there, she felt a keen sense of fear in her right hip and knee. Some of this she said was her mom's fear, while another part of the remaining fear was from the doctor who had cared for Jessie's mom during her last days. Jessie then removed the fear from her knee and hip, imagining it like smoke as it left her body.

Chapter Three

I noticed that Jessie was wearing a watch and a bracelet on her right hand. I asked about them. She said that they were her mother's things and that she had begun wearing them the day her mother was rushed to the hospital. The nurse had given them to her and she had "just put them on." I mentioned that it might be helpful to take these off since they were her mother's. She said she would think about it.

The next week Jessie came in and told me that she had been reluctant to take her mom's jewelry off, but when she noticed the numbness returning she did exchange them for her own watch and a bracelet similar to her mother's. She said that she felt immediate relief when she took off her mom's jewelry and began wearing her own. She heard her mom say, "Let go of the attachment, you need to let go of my stuff. It's not me." As she did this the numbness melted away. Jessie's consciousness, which had been frozen in some way since her mom's death, was finally liberated. The need for her mother's things dissolved, and for the first time memories flooded in, and as she remembered the qualities that her mother possessed, such as deep caring, and tolerance, she saw them in herself.

Jessie said she had equated keeping the watch with keeping her mom with her. She had initially put the watch on, in part because the battery in her watch had gone dead at the same time as her mom's stroke. She saw this as a metaphor for her life: she had been dead too, like her watch's battery, when her mother died, her world had stopped, just like her watch. She exclaimed that she was back on her own time for the first time since her mother's death, and she felt she could re-enter her own life now as well.

4

REINCARNATION AND REBIRTH: A BUDDHIST VIEW

> The reincarnation doctrine is not a matter of belief
> but a serious effort to conceptualize very concrete
> and specific experiences and observations related to
> past lives.
>
> Stanislav Grof[99]

Reincarnation and rebirth have been major tenets of Eastern religious systems and a part of certain Western spiritual traditions for over two thousand years.[100] This long spiritual tradition and history describes both the operation and beliefs regarding these concepts. Each concept has a distinct meaning. Generally speaking, the idea of reincarnation is widely held by Hindus, while rebirth is the preferred term used by Buddhists.

In reincarnation it is generally believed that when we die, our soul continues. As we take on a new physical form, the previous personality continues to grow or decline in that new body. Reincarnation believes in an eternal soul. Events from previous incarnations affect the new personality and create the kind of life the person will experience in the new life.

Rebirth in contrast, believes that a permanent entity or soul does not persist. What links one lifetime to the next is the mindstream. This aspect in the case of an ordinary person is propelled forward through successive lifetimes by karma and mental afflictions such as anger, greed, and ignorance. The mindstream operates in the same kind of way as our consciousness does when it continues from waking to sleeping. Dr. Ian Stevenson, author and researcher, explains rebirth:

> There is a constant flux of desire, action, effect and reaction, but no persisting soul...this newly born personality will relate to the first one only as a flame of a candle (before it finally extinguishes) can light another candle's flame.[101]

However Professor Robert Thurman Tibetan scholar and chair of Indo-Tibetan Buddhist studies at Columbia University shares a third view:

> Rebirth is involuntary. It's what happens to all beings who are reborn on the cycle of life—be they humans, animals, hell-realm beings or gods. In rebirth there's no choice. People are born in these states on impulse as part of a reactive cycle of action and its effects. Reincarnation, on the other hand, is when a being, usually a human being, develops free will in that cycle by being in control of their voluntary actions and impulses. They are therefore able to remain conscious through the transition from death to birth, and can choose the precise circumstances of their rebirth. In Mahayana Buddhism that attainment is simultaneous with Buddhahood. Strictly speaking, no one less than a Buddha can reincarnate. There are beings, however, who have a strong wish to reincarnate to perform certain tasks, and that intention might push them through their impulses, but it's not totally conscious and not infallible.[102]

Chapter Four

Again Dr. Thurman shares a different view, with Vicki Mackenzie, author of *Reborn in the West*, one that, when I first read it, made perfect sense even through it seemed to stand in opposition to what I had come to view as rebirth. He says:

> What goes from life to life is the most subtle level of the self. It's called the indestructible drop in tantra, and is also described as the extremely subtle body and mind. You can actually call it soul. Now Buddhists stupidly run around saying there is no soul and there is no self, which is a ridiculous statement. The Buddha's famous doctrine of selfishness had to do with the metaphysical status of the essence of the person. His whole point was that there is no fixed, rigid self—no absolutely unchanging, independent, sovereign self with your name and serial number engraved on it, which never changes and which is plopped from one existence to the next. What the Buddha constantly maintained, however, was that there is a relative, constantly living and constantly changing self. He said a person who controls the self is the one who is the master. 'Use yourself to conquer yourself ' he said. So for the Buddhist the soul is the most subtle level of that self. It is the extremely subtle body and mind that exists in the center of the heart chakra like a tiny drop. At conception the heart chakra (situated at a midpoint between the breasts) forms around it. And then at death it unravels as it leaves the body. In itself it is like a constantly self-renovating cell—it is like DNA.[103] You see, the impressions are encoded in it just like DNA chains. It's a very complicated thing, like on a subatomic level. Normally a person has no awareness of it, yet it is what constitutes a person's awareness, finally. And the key is, it's a continuum. This indestructible drop has encoded in it a tremendous amount of specific individual information, which is constantly changing. It 's being influenced by your experiences of this life.

> And it's what takes the code of whatever you have developed and learnt in this life into the next…Although one thing you have to remember is that this is like sub-subconscious. It is below even the subconscious.[104]

Very simply, what appears to continue are the countless impressions, characteristics of thoughts and behaviors from a person's previous incarnations. These characteristics create certain tendencies for experiencing the current lifetime, and they are like imprints that cause a person to revisit certain likes and dislikes when encountering different phenomena. These encoded imprints or patterns are what I call embodied memories that can be found within our body, mind, heart, chakras, organs, cells, and consciousness. Buddhist teachers and scholars like Dr. Thurman would appear to agree that something indestructible carries on encoded in the fiber of our consciousness.

> Past actions motivated by attachment, anger, and ignorance have left imprints of these on the mental continuum. These imprints cause attachment, anger or ignorance to arise again when we meet the various desirable, undesirable or neutral objects. These imprints are present because they have not been illuminated.[105]

These imprints continue within the mindstream until the patterns they represent are brought into conscious awareness, and they persist and recreate various emotional states when like scenarios in current lifetimes are encountered. Buddhism and Hinduism also acknowledge "that the conduct of one personality can affect the behavior, physical organism and life events of another later personality that is related to the first one through the process of rebirth."[106] This concept that the conduct of one personality can affect another may be the basis for understanding karma.

> For example, a big act of generosity, a big sacrifice, or the overcoming of a rage where you forgive someone instead, those sort of big shifts of the mind register as a kind of DNA increment of generosity.

> On the other hand, if you become incredibly greedy or murdered someone that would make a big DNA increment of avarice or viciousness. These deeper, more powerful deeds or thoughts would register something that would really have an impact in another life. In fact everything registers somehow, but it's like a tiny little side-chain in the molecule combinations, if we're using the DNA analogy. It doesn't mean that every little impression makes a big change. But the indestructible drop is very sensitive and picks up everything. That's what guarantees, in the Buddhist world view, the idea that every little thing will build into something. A tiny bit of generosity will build into a good fruit, or a tiny bit of morality, or meditative insight. Whatever it is, will build.[107]

In Buddhism, it is also believed that the last thoughts we have at death are the ones most strongly carried forward. If we die and are in an angry state this affects our mind and this mind state continues into the bardo and into the next life. If the death has been traumatic, fears and phobias can also be carried forward. This is why Tibetan Buddhists place so much value on a peaceful and fully conscious mind-state at the moment of death. Tibetan monk and teacher, Bokar Rinpoche elaborates:

> Because the state of mind of the dying person is very intense, the attitude of the person colors the mind. This has some consequences in the phases of bardos, and in future lives too. If, at the last moment, the dying person is in a state of tremendous anger and resentment, the impact of these emotions will be carried into the bardos. This could have very unhealthy effects in the course of the experience.[108]

The word bardo loosely describes the time between death and rebirth. The bardo state is like a dream, and it is created by our inner mental energy. Our mental energy, for instance, creates a sense of having a body, and in the bardo, as in a dream, we can become anything, a dragonfly, a tiger, or a person of the opposite sex. The unfocused mind will jump from one image to the next creating great instability, just like in a dream when our mind jumps from one story or image to another. This is why in Buddhist practice we endeavor to stabilize the mind and the unconscious, so that when we are in the bardo we have the possibility of directing our rebirth. Dr. Robert Thurman says,

> They say that when you're in the extremely subtle body / mind state of the between [the bardo] it's like being in a dream where your embodiment, because it is only created by imagery is very unstable. So if you have these unconscious images that helplessly emerge where you might suddenly like the idea of being say, a tarantula, you're in danger...The transition is so vulnerable, you see when you don't have control of your unconscious. That's why Buddhists spend so much energy in their life trying to influence this gene [the mindstream].[109]

A dying person's intense emotions are not only carried into the bardo but into the next incarnation as well. These imprints can cause us to have phobias, fears, and tendencies towards certain diseases or illnesses and cause us to gravitate towards certain types of relationships and life dramas. This may be especially true when death is sudden or traumatic. Buddhism understands that "even though the physical body disintegrates in the process of death, the continuity of the mind is not destroyed."[110]

Here is where the great debate about consciousness, the brain, and the mind begins. What is it that survives? According to Buddhist teacher and nun, Thubten Chodron, mind is described as having two aspects: gross and subtle. The gross mind is what ceases at death and the subtle mind absorbs this aspect into itself. It is the subtle mind that "bears with it the imprints of actions we have done (karma)."[111],[112] To continue, it is the subtle mind that leaves the body after death and moves into the bardo or intermediate state between death and rebirth before taking another rebirth and body The subtle mind is not considered to be a soul or self or real personality because it is not a "solid independent findable thing that can be isolated in a person."[113] The subtle mind is a stream of awareness that continues within consciousness not as a personality but as an array of impressions, inclinations, and patterns. Dr. Thurman describes this subtle mind as the indestructible drop.

The death and bardo process are elegantly outlined and described in the Tibetan Book of the Dead. As our consciousness withdraws, one by one the elements of our physical form are absorbed; as this happens, consciousness becomes finer, more subtle, and lucid as the gross conceptual mind recedes. Then the subtlest consciousness that rests in the area of the heart chakra is set free and revealed. It is said that in that moment the most important and powerful 'information' we hold comes forward to fashion our next incarnation.

> During the death process, the body loses its ability to support human consciousness. The various sensory faculties, emotions and thoughts retract into a latent state, a more simple, unmodified state of awareness emerges…At death, the stream of awareness that departs from the body is no longer human, though it does carry a vast array of latent impressions from the just ended life as well as earlier lives. These impressions are responsible for the type of experiences one undergoes during the intermediate period following death and prior to the next life.[114]

According to Wallace, after this interval has elapsed, if a person is incarnating as human again, the stream of consciousness joins with that of one's parents as conception takes place, and, as the fetus, develops these "latent impressions of human emotions, thinking and so on are activated."[115]

The Mindstream Continues
What I have observed clinically and experienced myself is that consciousness does continue beyond death, with all of its latent possibilities, problems and potentials intact. Emotional, physical, and behavioral patterns and symptoms resurface as our consciousness moves from one incarnation to the next. Old thought forms, emotions,

reactions, and circumstances experienced throughout the previous lifetime and at death actually affect our future lifetimes. Wallace writes that this continued consciousness [or mindstream] "carries innumerable impressions from an individual's past experiences, as well as personal characteristics and behavior patterns."[116]

These patterns have the potential to surface again and again if they remain unconscious. A person may repeat these patterns of experience until they are resolved and integrated. Marcus Daniels, writer, memory and trauma therapist notes, "The only reason the past can repeat itself is because there is a part of its experience that has not been fully felt–without reaction or judgment."[117] In Transforming Embodiment, as in Daniels therapeutic work this is true. Clinically there appears to be a need to remember and relive experiences fully with equanimity, in order to release and resolve our symptoms and difficulties.

I believe what clients experience in the remembering phase of Transforming Embodiment, are the imprints from other lifetimes upon their consciousness. Chodron says that these imprints are "the residual energy left on the mindstream when an action has been completed."[118] These imprints later ripen and influence our experience. Furthermore, it is understood that what we are experiencing now is a result of thoughts, feelings, words and deeds from previous lifetimes as well as from this lifetime.

These concepts have been borne out in my therapeutic work with clients, and students who have brought in emotional and physical symptoms rooted in previous incarnational experiences. I believe that imprinted information is held or kept unconsciously within the mind, the body, the chakras, the aura and the energy system, or mindstream. My own experiences and those of clients who have found other life memories within their physical organs, chakras and energy fields, support the basis for this belief. The process of holding these imprints may indeed be similar to how traumatic memories are held unconsciously in the present. I would suggest that since the memories retrieved in Transforming Embodiment are often traumatic, they might function similarly to repressed memories from this lifetime.

Each "memory" awaits a trigger that brings it into the light of day. These imprints or memories can be accessed, traced, reorganized and removed like repressed memories, when the strong emotions and the system of beliefs [119] that keeps the information functioning unconsciously is ready to be recognized, transformed and released. Memory triggers include people, places, and emotional states. Other triggers may be smells, tastes, kinesthetic sensations, and visual and auditory cues that are similar to the repressed experience.

People often experience deep emotions when recovering memories from previous lifetimes. Just like with repressed memories from the present, those from a past life can strike an intense emotional chord. These strong emotions can be used as pathways for discovering the ancient stories and traumas within us. Often, these memories are associated with strong emotional or traumatic events and even death experiences, which may account for their continued impact. "It seems to me reasonable to suppose that the intensity of an experience such as violent death can in some way strengthen or 'fixate' memories so that they are more readily preserved in consciousness or remain accessible to it."[120] Stevenson also notes, "Strong emotions influence the accessibility of memories; that is, their persistence in consciousness as well as their repression. We particularly either remember or forget events whose occurrence has occasioned us strong emotion."[121]

Strong emotions are keys to opening up memories from our past and other lifetimes. They provide a focus and level of intensity that is easy to follow as we journey into our body of experience.

Our ideas about death also change as a result of our experience of past life memories. This is especially true when we are reliving previous experiences of death. Many clients come away from sessions with a new hypothesis about death and the survival of consciousness. Ideas about time and space are also reinterpreted: time becomes fluid, like a river where we can move freely and space becomes a nonlocal experience. In Transforming Embodiment, consciousness is able to move through space and time, and these experiences change our perceptions about the nature of reality. Norbert Wiener, mathematician states, "We are not stuff that abides, but patterns that perpetuate themselves; whirlpools of water in an everflowing river."[122]

Many religions for generations have accepted that reincarnation is possible and that rebirth occurs. Science is now finding new evidence to support what eastern religions have known for centuries—that consciousness is indestructible and that it survives bodily death.

That the mind and consciousness are now being considered nonlocal adds more credence to the possibility that consciousness survives. Research and study into the nature of consciousness continues to be at the forefront of scientific and spiritual inquiry. Organizations like the Institute of Noetic Sciences and the Fetzer Foundation have been supporting research into the nature of consciousness for years. I believe that as the different disciplines of physics, neurobiology, spirituality, transpersonal psychology, mathematics, parapsychology, and biology converge, the mystery of what consciousness is and if it survives death may find resolution. By diving into our inner world and Self, we too can explore and find answers about the mysteries of life, death, and consciousness for ourselves.

5

"SOURCE:
A TIMELESS, SEAMLESS REALITY
UNDERSTANDING ESSENCE

The true original mind is open and clear, with no sense of self, person, or thing. It is one with the great void; how can it have birth or death?

Thomas Cleary [123]

All major groups of people and religions have described the universe and the life force that pervades it in similar ways. Christian, Buddhist, Hindu, Muslim, Jewish, and tribal cultures as well as Taoist mystics and Greek philosophers descriptions bear remarkable similarities. All of these wisdom traditions agree that while spiritual energy is ultimately beyond description, there are six key attributes that this energy possesses. Spiritual energy is present everywhere, is non-obstructing, utterly impartial, ultimately ungraspable, compassionate and profoundly creative.

The Tao
"To empty the heart of desire and thoughts, to be in the void, is to

emerge [merge] with the Tao. The Tao cannot be grasped by thoughts, it must be experienced directly with the heart."[124] Like the Tao,[125] the energy or essence of Source is veiled but it can be felt and understood directly. This essence can be sensed when we are in an open and reflective state, when we are out in nature, or when we are "in the groove" of any activity. There is a feeling of effortless effort that flows when we connect with this energy or essence. Time dissolves, and events and actions appear to slow down.

I first encountered this energy as a classical singer in 1975. One day, as I sang a familiar piece of music, everything external dropped away, only the line of the voice remained as it soared through me as never before. The environment shifted and what had been difficult became effortless. Years later I would experience this same feeling of peace and unity while sitting in meditation. Meditation practice proved to be a reliable avenue for experiencing this essence. This essence is everywhere around us and always with us. It is nondual in nature and when I rest within this energy there is an elemental unity or oneness within all things. All apparently distinct phenomena are folded into one deep continuum. This is called, in Buddhism, nonduality, or "the unity of self and other."[126] Mind and body are one and there is no distinction between the self and the other.

> Essence cannot be defined; it is beyond words, concepts, and descriptions. It is the context or space from which, within which, and to which all contexts and spaces arise. It is empty of any specific qualities and includes them all. It is the fundamental or absolute nature and foundation of all reality.[127]

This energy would be akin to a drop of rain falling into the ocean, unified and at one with everything. Verse 25 in the Tao Te Ching illuminates and explains.

> Something mysteriously formed,
> Born before heaven and earth.
> In silence and the void,

Chapter Five

> Standing alone and unchanging,
> Ever present and in motion.
> Perhaps it is the mother of the ten thousand things.
> I do not know its name.
> Call it Tao
> For lack of a better word, I call it great.
> Being great, it flows.
> It flows far away.
> Having gone far, it returns.[128]

In this regard, the energy of Source may be an expression of the Tao or the void.[129] The void is where I sit when I am working with the energy of Source. It allows me to perceive and it is from this place that intuitive and channeled information flows. The term *hsien*[130] is also a part of my perception of this energy, since I began channeling within a H'sien Taoist monastery where the holy mountain immortals were a vital part of our deeply yin meditation practice.

Natural settings, mountains, waterfalls, and sacred places restore and reawaken this intrinsic energy. Our minds and hearts can become empty and clear as we experience the natural world. The following image, *Mountain Ridges in Mists* by Art Wolfe, captures a quality of the Tao or the energy of Source for me. It is the clearest image I have found for the spacious mystery that I feel when I work with people. Perhaps through this image, a quality of the energy can be grasped, and convey the spirit of this energy better than my words.

Memory In Our Bones

This essence is all encompassing, pervasive, full of wonder, stillness, beauty, mystery, and compassionate wisdom. This energy touches our every experience and communicates with us directly through imagery, intuition, and metaphor. In these ways, I believe we can access it. This essence is paradoxical though because it is separate from us and a part of us at the same time.

> Tao is within us; Tao surrounds us.
> Part of it may be sensed,
> And it is called manifestation.
> Part of it is unseen,
> And is called void.
> To be with Tao is harmony.
> To separate from Tao is disaster.
> To act with Tao observe and follow.
> To know Tao be still and look within.[131]

When merged with the energy of Source, stillness and spaciousness flood my awareness. The stillness is peaceful and calm while the spaciousness is alive and full of movement. These two qualities exist simultaneously and are opposite yet inseparable in my experience.

> One of the most enigmatic of all transpersonal phenomena is the experience of the Void, the encounter with primordial Emptiness, Nothingness, and Silence. This extraordinary spiritual experience is of a highly paradoxical nature. The Void exists beyond form of any kind. While being the source of everything it cannot itself be derived from anything else. It is beyond space and time. While we can perceive nothing concrete in the Void there is also the profound sense that nothing is missing. This absolute emptiness is simultaneously pregnant with all of existence since it contains everything in a potential form.[132]

When experiencing Source there exists continuity, beginnings move to completion and become endings, and endings give rise to new beginnings. Like the image of the uleaborus, the snake that bites its tail, life becomes circular. There is a wholeness to life when viewed from this perspective of unending continuity. All things arise out of this continuity. "When we experience identification with the cosmic consciousness, we have the feeling of enfolding totality within us, and of comprehending the Reality that underlies all realities. The experience of cosmic consciousness is boundless, unfathomable and beyond expression."[133]

To experience the Energy of Source, I close my eyes, slow my breathing, and connect with the stillness within me. Entering into a light meditative state, I expand into the stillness and gently open and connect to a vastness of consciousness that transcends form.

As I breathe, I notice the ebb and flow of thoughts, feelings, and sensations. They drift into the background and without these normal attachments, my consciousness shifts. My thoughts get quiet and fall away, as I open to the spacious emptiness of Source. Every corner of my consciousness is infused with emptiness, which allows me to be free of the confines of my individual identity and to merge with the collective.

This transpersonal experience enriches my contact with clients and permits me to connect with their higher consciousness. This experience also allows for a connection to the collective consciousness. I know it as the Tao or Source and it this energy that is all around us that lets me connect with other Selves and the collective consciousness or universal mind.[134] Communication occurs quite naturally from this state of awareness because of the basic unity within the universe and because we are all connected. This communication can be through telepathic, clairaudient, clairvoyant, or clairsentient means.

Encountering Source: The Common Threads

Physical changes are common when encountering transpersonal phenomena. Shamans and healers have long linked deep physical changes with psychic or spiritual awakening. Moss experienced "a powerful current of energy that seemed to move with varying intensity both within and around my body."[135]..."the new me felt like an atomic reactor powered by energies so great that I could not have conceived them before."[136] For me, it felt like every cell was transforming as my body adjusted to the higher frequencies of energy and force that raced through me. I also experienced great heat in my body as a result of this accelerated cellular state.[137] This sensation Moss described was very much like the fiery pain I endured years earlier. This feeling of heat or fire is often linked to kundalini energy, which is sometimes called

Chapter Five

"the Fire, the Serpent Fire, or the Fire of Transformation."[138] Mookerjee describes kundalini as cosmic energy with a vast potential of psychic energy. It is a female energy in latent form, he says, that is coiled up at the base of the spine. He says that kundalini is not only in every human being but that it is in every atom in the universe as well.

> Kundalini is perceived as the creative energy of the universe...it may ascend spontaneously, triggered by unknown factors. When it is awakened, it rises in the form of active energy,...up through the conduits of the person's subtle body (nadis) along the way it opens up the psychic centers (chakras) of the body...During a Kundalini experience, there are often powerful sensations of heat and energy that seem to stream up the spine. Along with this rising energy the person may experience intense emotions, tremors, spasms, violent shaking, complex twisting movements and a wide spectrum of transpersonal phenomena.[139]

In a kundalini awakening waves of energy rush up your spine and powerful whip-like movements overtake you. And oddly there is stillness amidst it all. It is like living within a cyclone. Satprem, in *Mind of the Cells*, notes Mother's experiences, which were strikingly similar to my own, and those of shamans and healers saying "Suddenly, it seemed that Mother had entered the atomic level, that her body was living quantum physics. Overwhelming motion in perfect stillness—such seems to be the constant characteristic of the experience."[140] When connected to Source I feel an incredible vibration at the physical level, which carries with it a heightened sense of awareness. The vibration produces a sense of quickening and has a luminous quality to it. Mother explains this quality.

> The entire body became a SINGLE, extremely rapid and intense vibration, but motionless. I don't know how to explain it because it wasn't moving space-wise, and yet it was a vibration (meaning it wasn't immobile,) but it was immobile in space. This was

in the body, as if EACH cell had a vibration and there was but a single BLOCK of vibrations.[141]

The overall experience of the combination of stillness and movement develops a deeply penetrating mental and body state of awareness, encouraging a piercing kind of insight. A quality of settling in or deep relaxation accompanies this moving stillness, when I shift my attention and focus inward. I call this change of attention "going in". When I go in, the universe feels as if it distills into my body.

Merging with the sky and expanding into space, a deep connection to the earth ensues as well. It feels like sitting down into the most comfortable, old, overstuffed chair that fits our body, perfectly. We fill it, are embraced by it, and supported by it at the same time. This is how the earth feels to me. We become one spirit. This experience carries with it a profound sense of ease and tranquility and a depth that is fathomless.

Sitting at the Well or Touching Source

Clients say they encounter a sense of peace and serene quiet when entering my office. The stillness that takes place within me seems to refine the atmosphere and the environment mirrors the characteristics of Source. Source interacts with the environment and clients are able to relax when enfolded in the energy of Source. Clients also note that they feel a remarkable sense of safety that empowers them to do deep inner work; they would not undertake in a different setting. Clients may be perceiving the energy fields that are within the room.

People outside of my office have experienced this internal energy of Source as well. A body worker and somatic therapist once remarked that she felt as if she was touching the earth as she worked on my body. My acupuncturist shared with me that she notices great spaciousness within her treatment room and within me when she is giving me acupuncture. These women, like my clients, are experiencing Source, or this universal energy, through me.

The understanding that we are energy, as well as being flesh and bone, is more accepted than ever before. This knowledge sets the stage for a profound shift of consciousness and the vibration of the energy that surrounds us shifts too, as we do. We become more deeply connected to each other and our environment as a result. As more people feel and experience the kind of changes that allow them to touch Source, consciousness will be forever changed.

In the transformational scheme of things we are living in a time when life is moving at an incredible pace. The networking and global communication that computers have brought us may be a metaphor or blueprint for what we can achieve at an internal level. If we are energy manifestations and energy is awareness, presence, spirit, and magnetism, then what opportunities await us? The key obstacle seems to revolve around fear. Can we let go of our fears and accept the luminous nature of our true Selves? Can we allow the energy of Source to course through us to enlighten us? Can we then hold this universal energy of light, sound, and vibration so it can be a ray of hope and transformation? These are the types of questions that arise for us when we discover the true nature of energy—when we understand and experience Source for ourselves. And silence and curiosity may be our loyal attendants in this quest.

Memory In Our Bones

Connecting to your Aumakua

Take a few deep breaths and let go of any physical, emotional, or mental tension from your body, mind, or day. (Pause). Allow your breath to help you relax and do the grounding and protection exercises that you have learned. Begin to feel the energy within your being at the center of your chest. (Pause). As you connect you may feel tension, heat, or the beat of your heart. Whatever sensation you feel is perfectly fine as long as you remain calm and relaxed. Now, begin focusing your attention below your breastbone, see, and sense your awareness descending deeper into your heart chakra. (Pause). Allow yourself to merge with this center and move even more deeply into it—as if you were diving into a deep haven within your being. As you immerse yourself in this experience, envision a beautiful pearl resting deep within you. This pearl is the seed that embodies your inner wisdom, your wise inner guide, or aumakua. By connecting to this energy you can contact your deep inner knowing. (Pause). Now, imagine yourself reaching deeper within to touch this energy. As you encounter this inner wisdom, the luminescence which is your true nature showers over you. Let yourself be bathed in the radiance of this inner self that is all-knowing. Allow yourself to connect with this aspect of your being. Breathe gently and effortlessly as you let yourself merge with this inner Self. Rest there for a while, then allow your consciousness and awareness to resurface when you are ready. Allow this energy to be with you, as you move through your day.

This exercise reestablishes a relationship to your inner Self and knowingness. It may take some time to develop trust, as you may have your own unique resistance to work through, but it is important to understand that your aumakua, or inner wisdom, is a spiritual advisor that you have within you. There is no need to search outside of yourself, but you must be discerning and remember that the messages from your inner wisdom are never strident. If your inner voice tells you what you *should* be doing—you are most likely having a conversation with your ego self.

Part Three: Heart

6

OPEN HEART OPEN MIND—REFLECTIONS ON HEALING

> Healing is what happens when we come to our edge, to the unexplored territory of mind and body, and take a single step beyond into the unknown, the space in which all growth occurs. Healing is discovery. It goes beyond life and death.
>
> Stephen and Ondrea Levine [142]

What is Healing?

Healing is a transformative and transpersonal journey that takes us into our mind, body, and heart, and reconnects us to our authentic and multi-dimensional Self. It is a process that occurs when we look to our core for answers and open our hearts in friendliness to all our experience, including our symptoms, conflicts, problems, difficulties, and weaknesses. Healing asks us to look at our woundedness. If we open and relax our hearts and minds we are able to review actions from our past and present and with gentle incisive questions we can find the true causes of our pain. This journey into our selves is an organic free-flowing voyage.

Healing is also a deeply intuitive process that is guided by both our innate inner wisdom and our rational intelligence. When we are at our best, our rational and intuitive intelligences are balanced. Learning to slow down our thoughts and mind so we can listen to our intuitive Mind is essential. Healing becomes an adventure, an imaginative and creative process that happens as we sense the rhythms of our mind and body. When we follow these rhythms, a narrative unfolds and by touching into the imagery, energies and memories that reside within us are discovered.

Each of us is awash with images, symbols, imprints, and memories of other times and other selves. Connecting to the mind, body, and its energy centers and the imagery within will often surprise and amaze, as synchronicities and patterns that we may never have connected are seen with fresh eyes. Trust will grow as we listen to that quiet inner voice that lives within us. Lifelong patterns, affinities, and even symptoms will start making sense as we follow our mind, body, and the energy that flows through us. As we listen to our heart's song, in an open way, with a beginner's mind,[143] our world begins to change. In order to make this journey we need to develop spaciousness and quiescence and mental stability. Meditation can be a key to discovering these states. Discernment, having and maintaining boundaries, and knowing where we begin and end are essential. With discernment and the inspiration of our intuitive mind, our ability to interpret the messages of our innermost self increases.

This type of deep healing asks us to be accepting and non-judging as we "open our hearts" in friendliness toward our experience, symptoms, and problems. Opening the heart is essential, because as we open our hearts, our inner wisdom shines forth and truth is revealed to us. This opening also allows us to experience our pain and sorrow, grief and anger, gently, without aversion, and in so doing we learn acceptance and develop presence. Equanimity is discovered when we see that it is our beliefs that shape our emotions and that in a neutral state we are attending to even the most difficult issues in our life.

> Just as we open and heal the body by sensing its rhythms and touching it with a deep and kind attention, so we can open and heal other dimensions of our being. The heart and the feelings go through a similar process of healing through the offering of our attention to their rhythms, nature and needs. Most often, opening the heart begins by opening to a lifetime's accumulation of unacknowledged sorrow, both our personal sorrows and the universal sorrows of warfare, hunger, old age, illness and death.[144]

Illness occurs when our mind and body are out of balance or when we are within a process. When our mind is in conflict with a change that we are trying to make, illness may arise; however as we resolve the mental or emotional conflict healing often will spontaneously happen. Symptoms and body tensions may move from one part of the body to another and as we follow our experience.[145] Process manifests in this ongoing way, and naturally occurs when we investigate our symptoms and emotional states. As we process an event or experience, gradual changes take place, as we move from one state to another, in order to resolve a set of circumstances or symptoms. In this way, illness, emotional or relationship problems are seen as processes seeking completion. Completion encourages the resolution of the experiential gestalt surrounding a problem. This perspective of healing as a process is becoming more accepted, as seen in the works of Stanislav Grof, Stephen Levine, Stephen Gallegos, Arnold Mindell, Ron Kurtz and Greg Johansen.

Viewed in this manner, healing also becomes more of a journey than a goal. We move away from the idea of immediately taking an aspirin for a headache and begin to question why we may be having the headache in the first place. We are able to develop curiosity, openness, friendliness, compassion, and an ability to stay present with our symptoms and emotional states when working in this way. "By not running away from our experience, but staying with ourselves through thick and thin, we begin to accept ourselves in a new way and appreciate the basic openness and sensitivity at the root of our very being."[146] Welwood continues, "Befriending emotions opens us to ourselves and allows us to discover the intelligence and responsiveness contained in them."[147] This basic openness to our mind and emotions with heartfelt friendliness towards our experience is called *maitri* in Buddhism.

The healing process seems to unfold naturally when our present experience is accepted.[148] Accepting the present, our moment-to-moment experience, is integral in Transforming Embodiment because healing resides in the moment. By being in the moment we become aware of our experience, we can observe it without losing touch and can report upon it without coming out of the moment.[149] In this way our experience deepens and we move from the surface of experience to the core and the depths of our being.

Accepting the present moment and our experience takes great compassion and strength, because "presentness" can lead us into our pain, which can be, at once, physical, emotional, mental, and spiritual. Avoiding pain and suffering can deny the healing process however, so in Transforming Embodiment, we learn stay in the moment with whatever we are experiencing. This acceptance does not mean that we succumb to our illness and symptoms, but that we understand when to persevere and when to let go. We learn balance and with this we release the idea that we have to fight our illnesses as if they were battles. Compassion and gentle acceptance of the self arises when we remain present with what is right in from of us.

Being present helps us to understand and see the organic nature of the healing process. This fluid, mobile aliveness allows us to follow our experience, instead of leading it. Healing unfolds much like a flower. The focus changes from being outwardly centered to being inwardly centered and connected. From this inner perspective we can move through various experiences, images, sounds, smells, memories, habitual patterns and beliefs and gain insight from within. The act of following ultimately illuminates us.

Not knowing is essential when we are following our process. When we are in the state of not knowing we naturally slow down and become more attentive. This rouses our curiosity, which leads us to ask probing questions about our cares and concerns. The question focuses our attention and ignites the communication with our inner wisdom. "Not knowing what to do forces us to slow down, become more attentive and wait—which allows space for a larger intelligence in us to take over."[150] Without this sense of not knowing the dialogue between our wisdom Self and ego would not take place. Questions open the door to insight and by being open to the unknown, our inner wisdom can share insights and understanding about our lives and trails. With this view the therapist is no longer the expert; experience itself is the expert and the reality.[151]

Humor infused with forgiveness can help us immensely when working with habits and repetitive patterns. Humor gives us the opportunity to take a step back from our dilemmas, and observe them. It creates the needed distance from a problem, so that a fair appraisal of the situation can occur. Humor and laughter allow the heart to release the intense seriousness that often can accompany our problems and difficulties.[152]

Healing involves the investigation and transformation of symptoms and problems, and the discovery of the origins and belief systems that limit us and cause suffering. Healing as transformation means that pain is no longer our enemy. It is actually our ally and can be our teacher and show us how we can best heal ourselves.

> As we become conscious of the pain they [knots] have held, we may also notice feelings, memories, or images connected specifically to each area of tension. As we gradually include in our awareness all that we have previously shut out or neglected, our body heals.[153]

Pain can take us into our experience. We all know how pain and suffering can take us to our edge and ask us to go beyond our comfort zone. Pain and illness can be confusing and we feel our mortality when confronted with disease. Even the simplest flu can take us there. This may be why illness scares us so, because none of us wants to suffer or be confronted by our mortality. But when we reflect upon death it becomes a part of healing again. We see that we have the opportunity to transform our pain and our suffering, and to look at the countless deaths we have suffered in a new light. When we do this, our perception of the Self changes forever. We see that we are a combination of many selves, whose history is still alive within us, and by acknowledging these selves and releasing the pain from ancient lifetimes, we let go of the limits of our individual identity. We move into a more unified sense of being. We move, even if it is just for a moment, from a relative to an ultimate state of awareness, Stephen Levine notes that healing is the "letting go of the personal separatism, the self images, the resistance to change, the fear and anger, and the confusion that form the opaque armoring around the heart."[154] When engaging in the practice of Transforming Embodiment we have this kind of opportunity, to become conscious, to release ancient wounds and reorganize our very sense of Self. When seen this way healing is the growth that each person seeks.

By letting go, we are able to disidentify with our pain and suffering, our pain begins to soften and be released. As we open our hearts, our suffering is less individual and we see the universal nature of pain, which develops our capacity to be compassionate. Pain is no longer individualized, it becomes universal, and when seen in this manner, we are more capable of letting go, because the pain is not just ours, even though it ravages through our bodies. When we understand that there is no true self that is experiencing pain, we can see it for the physical constriction and mental and emotional conflict that it is and this awareness can bring about deep healing to the very core of our being.

Working with Heaven and Earth

The earth is our ground, and spirit is our inspiration. We are the earth's instruments for experiencing a wide variety of states and emotions and we are her emotional heart. The earth is a matrix of energy, a crystalline grid, a personification of form and the earth is our foundation and our point of connection where we can find stability and gain sustenance. We can dip into her energy at will and we can send our energy to her as well. The earth is conscious and human beings are a part of the earth's consciousness. This primordial feminine wisdom energy is a lineage that can be contacted by all of us; women however, have a very deep innate connection to this energy and the earth. We have a great capacity to embody this energy of love, wisdom, and fierce passion, to marry this energy to action when we are balanced and aware. As we do this, we find wholeness. The wisdom energy of the earth is our legacy and embodiment is the key, in all of its attributes, we must embody our truth and our wisdom self, and must speak, act and dance with the world from this place. Knowledge of this energy arises within us and flows within our very being. It is timeless, alive, and responsive.

Spirit is formless and unseen, yet the energy of spirit is always present and available to us. The practices of Transforming Embodiment seek to awaken and augment the energy of spirit within our consciousness. Spirit may be a veiled aspect to us at times, but it is our true nature and it is spirit that assists and guides the entire healing process, and spirit plays a dynamic and important role in the body-mind healing equation.

Love and the Body as Spirit

Transforming Embodiment encompasses a great love and appreciation for our physical bodies and our humanity. We do not seek to evade or deny our bodies, or the experiences found within them. In practicing Transforming Embodiment our bodies are viewed as a manifestation of spirit, which contains our inner wisdom. It is through our bodies that we experience potent emotions, feelings, inspiration, our hearts desires and aspirations; all our experience is played out through our body-mind and all can be transformed. The keys or answers to our most perplexing problems can be found within the body and consciousness. Cultivating and understanding all our emotions is the place we can work from, to most genuinely accept and love ourselves and our experience.

Our body and its emotions become our vehicle for experiencing ourselves in this broader and more loving way. Everything we need to know is right here, right now and right in front of us. There is no need to go anywhere else, to heaven realms or blissful states or to transcend or disassociate in any way. The task is to stay with what is. By staying aware of each moment, then moving to the next moment as it unfolds is at the heart of mindfulness in action. In this state we experience the reality of being present and in the moment. "Actually, one of the greatest spiritual insights is that there's nowhere to go."[155]

Heaven cannot save us. We can only save ourselves. This is often an unpopular view because we, as humans, wish to experience bliss and oneness, not the pain and suffering that embodiment includes. To be in the moment, to be conscious in the moment, means we will encounter our fears, anxieties, sadness, suffering and pain, as well as the joys and delights. The desire to deny our suffering and to participate only in the positive leads to an imbalanced view, and many limitations can arise.

By denying even part of our experience, we take ourselves out of the present moment. If our "negative" experiences are denied, we ultimately deny a part of ourselves, and it is often this denied part that is the most wounded part of being. By not including all of our experiences, negative and positive, we are not accepting or loving ourselves fully and we show no compassion to this wounded self. Love is the key to healing. To love ourselves in all our aspects is deeply important. This loving acceptance and openness allows us to find the keys to deep inner transformation and healing.

In seeking healing we must have the utmost love for our process and ourselves. We must be both tender and fierce with ourselves, and willing to ask the hard questions to discover the roots of our suffering and pain, but we must always temper our questions with love and compassion because they are our greatest tools. Love is the blinding light that illuminates us and it is love that heals us. Inner illumination and awareness through love is the key to dissolving the veils of illusions and attachments. Chögyam Trungpa Rinpoche says, "Developing tenderness towards yourself allows you to see both your problems and your potential accurately."[156] It is that tenderness, or love, that allows the healing in, so we can find peace. Peace=love and love=wisdom. Wisdom, compassion, and love reside side by side, ever entwined like lovers.

Blessings

In Hawai'ian shamanism, we use blessings as a form of love. Blessings are statements that admire, affirm, or appreciate a positive quality, condition, or characteristic. They are used to recognize and emphasize the positive. Blessings have been known to produce healing.

Years ago, I was cooking popcorn in a sauce pan, when I thought the popcorn was done, I turned the pan over and in so doing, scalding hot oil ran down my left hand and fingers. I glanced at my fingers, which were turning scarlet and instead of cursing, I immediately started to send blessings to my hand and fingers, as I went for ice. All evening I iced my throbbing fingers which were badly burned, and I continued to bless them.

I went to bed that night with an ice pack on my hand, and each time the pain woke me I sent my burned fingers a silent blessing. I sent blessings to my hand throughout the night with no expectation of what the outcome would be. In the morning when I awoke, I looked at my fingers, and instead of the watery blisters I had seen in the past when I had bad burns, my skin was the lightest of pinks. My littlest finger that had been coated in hot oil did not even have a single blister.

This experience showed me, in a very real way, how powerful blessings, right speech and love could be. By using blessings and by sending love, instead of anger, to my burned hand and fingers, the energy field relaxed, and took in the love and healing directly. I had wanted to test what I had learned in Hawai'i to see if positive thoughts in the form of blessings would help my injured hand, and quite simply love and blessing did just that.

Stephen and Ondrea Levine have experienced cancer, lupus and acute back pain together and say the following about love and healing:

> If you were to ask either of us, now fifteen years after her last cancer diagnosis, how Ondrea dispelled cancer from her body, we would each have to answer, 'Don't know.' But it seemed to be a combination of love and our willingness to focus a merciful awareness on the area to be healed—not ostracizing it or sending anger into the illness but inviting it into the preciousness of the moment.[157]

They continue:

> Some dynamic grace had allowed the heart to penetrate the body. A growing sense of the mystery embracing all that was silhouetted against the enormous energy of healing...Disorienting by its enormity at times, it was our love which again and again became the ground on which was being enacted

the 'great don't know' healing of her body. Now a few years later, the lupus, like the cancer, has retreated from her body, and all we are left with is the mystery and the love that goes beyond fear or 'knowing'.[158]

Like the shamans of Hawai'i, the Levines have found that love and an openness to the mystery play a vital role in healing the body.

Our Healing Potential

There is a potential for realization and enlightenment within everyone. We are masterpieces of possibilities and potentials that can be awakened. The nature of personal healing and ultimately the nature of reality can be found within each of us. We need only find the stillness within us, for it is within this silence that the answers to our most pressing questions about our lives resides. The great Tibetan meditation master and teacher, Kalu Rinpoche once wrote, "Truth is here, even here in this very all. Truth is in *you*. The supreme silence, Sunyata, infinity is in you. You are the silence, you are the truth; you are the Buddha."[159] Kalu Rinpoche is acknowledging that we all have the potential for awakening. Each one of us, from a Buddhist perspective, has this Buddha nature. "Buddha nature is variously described as the potential for full awakening, or as the essential perfection of each sentient being, that is temporarily hidden by the veils of delusion."[160]
Wallace continues:

> The idea of Buddha nature is that the essential nature of the mind is infinite purity, fathomless joy, power, wisdom, and compassion; right here, right now. We do not have to earn our Buddha-Nature or become enlightened to have it. We have it right now, it is common to all sentient beings.[161]

Buddha nature is each person's inherent potential regardless of culture or faith.[162] It is this veiled aspect that we aspire to consciously awaken within ourselves, this aspect of mind that is beyond duality, limitless, and full of wisdom. When we connect to this part of our being

Chapter Six

and listen, we can directly find solutions and healing that are perfect for our every situation and need.

How the Paradigm is Shifting

Over the past twenty years people have noticed that things are not as they used to be. Life has sped up, time seems to be moving faster, and we seem to have less of it each day. We have moved into an information age, one where communication is lightening fast. Computers, and digital networks move at ever increasing speeds. What was fast five years ago is virtually obsolete. These new technologies have created a vibrational change and this acceleration appears to be affecting many aspects of our lives. More than ever before we need to ground and center ourselves.

While we are in the throes of adapting to this new accelerated pace, we need to find new ways to stay connected to each other, our world, and ourselves. This is the dilemma. How do we keep pace, as we learn this new dance, especially when we feel out of step with the music? Each of us must find our own new rhythm and pace because as our outer world accelerates, so too will our inner world.

Perhaps this is part of what Yogi Sri Aurobindo was speaking about at the turn of the 19th century, when he wrote about a willed mutation of the species. He believed that we may be in the greatest adventure imaginable, or as others assert, we may be in the mouth of chaos. The latter statement is based in fear but some truth may be hidden in this dire assertion, a warning perhaps to not repeat the arrogance and corruption of the past.

As we move forward with blinding speed, we need to be like the martial artist who is in control of every move, balanced, and riding the energy that flows within and around us. Balanced action, deeply connected to the earth, is necessary for each of us to learn how to dance this new dance of acceleration.

This opens the door to a path of descent[163] rather than ascent. We have been sky or heaven centered for centuries and with the accelerated pace this focus only exaggerates the problem of staying connected. Descent changes the energy and the paradigm. It gives us the opportunity to reflect on the silence and the density, as well as the vibration and velocity, that this planet we live on emanates. Descent slows things down so we can sensitize ourselves to the ebb and flow of her tides and movement from within.

This movement and quiet resides within each of us. Like the still center of a cyclone we can find this stillness within us, as we connect downward and in. Reaching for so long to the sky and outside of ourselves has naturally given rise to—an ever-rising energy. This has unbalanced us. Now, we have the opportunity to blend these energies, as never before, and regain our balance.

We can move into a space of wholeness, not living the either/or of things, of only the feminine matriarchy of the distant past or the masculine patriarchy that we have known for centuries but a combination of both, where duality is relinquished, so we can marry form and formlessness. A marriage of earth and sky, the masculine and the feminine, a fundamental change from duality to unity. This is one gift that awaits us as the paradigm shift continues to unfold.

Spirit and Science

Jeanne Achterberg writes that spirit and science are reconnecting and with this renewed marriage a reordering of priorities naturally follows. She feels there is a deep need now to balance the male and female principles of wisdom and knowledge, intuition and intellect, compassion and power, synthesis and analysis, caring and curing, nurturing and fixing, and feeling and reason. From this unified perspective a new definition of health emerges, one that nurtures harmony and wholeness as well as transformation. "Every level touches every other level, and the connections are complex and infinite. Healing, or disease or disruption in the system reverberates to all levels."[164] Healing, which of late has been a linear and analytical process becomes a journey of deep transformation that is guided by both the intuition and intellect within this new paradigm. This is yet another gift of this rich time we are living in. In closing,

> A paradigm shift is much more than a change in ideas and how we think. It is a change in our views of reality, identity, social relationships, and human purpose. A paradigm shift can be felt in the body mind and soul.[165]

This is what I believe we have been in, a paradigm shift of great proportion that radiates into every level of our lives, relationships, and even through our institutions. It is global and personal and is felt on every level of our being. As we turn away from fear, the old structures we have known will change; this is a part of the natural evolutionary process of moving from fear to love and it will be revolutionary in its scope. As we truly learn that we are all one people and that the differences we have envisioned are merely illusions, our world, as well as ourselves, will change.

The Non-Hierarchical Nature of Healing—The Spiral vs. the Pyramid

We are experiencing a paradigm shift, this shift is affecting healing in deep ways. Whether it is mental, emotional, or physical healing we are seeking, I have found that it is no longer a linear pathway. It is a process that is a multi-layered dialogue between the many aspects of our body, mind and spirit. It is informed by energy, imagery, info-energy within the organs and cells, our embodied and unconscious memories, stored consciousness, environmental factors and the collective unconscious. Our relationships, family, work, beliefs, memories, emotions, and feelings about all these things affect us.

It seems that talking about these issues is no longer enough in many cases; the body, mind, and spirit conversation needs to be included in the healing process. And as we work with the body, and the memories, and imagery that reside there, we can feel that the energy within us moves from one area to another as we unravel the mental conflicts and twisted emotions that organize our physical symptoms and perceptions. The energy itself, if we allow ourselves to follow it, takes us on an inner journey from one place to another in a non-hierarchical way. The links and connections are no longer defined by graded steps. Certain requirements need to take place before we can go to the next step in this paradigm. "This is not a linear progression, but a process of expansion that does not so much change levels as include greater depths."[166]

While the Levines are speaking of the levels of conscious connection within spiritual relationship, this description is an apt one. In this new paradigm I am describing and have encountered, levels and linear progression are replaced by an expansion that is more sweeping and ever deepening. The image of a pebble being dropped into a still pond and the rippling affect this action produces is a good image to describe what I am trying to convey. Levine also describes a fifth realm of consciousness and says, "It is that which goes beyond levels. It is the truth that remains when all dualities...dissolve back into themselves, not relating from them or even to them but as the space in which they unfold."[167] This realm of consciousness may well be where the energy of the channel arises.

Twenty years ago Marika spoke to a group about this change and said, "There are no levels." She continued by saying that a shift was occurring that was moving away from a linear hierarchy to more of a spiraling form, or circularity, which expands outward and becomes more encompassing at the same time. She expressed that a system without levels naturally becomes more inclusive, varied and balanced. Like the old class systems based on a person's station, the old view of hierarchy leaves many people out of the mix. A system that is circular or spiral gives rise to freedom and more diversity. Our experience becomes an important part of the process.

Life and healing in the last fifteen years appear to be taking on a more spiral or circular quality, one that may be more feminine in character. Jeanne Achterberg, in her book *Woman as Healer* recognized this change from a masculine and linear perspective to one that is nonlinear and decidedly more feminine.[168] With this understanding an interconnectedness of multiple layers of experience becomes possible. Body, mind, and spirit are no longer separate but are seen as an interconnected network, from which a new complexity emerges.

> A network is different from a hierarchical structure that has a ruling 'station' at the top and a descending series of positions that play increasingly subsidiary roles. In a network, theoretically, you can enter at the nodal point and quickly get to any other point; all locations are equal as far as the potential to 'rule' or direct the flow of information.[169]

Levels of experience are replaced by layers of experience that we must traverse. The latter appears to be a fuller, richer and a more encompassing approach, and it gives rise to a natural compassion that is a part of healing.

I can attest that healing is often complex, varied, and surprising when we work with the breadth of our being and within the body consciousness to find healing at its deepest roots. Dr. Stephen Gallegos affirms that hierarchies cannot return us to wholeness, nor can thinking, which constructed the hierarchies in the first place. We must use all the tools at our disposal and the body in all its complexity and beauty as our vehicle for awakening. This pathway often takes us on decidedly nonlinear and non-hierarchical journeys.

Rewriting Spiritual Contracts and Changing the Code

Many people are writing about spiritual agreements these days. For over fifteen years I have been working with people as they have explored and rewritten these contracts. Spiritual contracts are agreements made between individuals before incarnation takes place. We share common goals, interests, and history with these people. They may be our lovers, siblings, spouses, and parents or even in some cases our enemies. Belief systems and mutual experiences we have lived through in the past together hold these contacts and contracts in place. Often there is something that needs to be learned or resolved and this is why many spiritual contracts continue between people. When we incarnate we are attracted to situations and people that will help us remember and release these ancient histories that bind us together.

In the Buddhist tradition there is the concept that we choose our parents. It is thought that during the act of sexual intercourse our consciousness is impelled to join with certain individuals, who will become our parents. We may have specific agreements that we make with our parents, both in other lifetimes and during the time between lives. In my personal and clinical work, I discovered how these spiritual contracts are held and how they hold a powerful sway over our behaviors, relationships, and sense of self.

My direct experiences with pre-incarnational memories have brought me to understand how these contracts are conceived and how they can be transformed and laid to rest when necessary. Spiritual contracts are held deep within our very bones and cells. When ready, new knowledge about these agreements bubbles up, as from a spring, when we ask potent questions about why we respond or react the way we do. Not all of our reactions are linked to experiences from this life and spiritual contracts can help us understand our roles in our family or with friends and lovers.

Agreements are often made between family members and loved ones based on past lives spent together, while other contracts focus on current spiritual questions that we are exploring in this lifetime. Agreements are like pacts that individuals or members of a group can make with each other. These bonds or contracts can be with people that we will later be in relationship with. Agreements with the ones we love can be the hardest to imagine changing, because we fear breaking these contracts may harm or alter our relationships in some fundamental way. This is not the case. The rewriting of contracts deepens our understanding of our shared experience and the roots from where our relationships develop. Growth, freedom. and peace for all parties can occur when we revise or rewrite these contracts.

In 1989 I was working with Sophia, who was working through a variety of relationship and family issues. One day she began to speak about a problem she felt was a spiritual agreement that she made with her father before this lifetime. Her belief was that children were born to serve their parents. She said she had learned, from another teacher, that kids have to help their parents, even if their parents are unavailable and unsupportive. She noticed deep anger as she spoke of how dad had never been much of a father to her. She felt completely limited by this belief and the feelings that accompanied it. She also felt that this was a non-negotiable item within her life, as though this agreement had been written in stone. It was a commandment she had to live by, she explained.

Obligations can lead to many difficult emotions: anger, resentment, or a feeling of helplessness, as in the case of Sophia. Unconscious emotions can keep spiritual contracts in place, and unexplainable symptoms and emotions, such as depression and anxiety, may surface due to these continued obligations.

My attention shifted as the energy of Source and Marika conveyed to Sophia that any contract could be rewritten if one has outgrown that agreement. Sophia's eyes widened as amazed relief washed over her face. Never before had she imagined that this could be so. She told me later that she was so surprised and stunned, that even thirteen years later her body remembers the relief she felt that day. Relief, she said, felt like massive rays of sunshine pouring forth from a cloudbank after a storm, and the emotion accompanying this was one of total freedom. This simple concept, that we are not bound forever by these contracts that we make with others, and that change is always possible, was a real turning point for her. This simple understanding freed her and released her from the obligation and duty she had felt over-burdened with her entire life.

She has since shared this channeled information with her own clients and on every occasion, great relief was experienced when people understood that these agreements were negotiable and could be rewritten. She remarked that just uttering the words has an affect. It seems that the info-energy of the words is heard directly by the cells within the body and consciousness, and the vibration of the information itself brings about change almost immediately.

When the transformation of the energy surrounding a life challenge or problem takes place, mental and emotional release will result. Relief may come in the form of a deep exhalation of breath, as body tensions wash away and are released, or as laughter or tears. Relief and release are married when we work with the mind-body and these potent agreements. Mental and emotional relaxation also transpires when we release these contracts once and for all.

Prior to the release of a spiritual contract we are able to re-negotiate with the other person's spirit and consciousness. In some cases this may include an actual conversation. but this is rare. This work is usually done individually and energetically. Clients have found that a quiet mental conversation, mind to mind, is very effective. It is not necessary to confront the other person and say, "this is what I am doing..." In fact, this can cause harm and is not recommended. I have found that when we are ready to rework a spiritual contract the energy of the others involved is ready as well. Even if the other person is not consciously aware of what we are doing, they will feel a distinct change in the energy surrounding our relationship, usually for the better. Spiritual contracts cannot be changed without the assent of the other person's higher Mind. Late one day in 2002, Sophia called me in a panic.

This was very uncharacteristic of her normally calm demeanor. She explained that she had become the head of a professional organization and that she felt under attack, at a psychic level, by a group of the membership. She had never felt this way before, but she was certain that some people in this group were attacking her. I immediately opened the channel and they (the energy of the channel) gave her a powerful protection visualization involving certain Buddhist deities to protect her. I asked if she could visualize them, she said she was unable to focus on anything, so I put the protection in place for her. She calmed down almost immediately, her breathing slowed and her voice changed timbre and she told me that she felt a change as soon as I placed these energies around her.

As relaxation reestablished itself we were able to begin working with the origins of this conflict. Sophia found out over the next month the causes of the hostility that pervaded her interactions with this group of people. Lifetimes of pain and harm surfaced, and as these memories and the events surrounding her experiences in both the past and present interfaced, the spiritual contracts that were stamped upon her psyche became clear to her. She diligently peeled away the layers of trauma that had been inflicted upon her, and that she had inflicted in turn. Incarnation after incarnation were clarified and cleared.

In the end, she understood the beliefs and contracts that were at play, and as she released these old covenants her world began to change in the present. She ceased being afraid of these people, who had once terrified her, and was able to hold her ground on key points of importance to herself and within the organization she served. She was able to conduct business without the interference she had once encountered, and her mind was restored to its former state of peace, for as she reworked and freed herself of these old entanglements, her present world was transformed, and she was able to complete her service with more ease.

Another Connecting, and Grounding Exercise

Allow yourself to take a few deep breaths, and come into contact with your body, and any tensions you may feel at this time. Take another deep breath and as you exhale release all tension from your body. Just relax and let any tension just drain out the soles of your feet. Take a second deep breath and this time release any emotional tension, or feelings and come fully into the moment. Know that with each breath more spaciousness and relaxation is created. Take a third deep breath and as you exhale let go of any mental tensions, cares from your day, and allow any concerns to just float away with your breath, like a leaf on the wind. Gently and effortlessly let go of all the tensions in your being. Just for the moment allow this peace to pervade your being. Now imagine a golden ball of light above your head, see, feel and sense this light moving into your body like water being poured into a glass. See and feel it fill every corner of your being, let this light melt into your body, and flow through your being all the way down to the soles of your feet. Then see it move outward like the roots of a tree or as one great tap root, see it descend into the earth. As this light moves down into the earth, let your body relax even more and feel yourself settle into an even calmer and more relaxed state of being. Imagine that you can connect to the earth that you are resting upon. Feel the pulse of the earth flow through you as you breathe in and out. Let your breathing be soft, let your belly be soft, let your mind go. No focus, no agendas—just allow yourself to be one with your breath, just follow your breath as it rises and falls with each inhalation and exhalation, just be present with your breath and the pattern of your respiration, your life and heart.

7

WORKING WITH THE SPIRITUAL SELF, HUNA, CHAKRAS AND ENERGY

Two people have been living in you all your life. One is the ego, garrulous, demanding, hysterical, calculating; the other is the hidden spiritual being, whose still voice of wisdom you have only rarely heard or attended to.

Sogyal Rinpoche [170]

The Spiritual or Wisdom Self

The spiritual Self is only one of many terms used to describe the experience of inner wisdom and connectedness that each person possesses. The spiritual Self is the transcendent aspect of self that carries the wisdom of the being. This aspect of the personality has an individual's highest good in mind at all times and it is this aspect that guides and inspires us.

This wise inner Self resides within everyone and contact with this aspect of mind is possible. It functions as our higher consciousness, and as a spiritual teacher or guide might. Sogyal Rinpoche calls this aspect of the being the wise guide. Jung used the term Self and Assagioli used the term spiritual Self to describe this quality of inner wisdom or higher consciousness. I have found this aspect to be beyond thoughts, words, and actions; it is a direct knowingness of pure being and the intuitive spark that inspires us. To students of Huna, this Self is called aumakua and is seen as a teacher, or totally trustworthy guiding spirit. Aumakua is also the intelligence that runs through life.

I have recently begun to use the term 'wisdom self' to describe this potent inner knowing because this aspect of our being is beyond the boundaries of spirit alone. It is within us and beyond us at the same time. It is timeless, eternal and as we come out of eternity, to dance with the beauty and rawness that is our human existence, it is this energy that enlivens and guides us. We are bridges between spirit and matter and we embody both these aspects; based on our individual beliefs, we may merge into eternity again. Consciousness is infinite and immortal and our capacities and capabilities far outreach our current knowledge. Many traditions and even sections of psychology believe in this aspect of our selves.

Wise Guide

Sogyal Rinpoche maintains that meditation is a powerful means for cultivating the wise guide.

> As you listen more and more to the teachings, contemplate them, and integrate them into your life, your inner voice, your innate wisdom of discernment, what we call in Buddhism 'discriminating awareness' is awakened and strengthened, and you start to begin to distinguish between its guidance and the various clamorous and enthralling voices of the ego. The memory of your real nature with all its splendor and confidence, begins to return to you. You will find, in fact, that you have uncovered in yourself your own wise guide.[171]

Rinpoche teaches that qualities attributed to the wise inner guide are a "continual joyful, tender, sometimes teasing presence, who knows always what is best for you and will help you find more and more ways out of your obsession with your habitual responses and confused emotions."[172] This description is similar to the gentle, playful, and humorous qualities I encounter when contacting Source, or this primordial wisdom, my inner Self, and clients' inner Selves as well. Source, or this aspect of Self, is extraordinarily compassionate, ever-present, and willing to reach out, at a moment's notice, with a steadying hand, to aid us. This spiritual Self not only inspires life, but also steers a course that relates to our life purpose, goals and ultimate healing.

Sogyal Rinpoche gives advice on working with what he calls the wise guide.

> As the voice of your discriminating awareness grows stronger and clearer, you will start to distinguish between its truth and the various deceptions of the ego, and you will be able to listen to it with discernment and confidence. The more often you listen to this wise guide, the more easily you will be able to change your negative moods yourself, see through them, and even laugh at them for the absurd dramas and ridiculous illusions that they are.[173]

I have found this to be true both personally and clinically. As a relationship is established and developed between our ordinary consciousness and our inner wisdom, discernment naturally occurs. With practice and patience we can learn to distinguish the voice of our ego from the voice of our inner wisdom. The ability to distinguish the false voices of the defensive ego is imperative, in doing any type of psychological or spiritual practice.

Aumakua

Aumakua, or *Kane*, are the terms used in Hawai'i to express the concept of a spiritual Self. In psychology, aumakua would be the equivalent to the superconscious. Intuition arises from this Self.

Dr. Serge King, author, teacher, and shaman, says "The aumakua can also be called the 'Source Self' since it is the source of individual life, purpose and expression."[174] Aumakua is the 'spiritual essence of the individual 'according to King. While aumakua is like the spiritual

Self, it is also larger. It is a deep expression of Source and in Hawai'i, prayers are sent to aumakua for help and guidance.

Aumakua resides within us and brings inspiration and guidance into our lives. It is the wisest part of our Selves, and yet it can be the most difficult part to find and develop. However, if we release the judgments, expectations and limitations of the ego, or small mind, communication with our aumakua begins to flow. Intuition develops as we nurture this rich inner resource, which can communicate to us through images, dreams or as a quiet voice.

Huna and The Three Selves

Huna understands that our habits are based on our beliefs and that ideas generate the circumstances which we experience in life. A key principle in huna states that the world is what we think it is. In this tradition, man is thought to be a spiritual being made up of three aspects. Ideally these three aspects function as one; in Hawai'ian that combined aspect is known as *kanaloa*. When these principles work together, anything is possible.

These three aspects, known as *ku*, *lono*, and aumakua can be correlated to modern psychological terms. Ku corresponds roughly to the subconscious. However, unlike the subconscious in modern psychology, the ku is linked to the body. Lono is the equivalent of the conscious mind and aumakua is similar to the superconscious. These three selves are interconnected; we only separate them to communicate with each of them individually. Ideally, the three selves function together, each doing their own jobs, yet acting as a team. If conflicts develop between the three selves, physical illness, emotional pain, and mental confusion may result. So, in Huna, we learn to communicate with these different aspects of the self and understand their distinct functions and abilities.

The ku is associated with the body, memory, habits, and instincts. It stores all incoming information: words, feelings, emotional responses, body signals and language, and psychic information from others and from the world. It is our memory keeper. The ku is like a tape recorder that gets turned on at birth and records all of our experiences. Huna believes that the *ku* is the holder of memories and emotions from this life as well as from all previous lives.

Chapter Seven

> Essentially the functions of the ku are to maintain the integrity and oversee the operation of the body, to receive perceptions and transmit them to the lono, to store memory, to generate, store, distribute and transmit energy, and to follow orders.[175]

The ku also maintains involuntary habits, such as breathing and heart rate, and forms habits from repetitive behavior and experiences.

According to Huna practices, in order to change habitual patterns, the ku must be convinced that the change will be positive and fun, because the ku is motivated away from pain and toward pleasure. If this part of the self understands that a new behavior is going to be pleasant instead of painful, it will gladly make the required change with the proper motivation.

When motivated, and when the three selves are unified in their desire to make change, the ku can even change physical symptoms. As an example, when I was twenty I went to my allergist, who proceeded to give me my prescribed dose of allergy shots. Within minutes I was in a full blown bronchial and laryngeal asthma attack. Unable to breathe, I was rushed into a room and given adrenaline to relieve this attack. The medication sent my heart into overdrive, racing like a wild horse, completely out of control. I was monitored for the next hour or so, and when my heart and breathing finally began to regulate themselves again I was sent to see a doctor. When he began to question me about my day's activities, I told him I had been weaving in an old building. He disapproved. He then asked if I still had my cat, to which I responded, of course. He told me I would have to get rid of my cat and that I must go home immediately to rest. I had tickets that night for the opening of the San Francisco Opera with Joan Sutherland and Luciano Pavarotti singing, and I was not going to miss this performance, so I decided to make a change. With the power of all my frustration and anger at the bumbling care I had received that day, and my fury at having so many limits set forth by this doctor, I firmly told him that I would *never* have an asthma attack or allergies again and walked out.

This combination of strong emotions and the well-formed desire to be relieved *forever* of the limitations and fear that asthma created in my life changed in that moment. My ku heard me loud and clear and, as the ku is able to do, it changed my physiology to match this new belief system that I had expressed so powerfully. This is how change can be made on a physical level. *Mana*, or internal energy, is generated and with it a new direction is given. When all three aspects of the self work together, one can change one's world! To date, twenty-eight years later, I am still allergy-and asthma-free.

I was vehement about going to the opera, weaving, and keeping my cat, as each of these things gave me great pleasure. This illustrates how the ku will gladly move from a painful situation or habit to a pleasurable one, if properly motivated. The building of mana, accompanied by visual images, words and statements directed toward the ku, can enhance this process.

It is important to realize that the ku also takes what we say quite literally. For instance if you say,"...makes me sick" or "so and so is a pain in the neck," the ku hears that message and whenever that stimulus is encountered, we might get sick; or notice a pain in our neck. In Huna, we become acutely aware of how we use language.

The conscious self is known as lono in Huna; lono was born to make decisions. This aspect of self directs, analyzes, and interprets information from the ku. King describes lono, in this way: "It is that aspect of the mind which focuses on the physical reality, analyzes it, integrates it and forms beliefs, attitudes and opinions about it. It is a receiver of subtle and gross information and a director of action."[176] It is this part of the self that helps us consciously modify our beliefs. Lono has the ability to review and decide which beliefs held by the ku are relevant to the personality. Creative imagination is another important ability the lono possesses. "It is by the use of this faculty that the lono develops new skills, expands it [its] awareness, solves problems, changes beliefs and directs energy."[177]

The lono is motivated to move away from powerlessness to power, from insecurity to security, and its basic function is to make decisions. If lono can be shown that held beliefs are maintaining a state of powerlessness or insecurity, it will gladly change these beliefs, habits, and circumstances. We enlist the powers and abilities of the lono to change our beliefs, provided the new beliefs are empowering to the self.

The ku communicates with lono by offering up feelings, emotions, and memories.[178] It is the lono, however, that has the opportunity to change the response to our feelings, emotions, and memories. Lono can follow these beliefs through, ignore them, or redirect them.

Lono's job is to make decisions about our habitual reactions and when needed, it creates new responses by engaging the will and consciousness. Lono is responsible for setting up new patterns for the subconscious and it instructs the ku in new ways to respond. If emotions and feelings are not understood, the lono may feel powerless, and at this juncture the ku may begin to take over the process and run the show. If the lono does not make decisions, which is one of its primary functions, the ku will rely on past habits and experiences to shape responses. Responses and reactions are then based on past experiences alone stored within ku's memory.

The third aspect of the self, aumakua, corresponds to the superconscious[179] in psychology. It is this part of the self that organizes and integrates all of our inner aspects into a cohesive whole. If life were a movie, aumakua would be the producer, acting as the unifying force that brings the other elements together, creating unity and wholeness. Aumakua is like a teacher, or guiding spirit, who illuminates us and represents the creative aspect of the self. It brings us dreams, inspirations, creative ideas and visionary experiences, and inspires intuition, hunches, and synchronicities. "As a teacher, it is considered to be the source of all knowledge of which the individual might ever have need or desire."[180]

Aumakua has the broadest view of the three aspects of self, yet it gives no orders. It dispenses knowledge and respects our free will and freedom of choice at all times unless we are in deadly peril.

> According to kahunas, then, a person who expects a guiding inner voice to make decisions for him will end up listening to his own beliefs and habits of thought. The kahunas instruct students to beware of inner voices that attempt to command thought and action, for these are not from the 'higher Self.'[181]

The decision-making process itself is always guided by the lono which analyzes and correlates data from outside sources, including aumakua, in making decisions. Aumakua works with the other selves and will not interfere unless we drift away from our life purpose, or if events brought about by the lono might lead to death, or injury. Aumakua respects our independence and will only guide us back to our life purpose and no more. It does not dominate us. Aumakua seeks harmony and unity and is motivated away from disharmony; in this way aumakua can help us achieve greater balance and peace.

There is fourth aspect called *kanaloa*, that relates to aumakua. Kanaloa is a companion spirit to aumakua. Kanaloa is equivalent "to one's essential identity or core Self."[182] For me aumakua is formless in nature while kanaloa is a part of form.

In Hawai'ian, ku, lono, and kanaloa are depicted in tikis or carved forms; aumakua is not. The tiki of kanaloa has a high headdress that reaches down to the ground, symbolizing "the power of creative thought and direct involvement with the physical world."[183] Kanaloa's eyes are wide open, symbolizing complete awareness. The tiki is carved with two sets of eyes, so it literally has "eyes in the back of its head," and thus can perceive all things. Aumakua perceives in this same way.

Hawai'ian Style Healing

> All healing, in the kahuna view, is really nothing more than the result of natural communication with the aumakua, of allowing its source energy to flow freely along the original *aka*[184] pattern. All illness or distortion of any kind results from interference with that flow.[185]

In the huna tradition illness is caused by tension that is the result of conflicts of thought. "Healing occurs in kahuna healing when a person is helped to re-attune this natural flow (of mana) by removing obstructions, distortions caused by conflicting thought patterns."[186] Within this tradition, there are a number of methods that can be employed to create healing. There are three areas that we can work with: matter, energy, and current manipulation. We are able to influence matter with diet, medicine (including herbs), ritual, fasting, and by using highly charged energy devices, such as crystals, or orgone devices like those developed by Wilhelm Reich. Traditionally massage, *lua*, a form of hand to hand combat used to release emotional energy, and *hula* (which means "to raise the sacred flame,") are used when the energy of a person needs to be affected. Current manipulation is based on the idea that currents of energy run through us (as in Chinese, Japanese and Tibetan medicine). Hawai'ians use *kahi*, which is a light hand work done with a open palm on areas of tension within the body, or *kaomi* which uses specific points, as in acupressure. Kahi is effective based on the amount of *mana* the healer's hands emit.

Field manipulation or *manamana* looks like kahi, but the practitioner's hands never touch the body. Hands are held about one foot away from the body and mana or energy is emitted from the practitioner's hands and transferred to the patient. It is also possible to discharge excess energy from the body with this technique. This is similar in effect to how acupuncture needles are used to either build energy or remove excess energy from the body.

There is also the manipulation of thought that can work wonders. In this technique, seven basic principles are employed to guide our mind; and guided visualization often accompanies this form of healing. The basic principles are *ike* (awareness), *kala* (freedom from limitations), *makia* (concentration, planning, setting new goals and beliefs), *manawa*, (presence, and establishing new patterns of thought and behavior through persistence), *aloha* (love, forgiveness, trust), mana, (energy, confidence, and all power comes from within us and) and *pono* (flexibility and knowing there is always another way to do everything). Each of these principles can be used to dispel its opposite; ike is used for ignorance, kala for limitations, makia for confusion, manawa for procrastination, aloha for hate and distrust, mana for fear and pono for doubt.[187]

As an example, I used to get fever blisters when I ate chocolate. My conscious mind knew that chocolate was high in the amino acid that inhibits the production of lysine and that this increased my chances of getting fever blisters. It also knew that when I ate chocolate I would get a fever blister on my lip. So for seven years this self-confessed chocoholic never let it pass her lips, until one day at a lunch after my first huna training. I asked a friend if I could have a bite of her chocolate mousse and she agreed. My husband looked at me; with trepidation, but I didn't let his doubt stop me, I was going to see if what I learned could be applied. Remembering that the body consciousness is motivated away from pain and toward pleasure, I went to work.

I began to work with my ku, like a cheerleader, I began telling my ku that chocolate was the perfect food, that chocolate mousse was rich, luscious and delicious, and that it was full of pleasure and delight. As I did this I built my mana with my breath and sent it forth, as I took a bite of the most delicious mousse I had ever tasted. This confirmed the energized thoughts I had been sending my ku. I knew that this was far more pleasant than fever blisters, and now my body consciousness or ku, knew it too. I finished the bite, continuing to tell my ku what a wonderful taste and experience chocolate was. Since that day I have never had another fever blister from eating chocolate.

This demonstrates that by tapping into Source via the breath, and through the building of mana, I tapped into aloha and was able to heal the conflicting thoughts that my conscious mind held. Using the healing principles of Huna, I was able to change the ideas and beliefs within my conscious mind to create a new pattern for my ku or body consciousness to follow.

Oriental Medicine and Energy

To the scientist, energy is no more than the force or substance that is released, for instance when a chemical reaction takes place. This is how neuroscience perceives energy. But energy is more than that: if we sit quietly, allowing our thoughts to settle in an open and receptive state, it is possible to perceive this energy as it moves and flows within our body. There are many names for this energy: in Hawai'i we call it mana, in India it is called *prana*, in Tibet *lung*, in China *chi*, and in Japan it is called *ki*.

Energy travels or flows through channels, or meridians within the body and chakras. This energetic system of channels has roots that are thousands of years old, dating back to ancient China, India, and Tibet. Chinese, Japanese and Tibetan medicine are all based on the principle that energy flows through the body and that these rivers of energy can be tapped into to support the body's organs and general health.

In acupuncture, the meridians are associated with different organ systems, extraordinary vessels, and channels. Very simply, these meridians can be tapped into at certain points on the body to balance the chi within the system thus supporting the various organ systems. This is accomplished by removing excess chi or by tonifying or building the chi. Where and if this needs to be done is governed by the twelve pulses, tongue diagnosis, as well by asking the person about their symptoms, and listening to the body, which includes hearing and smelling.

> Chinese medicine, one of the oldest, longest tested and most powerful and trusted medical systems in the world, views the body as an eco-energetic system. It speaks of vibrational subtle energy that must be integrated into the cellular matrix by passing through a specialized step down system of 'transformer stations' that yogic tradition calls chakras.[188]

This form of medicine arose out of a meditation tradition where yogis and contemplatives perceived the working of the body from an internal level without cutting into the body. The interesting thing about this approach is that the energy is perceived first and the cellular or molecular level is secondary. Francisco Varela, in the book *Healing Emotions,* asked the Dalai Lama why this is so, since in the West the cellular is the most immediate and important.
His Holiness replies,

> One reason could be that lung, or energy as defined in the Buddhist Tantric literature, is the mount or the vehicle through which consciousness and mental events occur. But it's also the case that you can follow this energy even to the most subtle levels of consciousness, and at that level you've really left behind the gross physical level of cellular activity. By understanding and manipulating these energies, you have a direct effect on the mental states, which is why the yogis emphasized their importance. Further, influencing your mind or changing your mental state can also affect the physiological state of

your body. It doesn't work the other way around. A change in a physiological state does not necessarily affect the mind, especially at the subtle levels.[189]

Everything is energy, our minds, and our bodies. So, if we make a change at an energetic, mental, or emotional level we can affect our health and physiology. In this way the chakras become a useful tool for inward exploration and outer healing. By understanding the traits, psychology, traumas, and patterns that each of these centers holds, we can heal our mind and body.

A Brief Discussion of Chakras: A template for deep inquiry and psychological work

Our chakras can be used as a blueprint for deep inquiry and for understanding the psychology of our inner being. This system of psychological referencing was founded in Indian yogic traditions, and in Transforming Embodiment the chakras are used as a framework for investigating symptoms, emotional and relationship issues and belief systems.[190]

Traditionally, there are seven major chakras located along the spinal column. Each chakra is associated with different themes and corresponding emotions, and each has a distinct focus. Each chakra is also associated with certain psychological patterns, traumatic experiences, belief structures, and emotions. The major chakras are linked to emotional states, our physical health and to the different major endocrine glands in the body. Traditional eastern medicine sees these energy centers as being connected to the immune system as well.

The flow of energy within the chakras is vital and continuous. Chakras are never closed, for if they were we would die. However, their level of activity may vary. "Extremes of overactivity or underactivity produce the imbalance that leads to disease."[191] Illness and stress can impair the energy flow within the chakras and subtle body[192] and disease can manifest if the imbalance continues over time. There are many minor chakras within the energy or subtle body as well, but our focus will be on the seven major body chakras and three chakras outside of the body, that align with the central channel or spine.

Chapter Seven

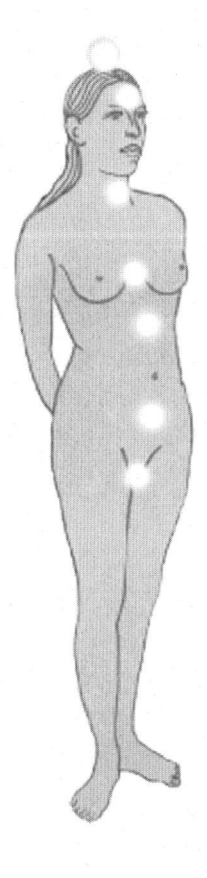

When certain problems arise in our lives there is a direct association to the different chakras within our subtle body; knowing the traits and qualities of these centers can provide us with a template when doing inner work.[193]

For instance, traditionally, the area of the mid chest at the sternum is linked to the heart. Very simply, issues centered in this area involve love, trust, and self-esteem. When this area is examined, issues of betrayal may also arise. Diseases of the breast, heart, or lungs might surface if this area is afflicted, by great unconscious emotional pain or ancient trauma. Chronic upper spinal misalignments can all be linked to issues of the heart chakra. Symptoms, emotions and beliefs can be directly correlated to the different chakras or energy centers. "The experience encountered at these focal points can be followed outward into any area of human thought or endeavor."[194]

The chakras are interlinked and are only considered separately to understand and examine their individual characteristics. When we look at them from an energy standpoint, the chakras are a dynamic, interrelated system. One might imagine the chakras as a beautiful string of jewels, each with its own color, shape, size, sound and vibrancy and movement. However, if we were to take such a necklace apart, each stone would be lovely, but it would be incomplete. The harmony would be changed; it would be like listening to one note of a chord played by one instrument instead of a full chord being played by an orchestra.

The first chakra is located at the base of the spine, at the perineum. Issues traditionally associated with this area relate to survival and fear. In my practice, I've noticed that this area is associated with trauma, boundaries, eating disorders, financial issues, sexual abuse, abandonment and neglect, as well as basic food, shelter, financial, comfort and procreative needs. Issues about protection, safety, and one's ability to be connected to living on the earth are also associated with this chakra. This chakra is aligned with the adrenal glands and kidneys, as well as the blood, immune system, bones and joints.

The second chakra is located a few inches below the navel at what is traditionally, the *hara*, or *da dien*. (Hara is the Japanese word and da dien is the Chinese word for this area of the body). The hara or da dien is thought to be the center of the body in these traditions. "It is thought to be the center of gravity and the point where equilibrium is found."[195] Traditionally this area is associated with sexuality and deep emotions.

Chapter Seven

Beliefs about self-definition and ideas of how we see ourselves as men and women dominate this area. Relationships of all kinds, and the dilemmas they bring, such as emeshment[196] and shame, are associated with the second chakra. Gender issues, as well as issues about children and family, are also noted in this area. Traumas to this area can include rape, sexual or emotional abuse, abortions, and miscarriages. The gonads or ovaries are linked to this chakra, as are the uterus, prostate, testes, and penis.

The third chakra is found at the solar plexus, just below where the ribs meet. Central themes within this chakra include issues of power, ego, control, anger, self-esteem, and being capable and assertive in the world. I have also noticed that issues of manipulation, victimization and the use or abuse of power can be found in this area, as well as problems with will and willpower. Problems with digestion, both physical and mental, can also be seen here. This chakra regulates and is connected to the pancreas, liver, and stomach.

The first three chakras operate unconsciously, from instincts, but as we move to the heart chakra (the fourth chakra) at the center of the chest just above the diaphragm, the energy and focus change. The energy of the heart chakra feels less dense, and it vibrates differently than the lower three chakras. The transition and sensation may be quite subtle, but the difference is distinctive. The heart chakra acts as the bridge between the upper and lower chakras, and brings with it a sense of compassion. An image sometimes associated with this chakra is an equal-armed cross, further symbolizing the idea that this chakra acts as an intersection, or crossing point. Issues of love, trust, intimacy, self-acceptance, betrayal, empathy, grief and nurturance reside within the heart chakra. This center is associated with the thymus and with the heart, lungs, breasts, and upper back.

For example, if a person is suffering from a "broken heart," this is the area to investigate. If a client feels a sense of abandonment as well, the first chakra needs to be explored. If this suffering stems from a relationship, the second chakra would also have to be examined. This example is a simple demonstration of how the system is interconnected and cannot be seen merely as parts, but as an interactive whole.

Moving up the spine, the fifth chakra is found at the throat and neck and is chiefly associated with communication and creativity.

In yogic traditions, this chakra is also connected to listening, receiving nurture and attention. Blocks in creative expression, because self-judgment or criticism is strong may find understanding and relief when the fifth chakra is studied. Beliefs about communication patterns that create misunderstandings can also be associated with this chakra. The thyroid gland is linked to the energy center of the throat and the neck is also associated with this chakra.

As we continue to move up through the chakras, the energy becomes still subtler. One can sense and feel the energy become less dense, similar to how air is rarefied at higher elevations. This is especially pronounced if the chakras are open and unblocked.

The sixth chakra is found at the brow, just above and between the eyes. This area is often called the third eye. This chakra is strongly associated with intuition, introspection, the balancing of rational and intuitive intelligence and the left and right brain. Imagination and visioning are also included in my understanding of this chakra. Limiting belief systems concerning the intellect, and especially the intuition, are often seen in this chakra. This chakra is associated with the pituitary gland, the eyes, the ears, and brain.

The seventh chakra is located at the top of the head. In yogic schools this is the last major chakra. This crown chakra is linked to spiritual awareness, autonomy, interdependence, self-knowledge and union with our wisdom Self. Issues concerning independence and transpersonal or spiritual understandings may arise when investigating this chakra. Feelings and experiences of spiritual isolation or punishment may also be encountered when examining the crown chakra. The pineal gland is linked to this chakra.

Psychic schools of thought reveal that there are three more chakras that exist outside of the physical body. They provide additional information on how a person relates to being in a body, as well as, how they feel about being connected to the cosmos and the earth.

The eighth chakra is found above the head at a distance of twelve to eighteen inches. This chakra concerns the distribution of energy into the body's energy centers. Issues of how much information we feel we can take in, hold, and maintain, or how much we are willing to let flow into our chakras are some of the concerns found in this area. The ninth chakra is the place where the universal and personal spiritual

Chapter Seven

energies meet. Issues related to spirit, god, and again, our ability to hold, share or express this energy can be found within this chakra, which is located up to thirty-six inches above the crown chakra. The tenth chakra is below our feet and concerns grounding, presence, embodiment and our connection to the earth and our bodies. This chakra is found between six to thirty-six inches below our feet. Issues of the tenth chakra include grounding, presence, and embodiment issues. as well as our willingness to be in a body. Spiritual contracts that were formed before we were born can also be found within this chakra.

Ideally the flow of chakra energy moves from the right shoulder over the head to the left shoulder. This is how the energy of our aura flows as well. The chakra system is interconnected in the following way: starting at the heart chakra at the center of the chest over the sternum, the energy pathway spirals out and up, traversing across the right breast, to the throat. From the throat the energy continues the spiral down the left side of the body to the solar plexus, where the ribs meet. From the solar plexus the energy ascends up the right side of the body to the third eye, or brow. Once again the energy moves down the left side of the body to just below the belly button, the spiral continues as the energy climbs up the right side of the body all the way to the crown of the head. The energy completes the circuit as it descends down the left side of the body to the base of the spine where it finally comes to rest. So, the third chakra, and the throat are connected, as are the second, and the sixth chakras, and the crown chakra and the first.

Everything emerges from the heart and moves out from the center of our being. Issues surrounding communication and power of the fifth and third chakras are connected, as are issues of visioning, dreaming and relationship, which correlate to the sixth and second chakras. Issues of survival and independence of the first and seventh chakras are also interconnected.

The first, third, fifth and seventh chakras are associated with a single area in the body: the perineum, solar plexus, throat and crown. While the second, fourth and sixth chakras relate to areas where there are two parts of the body emphasized—the right and left brain, the right and left breast or the right and left ovary or testicle. A pattern of individual then dual energy exists as we move from one chakra to the next. The drawing below illustrates the flow of the energy as it travels from the heart and shows the connections between each of the chakras.

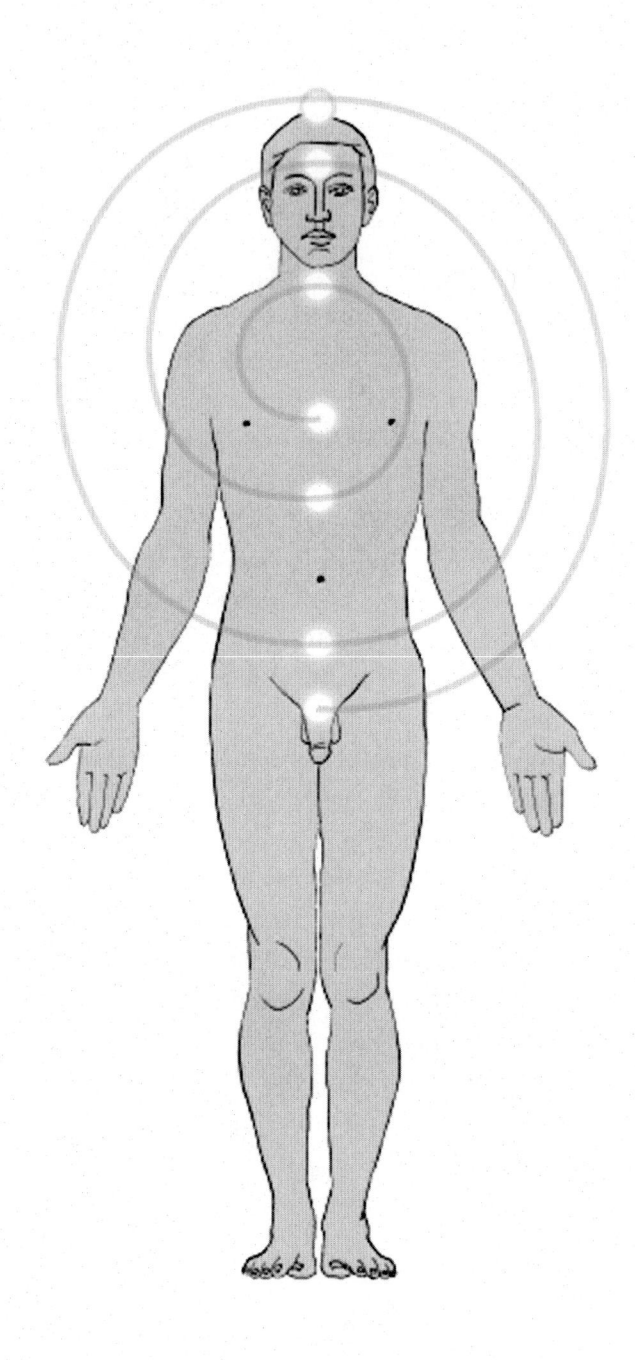

Chapter Seven

The chakras can be a vital resource for information and stored memory patterns, and great relief can be achieved when we investigate our chakras. This can be done in a systematic manner starting at the root or base chakra and moving up through the individual energy centers. Each chakra can also be explored as issues come up that correspond to the psychology or issues within the different chakras. There are also intuitive exercises that can be done to energize, regulate, and balance the chakras and to bring the imagery and memories held with them into clearer view. Practices and meditations using light and sound have deep effects upon the chakras and a corresponding potent effect on our psychology and soma. I have witnessed profound changes as my students have explored their chakras and energy systems using both light and sound.

As noted above in the description of the chakras, we can see that different organs and the endocrine system are associate with different chakras. Dr. Paul Pearsall concurs that the seven transforming energy centers of the body correspond to both physiological, endocrine and neuro-emotional systems within the body. So, by affecting change within a chakra, we can change not only our beliefs and memories, but our health and well-being as well.

Dr. Brugh Joy's book *Joy's Way* and Jack Schwarz's books *Voluntary Controls* and *Human Energy Systems* are three classic texts that discuss the chakra system. Dr. Joy's book has some excellent drawings of the chakra and energy system; he describes the secondary chakras as well. Anodea Judith's *Eastern Body, Western Mind* is a comprehensive guide to the chakras and very well-researched book.

Infinity Breath Meditation

Begin by focusing your attention on your breath. Feel the rise and fall of your belly and chest as you breathe deeply in and out. Feel the temperature of the air as you breathe in and out through your nose. Notice how your breath caresses your throat, bronchia, and lungs as the air passes in and out. Focus too on your heart and its constant rhythmic pulse as blood courses throughout your system, nurturing every cell in your body. Sense your chakras starting at the base of your spine and moving up one by one, all the way to the top of your head. Feel the energy of each of these centers, and when your attention reaches the crown of your head feel the energy move upward, out of your body through the eighth and ninth chakras that are above your head and, like a fountain, feel that energy wash over your entire being. Now focus your attention on your feet, and extend that attention all the way down to your tenth chakra, just like in your grounding visualization, imagine your mind and energy extending into the earth to its core. Notice your body as you do this and stay with the breath. Now bring your attention back to your center, to your heart, chest, and lungs. Feel yourself breathing and being breathed. With your mind on the center of your chest, imagine a strand of golden light extending from your heart through your heart and down your back, all the way into the earth forming the bottom half of a figure-eight as this strand of light dives into the earth as deeply as you can imagine. Now on the in-breath follow this strand of golden light as it completes this lower figure-eight and comes back to your heart. Breathe this half of the figure-eight for a few moments to familiarize yourself with its movement. Then follow this strand of golden light as it travels from your heart, up your spine and neck, out of your body and over the crown of your head forming another large arc. It continues along this arc above your ninth chakra and flows over your face to form the other half of the figure-eight before it descends back down into your heart. Breathe and follow the pathway of golden light as it moves over your ninth chakra and back to your heart again for a few breaths. Once you are familiar with these two movements we are going to merge them into a large infinity. Breathe in and as you exhale imagine golden light moving from your heart, down your back, and legs and out the soles of your feet. See this light dive into the earth as deeply as you can imagine. Following the arc of the lower figure-eight, breathe in and see this strand of golden light ascend up the front of your body all the way up back to your heart. Relax for a moment and breathe naturally. Then take a deep breathe in and see this strand of light flow up your spine, neck, and up the back of your head. See this golden light flowing upward and out, forming the second arc of the figure –eight well above your body. As this light passes over the crown of your head, exhale and see this golden light wash over your face as it travels back to your heart. Breathe the light in this way until it becomes one breath.

9 th chakra

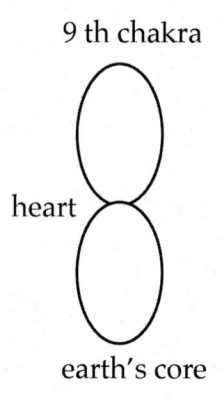

heart

earth's core

This practice marries the energy of the earth to the energy of spirit and it uses your body and heart as the vehicle, as your breath travels along this pathway. It allows you to experience spaciousness, and connected awareness and builds a bridge between heaven and earth via your being. It nurtures your self, the earth, and the universal energy that surrounds us. Practice this for 10 minutes at a time; if you get light-headed stop and re-ground. Let the flow of energy be very natural like a baby's breathing when it is asleep. Be gentle with yourself and this new breathing practice.

INTERLUDE

HEALING THE ORIGINS OF RELATIONSHIP PATTERNS: A JOURNEY ACROSS TIME

Our chakras, energy systems, and body are conscious and deeply alive. If we wish to, we can access the entire history of our being through the body and chakras. By gaining access to this body of knowledge we can answer our most perplexing questions.

Marika 1998 [197]

Introducing Sara

Sara was working as an artist and ran a successful wholesale and retail business when we first met. She originally came to New Mexico to study massage and natural healing, but later, after finishing school, she was drawn to the art of ceramics. Sara was a student and client on and off for ten years and took a variety of classes[198] with me, as well as working privately when the need arose. She had a daughter a few years after we met and was also an independent single mother.

Over the years we worked on a variety of relationship issues and obstacles she faced. Sara became aware of some of her patterns and saw how her parents relationship had deeply affected her. She realized that she repeated many of her mother's patterns and chose men who were unavailable to her, like her father had been with both her and her mother.

She changed many behaviors and unwound a series of memories and emotions from a past life where she had been married to a man, who she did not love, and who later kept her prisoner. Remembering this, she grasped why relationships had been so unsatisfying and unfulfilling for her.

This interlude tells that story of Sara and Lee and how Sara uncovered the roots of her unyielding dread that surrounded her new relationship with Lee.

Sara experiences her past life memories as if she is viewing them on a screen. As we will see, there is some detachment as she views her experiences, however when she remembers Lee's death, in this previous lifetime they shared, her experience changes. She opens herself to the memory fully, and in so doing she touches and feels her original grief anew. At this point her position has changed from that of a watcher, to a participant. In doing this she is finally able to feel and release the trauma, sadness and loss that bound her to that lifetime, and its emotions and beliefs.

Highlights from Sara's Previous Sessions

Sara is presently in a long distance relationship with Lee. Lee frequently leaves her to go back home to work in the Virgin Islands, or to travel for pleasure or on various work assignments. They have split up a number of times over this issue. Sara says that he seems to only be able to be in their relationship for short periods of time before he has to go.

In a previous session, Sara remembered a past life where she and Lee were lovers, they lived on the coast, and he was a sailor. They loved each other but in this past lifetime he went off to sea and Sara found out she was pregnant after he left. Sara vividly remembered how she watched the boats and the sea and waited for him to return. She gave birth to a baby girl in this past life and the predominate feeling she remembered was of waiting—always waiting.

Interlude

In the present, Sara feels a deep connection with Lee and feels that he may be "the one," even though he leaves her and has been with other women. Lee continues to return to her and she takes him back each time, which she says is uncharacteristic, because she would normally throw a man out if he did such things.

Sara's Session

After doing her grounding, protection and connecting to her inner Self, Sara tells me how she always feels a strong sense of dread when Lee leaves, and that it is different than how she has felt in the past when lovers have left or relationships have split apart. She wants to understand why she feels this dread so strongly.

E: As she is voicing these words, images begin to come into my mind, giving me the impression that Lee did not return from his sea voyage. I recognize that this may be why Sara feels such dread each time Lee leaves her in this life. I notice these images and feelings and let them go.

E: Let's go back to the lifetime we worked with last week and see if you can follow that story forward.

S: I'm going to see Lee soon and I want to complete this. I don't want to hold on anymore, it hurts too much. I *can* stop struggling with this relationship. I just have to trust the love, the deep love we share. I feel the strength of that love, it's never left me, even if Lee leaves. That's our bond. It's funny, I was watching Lee sleep the other night and he looks very similar to how he looked in the "past." I looked at him and realized how much I love him and how deep our bond is. So why is this so hard?

E: Let's see why that is. Take a few deep breaths and move back to the point when you were waiting by a sea wall with your little girl.

S: Yes.

E: Her voice deepens. Sara sounds relaxed as she says yes. The pace and timbre of her voice are accompanied by a shift in her energy This signals to me that she is moving into an altered state and closer to her past life experience. I give her a few minutes, so she can deeply connect with her inner world and experience of last week. I gently breathe with her matching my breath to hers. The room becomes very still and quiet. Our rapport deepens.

The energy within the room at this time vibrates much slower than when we began, as the energy in the room settles and slows down.
E: Sara, can an you allow yourself to move forward, see yourself older and your daughter grown up? Notice the scenery around you, what are things like, where are you, and has your man come back?
Time passes as she focuses inwardly and settles back into her experience of this previous lifetime.
S: I'm alone.
E: Can you see what has happened to him?
S: In this lifetime, every time he leaves I get this sinking feeling.
Sara has flipped into the present, demonstrating that she is not quite ready to work with what happened in her past. We change course and follow this feeling.
E: Allow yourself to be open to any experience that pops up. Where is the first time you ever felt this sinking feeling? Allow yourself to float and hold that question gently in your mind. Go to any place where you have felt this sinking sensation before.
S: I remember having an experience of drowning once. In this life, I've always been terrified of the water, but I learned to swim when I was 21. A girl friend taught me to swim and we would go to a reservoir, and I remember being afraid especially when we would swam across to a little island. One time when we were swimming to this island, I opened my eyes and saw a face beneath me in the water and I had the feeling that it was being pulled down.
This image of someone being pulled down may relate to Lee and his not returning in their past life together. Sara's inner knowing is bringing her present-day experience of drowning into the session.
E: Good. Can you go back in, to the past where you are waiting and see what happens next?
S: Yes.
Again she takes some time as she opens and explores inwardly.
S: He didn't come back—not because he didn't want me—he just didn't come back.
E: Oh, (pausing). Can you follow him, and go to him with your attention? Follow his life forward now, from when he left and tell me what you see.

Interlude

Remembering how deep her bond with Lee is, I sense she will be able to travel to him in this way. By following him, she can understand the dread she feels each time he leaves her in the present. Their love will allow her to follow his experience.

S: He's in a hurricane or some very bad weather. He never made it anywhere.

E: What do you mean he never made it anywhere?

S: I think the whole ship went down. I don't get the impression that they made it back to shore. It's like there is some kind of barrier and they never make it back to land. I see the ship's wheel is spinning and there is no one at the ship's helm.

E: Come back to yourself on the shore now, what is happening for you, how are you doing?

Time passes again as she works with the question.

S: On some level I knew that he died on that voyage. We had such a deep love, I felt it, my body felt it and I decided to stay alone. I never married or anything. Even thought I felt this I always hoped he would return.

Her voice sounds very remote as she describes her life. It is quiet and a bit distant. This knowing she speaks of is the knowingness of her inner Self, which is connected to her body consciousness that registered Lee's death.

E: You raised your daughter?

S: Yes. (She begins to cry.)

E: Is this death why it's so scary when Lee leaves in the present?

S: Yes, I think so. (Her weeping deepens. She weeps for quite some time, remembering and grieving her loss.)

I breathe with her and move across the room to hold her as she cries. As I hold her, I can feel that her inner world is shifting. This shift feels like I am holding onto something very shaky yet strong, like a newborn lamb or colt that is getting its legs under it for the first time. It feels as if this shift is happening quite naturally. As I continue to breathe with her. I sense Sara understands that her lover left because it was his job as a sailor, not because he didn't love her. I also understand that she has begun to accept that he did not return because he died, and knows now that he did not abandon her.

As she reexperiences this loss, I feel her sadness in my own heart and wait until her crying calms and eases, before I move back to my seat.
S: In that lifetime he said he would come back and he never made it. He never came back, so it was just my daughter and I, alone.
E: Like you and your daughter in this lifetime.
S: Yes. (She weeps.) Um. Wow. (Time passes.)
At this point Sara is visibly grieving and reorganizing at the same time. Her tears demonstrate her grief and the way she says Um brings with it a distinct feeling of understanding. She grasps perhaps for the first time the interconnectedness of the two experiences and lifetimes.
E: What else happens?
Sara shifts her attention again and "goes in."
S: I raised my daughter, I loved her so much—she was a part of him and such a gift. Time passes and we're in town, and I see her with her betrothed. She's all grown up. I realize I'm going to miss her. I took good care of her and myself, but I feel kind of empty. I'm not a broken woman, I have a lot of strength, but I am not going to be with anybody else.
Sara flips back into the present and continues to make connections.
S: It's really interesting, when I think about it, Lee's father died when he was 26 or 27 and for his mother, that was it. There was nobody else, she's about 66 now and she's still working, a real independent lady. Lee really respects that his mother has only been with his father and apparently he was the first man she had ever been with and she stuck with him through and through. I think Lee sees that in me.
E: Interesting. So you were strong and alone, and independent like Lee's mother in the present?
S: Yeah, I was, and I'm remembering that.
E: Good, but we need to look at that feeling of emptiness you mentioned. Go back in if you need to and see if there anything else.
S: There's a hole in my heart.
E: Really, can you ask what you need to do with this hole in your heart?
Time passes.
S: I need to remove the image, I'm lifting it out, the heart with its hole. (She pauses) I burned it and it disappeared ashes and all.

Interlude

E: How's that feel? How's your heart now?
S: Better, lighter.
E: Do you think you can enter into this relationship whole-heartedly? Check with your heart.
S: Ummmm.

Her voice lowers and goes down as she says "Um." She seems to sink back into her inner world, truly feeling the question. Her voice and being sound very relaxed.

S: Um hum, I can.
E: There's the healing, I think.
S: Um hum.
E: How's that feel?
S: It feels good.
E: Does it feel more complete than it has before?
S: Oh yeah.

I ask these questions to ground or affirm her new feelings. Sara sounds really relieved. Her voice is lower, her body is more relaxed than when she came in, and it seems like something has truly released. I sense that the fear that Lee will die when he leaves her has been resolved. There is a palpable sense of this and a feeling of relaxation in the room.

E: Is there anything else, you want to share?
S: I feel I have a whole new understanding. He didn't want to leave me, he just went off to do his job and for the adventure of it. He loved me though very much.
E: This is very similar to how it is now, isn't it?
S: Yep. He has come and gone so many times, it is similar. Huh, but since he's been here this trip, he's been going to work and coming home. It's felt a little safer. We have a family kind of and it's really nice; I've been glowing and Josie loves it. But there's been this nagging fear that he will leave and not come back. That's changing now, I can feel it changing inside of me. I understand what happened he drowned and I was alone but we can go on from here.
E: You're letting go of your fear.
S: Maybe. I feel much better about things.
E: Good work Sara.

Updates and Interesting Correlation's

Sara tells me a few weeks later that hurricanes make Lee very anxious. During a recent hurricane alert, even with the hurricane far out to sea and not a direct threat to the Virgin Islands, Lee became very unnerved. She adds that it now makes sense to her why Lee also hates sailing, and is so afraid of hurricanes.

March 1995

Sara and Lee have split up again and she is back from a trip to the Virgin Islands. Over the past six months, their relationship has gone through a series of extremes, from Lee wanting to marry Sara—to the point of him asking her to leave, saying he did not want to be in relationship with her the way things were. She shared this view and understood that they were not ready to be together in a long-term relationship.

Just before leaving to return home however, Sara became pregnant and miscarried. During her pregnancy and miscarriage, Lee became very tender and supportive. Sara felt the pregnancy and subsequent miscarriage, and Lee's ability to be with her during this time, were very important, and needed to be experienced by them both. She is uncertain as to why she believes this but she feels it nonetheless. It was very difficult for Sara to leave Lee with the tenderness reemerging in their relationship, but she knew it was the right thing to do. Since her return from the Virgin Islands, she has come back and done additional work with me regarding their break up.

In session we worked with her earlier feeling of waiting and Sara has understood and released her habit of perpetually waiting in her relationships. She sees how this has been pattern in both her present relationship with Lee and their past life relationship when he was a sailor. Always having to wait she feels, is what fueled her deep anger with Lee over the past few years. Her anger, being left and abandoned and the uncertainty of waiting were all connected. While she may have "known" that he had died she realized she still held onto the hope that he would return. In this session she decided that waiting was no longer an option and decided to move on.

July 1995

Lee contacted Sara again and they have been talking over the phone for the past three months. He has been with a former girlfriend again, but this time he has found it was an empty and shallow affair. This new feeling of emptiness prompted him to contact Sara again. For the first time, perhaps, Lee knows that there is something special between them. He expresses this to her, but Sara's position is very different.

She has been clearing up the things in her life that have been muddled, her difficult relationship with her daughter's father, and issues with her family of origin and those from her relationship with Lee. She has much clearer psychological boundaries and knows what she wants, what she will take, and what she will not put up with. While she is hopeful about her relationship with Lee, she is much more centered in the moment and is not waiting any more.

This is a very important change for Sara. She is able to be more present, not dwelling on the past, or Lee's faults and her difficulties with their relationship. She also is no longer willing to be a bystander within her life or her relationship and is taking a more active role now in creating a healthy relationship for herself.

She has set up clear guidelines for their reunion in the fall. Lee has stated he does not wish to be separated from her again and has mentioned marriage once more and appears sincere. She, in turn, has brought up the difficulties they had experienced previously, and Lee's response has been new, saying that they will work their problems out together.

January 1996

Sara and Lee have split up again, but this time she kicked him out. She packed his things and told him to get out. He left for the Virgin Islands the next day. This was a real turning point for Sara and tests her old pattern of waiting to its depths. She finds that she really cannot wait anymore and that she would rather be alone than be with a man who displays such mixed emotions. His on again—off again behavior finally has worn thin, she says.

April 1996

In April, Lee was back in touch with Sara, saying he wanted to start over and asked her to come to the Virgin Islands, alone. She decided to try one more time and went to see him for two weeks without her daughter. They had a wonderful time. Lee has re-examined his wants and needs in relationship and grown from this process of self-examination, Sara realized. Since Sara's return they have continued to talk via long distance and have worked out many of their initial problems.

Sara says she is no longer angry with Lee, as she was in the past. If she gets angry with Lee now, she says that her anger is less intense and it is appropriate to the moment and no longer burdened by her past and the unresolved traumas from her distant past. When Sara released her emotions, this release allowed for the field of energy surrounding their relationship to open and expand, thus relaxing the field energy and giving Lee a chance to change in response to Sara's changes.

This process of energetic resonance or response is very interesting and occurs on many occasions when one person within a relationship makes a change. I do not know how this happens, but when one person in relationship makes genuine deep change, it somehow resonates within the other partner allowing them to become more able to respond and to make a change within themselves.

June 1996

Lee asked Sara and her daughter to come live with him. Sara feels they are finally ready for this next step in their relationship. Sara packed her belongings and she and Josie moved to the Virgin Islands in July. Interestingly at the same time, after a long time on the market, Lee's house has finally sold; giving them the ability to move into a new place of their own making, truly a fresh start. Sara is very happy and so is her daughter. Lee says he wants to spend the rest of his life with them.

December 1996–March 1999

On Christmas Eve 1996, Lee asked Sara to marry him. She said yes. Lee and Sara purchased a house in December of 1997 and at the end of August in 1998 were married. They continue to have their ups and downs, but are working things out together. Lee has realized that his love for Sara is very deep. He also understands how he has taken her love for granted in the past, assuming that Sara would be there no matter what. He has learned that he has to be there for her as well, and is changing, so he can be there for the woman he loves.

Conclusions

This example shows how the remembrance and reliving of important "memories" and "feelings" from another lifetime can help to resolve emotional and relationship conflicts in the present. It also shows how a feeling within the body can guide you to the origins of a problem. The "sinking feeling" Sara felt led her to uncover both her feelings and memories surrounding her fears of abandonment, death and her dread that something might happen to Lee. The dread associated with the sinking feeling was Sara's way into her experience. The dread was the hardest thing for Sara to face, because it required her to face her grief and her anger over Lee's death in the past lifetime they had shared. As she remembered that moment and was able to relive her feelings and be comforted, the dread and the sinking feeling that accompanied it released. With the grief resolved, Sara was also able to process the depths of her anguish and sadness, which further released the shock and trauma of Lee's death from her mind and body; and as time passed we were able to work with another dimension of her anger, surrounding waiting, frustration and stagnation.

Remembering the origins of her frustration with waiting helped Sara resolve her anger that she felt when she was waiting for Lee. Sara saw how her impatience with waiting created her feelings of anger and created great friction in her relationship with Lee. She experienced other releases when she realized how futile this pattern of waiting was, when she kicked Lee out in 1995. She saw anew that this pattern of waiting created her reactions and it was at this time that she learned she could stop reacting in this old way. This experience and the others I have briefly described at the end of the case study have allowed Sara to finally be at home with the man she loves.

Part Four: Mind

8

WHAT IS MIND? WHAT IS MEMORY? EMBODIED MEMORY AND IMAGERY'S ROLE

Assumptions that the brain thinks independently of the body and heart,...and that our cells cannot remember are not in keeping with either the newest scientific knowledge from cellular biology or the oldest wisdom of ancient traditional medicines.

Paul Pearsall [199]

What is Mind?—Body-Mind Connections

When most people think of the mind they think of the brain. This is the place where thinking goes on, it is the place where memories, feelings, perceptions, and imagination are stored. To bring an idea or object to mind is to remember it, so memory has been connected to our mind and brain. But is the mind confined to our brains? This is a question that spurs wide debate within the fields of science, philosophy, psychology, and religion. Like never before, this is an area where deep inquiry and interdisciplinary study is occurring. The Mind Life Conferences between His Holiness the Dalai Lama and Western scientists from a variety of fields are giving us new insights about the nature of mind and consciousness.

More and more, people are beginning to believe that the mind is not just held in the brain, but is now being seen as an interactive, complex network that links both the psyche and soma. Neuroscientist Dr. Candace Pert, who discovered the opiate receptor in 1972, sheds light on this eternal question:

> The mind, then, is that which holds the network together, often acting below our consciousness, linking and coordinating the major systems and their organs and cells in an intelligently orchestrated symphony of life. Thus, we might refer to the whole system as a psychosomatic information network, linking the *psyche*, which comprises all that is of an ostensibly nonmaterial nature, such as mind, emotion, and soul, to *soma*, which is the material world of molecules, cells and organs.[200]

Dr. Pert, when she began her career, thought that the mind and brain functioned separately from the body; through research and discovery, she now sees that they are inextricably linked. Her discovery of the opiate receptor led her to this new view. As she mapped this chemical and traced its origins, she found it not only in the brain but in the body as well. She saw that the mind, body, and emotions were all interconnected and that chemicals once thought to be only in the brain actually roam the body.

Psychoneuroimmunologist Dr. Paul Pearsall suggests that there is not only a mind-body link, but that it is governed and perhaps centered in the heart, with the circulatory systems being the means of transporting information throughout the system. He states, "The 'Mind' as I have proposed it, is an interactive, energetic, dynamic, remembering system functioning as a single whole, coordinated by the power of the heart and maintaining the connection between the brain and the body."[201] In Hindu there is a Sanskrit term, hridaya, that means heart-mind, so the ancient traditions understood this synergy between the heart, body, and mind that science is now examining. This "mind" that remembers is centered not in the brain but within the whole organism, with the circulatory system and heart acting as the transport vehicle for a mind that is systemic.

Long-time researcher, Valerie Hunt, Ed D., believes that the mind is not in the brain, but that it is an energy field that has a specific and individual organization. She believes that each person has their own energy signature and that the mind field carries memories and soul memory that includes everything that a soul has ever been through. In 1998 a lecture at the 2nd International Psychology of Consciousness, Energy Medicine and Dynamic Change, Hunt expressed the following: "The brain remembers and has a record of all the experience this organism has had in the material world, as this thing, from the time it was conceived to when it dies." Dr. Paul Pearsall stresses that "the brain is beginning to look more like an energetic manifestation and holographic info-energetic system, parts of which can be found throughout the body and within every cell."[202] More and more scientists and researchers are seeing not only a link between the body and mind, but they are seeing links between the body, mind, our cells, emotions, and memory, as well.

More than ever before, we can consider that the mind, body and emotions as one interconnected and active energetic system, with the mind being systemic in nature. Early in her career, Dr. Pert thought that emotions were in the brain alone, but as her research developed and progressed she understood more and more that emotions flowed within the body as neuropeptides, or as she would later call them "molecules of emotion." She now believes that the mind and body are one, linked by our emotions. "Mind doesn't dominate body, it *becomes* body—body and mind are one."[203]

> We know that the immune system, like the central nervous system, has memory and the capacity to learn. Thus it could be said that intelligence is located not only in the brain but in the cells that are distributed throughout the body, and that the traditional separation of mental processes, including emotions, from the body is no longer valid. If the mind is defined by brain-cell

communication, as it has been in contemporary science, then this model of the mind can now be seen as extending naturally to the entire body. Since neuropeptides and their receptors are in the body as well, we may conclude that the mind is in the body in the same sense that the mind is in the brain, with all that that implies.[204]

What Is Memory?

Conventional wisdom has believed that memory was a function of the brain. Memory is defined as "the mental faculty of storing past experiences and recalling them at will."[205] Memory is also thought of as something remembered. There are two types of memory: explicit memory, which is conscious, like what we ate for dinner; and implicit memory, which is procedural, like how to drive a car, and unconscious. Memories are constellations of images, feelings, emotional responses, and sensory experiences, like smells and sounds. Western psychology submits that three types of memory systems exist: sensory, short term and long term memory. Sensory memory "serves as a temporary storage system for basic information brought in from our basic five senses"...Within this form of memory "our eyes, ears, and other physical senses have their own unique, individual forms of limited sensory memory."[206] Short-term memory is defined as "a system that holds small amounts of information for brief periods of time—usually four to seven seconds"...Short term memory "is limited to seven items or brain bits of information at one time."...Long-term memory holds "vast amounts of information for long periods of time."[207]

According to cardio-energetics, there is a fourth memory system that incorporates the above three and transcends them,

> It suggests that memory is not limited to the two body systems most scientists are willing to agree have a memory—the nervous systems and immune system. In addition to the immune system's cell's memories and nervous system's sensory, short- and long-term memory, cardio-energetics proposes a 'spiritual' or info-energetic memory made especially to store 'fifth force' or 'L' energy, events.[208]

This fourth memory system could be equivalent to the body of experience.

Body-Mind and Memory

> It's true, we do store some memory in the brain, but by far, the deeper, older messages are stored in the body and must be accessed through the body. Your body is your subconscious mind and you can't heal it by talk alone.[209]

This is very close to how the Hawai'ian shamans think about the relationship between our memories and our minds. They, too, believe that memory is stored within the body and that an aspect of mind similar to what western psychology calls the subconscious carries a record of all of our experiences. This differs from the body-mind view in that the shamans of Hawai'i believe that our memories are representations of beliefs.

I agree with both Dr. Pert's observations and those of the Hawai'ian shamans I studied with, as well as with Peter Levine's idea that memories are like a mosaic or an aggregate of many different elements of experience, woven together into a whole. What I have also come to understand is that memories are embodied. They reside in all of our cells, bones, and tissues as well as in our brains, organs, and energy body. Like the Hawai'ians, I believe that memories are constructed whole gestalts linked to images, feelings, emotions, and actual events. Unlike Peter Levine, who believes memory is not a coherent and continuous record of what actually has happened, I think our memories are both a record and a complex interwoven system.

Memories are ephemeral and holographic. They are 'there' but we can't touch them except through our senses and feelings. When we try to remember a friend's face, we see it, and with that image we can be flooded with more images, sounds, shared experiences, memories and feelings. Pearsall says that if we try to remember a loved one's eyes, for instance, we most often will recall the whole person, so he believes that memory is more like a hologram than a one dimensional picture.

Neuroscientists have not been able to find a central memory center within the brain. Memory appears to be everywhere, and yet it is nowhere. Like the Zen masters who try to find a Self, which is not findable, the neurologists and scientists have been unsuccessful in finding a central hub for memory within the brain.

The body and heart are both areas that store memory. Energy cardiologists believe that the heart may be the centralized location for memories. The chakras and energy field or aura also house very dynamic memories. The Hawai'ians believe that the totality of our experience, including our beliefs, feelings and emotions surrounding our experiences reside in the aspect of mind that is body-based. My belief is that we are awash with memories that are stored within our cells, bones, tissues, organs, chakras, energy field, and psyche—a symphony of history.

Felt Sense, Emotions, and Memory

Our feelings and memories are interconnected and both deeply affect our health and well-being. By using our emotions surrounding any given experience, we are able to access a wealth of imagery, feelings, and perceptions about the events that confront us in our daily lives. Our emotions are a gateway opening the door to our inner reality. Within this inner world lies the felt sense. The felt sense is a physical experience, not a mental one, and it is a reflection of our internal body sensations. If we think of a conversation with our boss that didn't go well, afterwards we may feel a knot in the pit of our stomach. This would be a part of our felt sense. Along with this physical sensation, body postures, words spoken and our emotions are all a part of this experience. By working with the sensation within our body, we are able to access the gamut of our emotions and memories of the conversation. That is the beauty of working with the felt sense, because it organizes so much information for us. And our emotions are a way that we find and locate the felt sense within our body; by tuning into where we feel the emotion we are able to find the felt sense attached to the experience or event.

The felt sense is nonlinear, and unifying and it serves us by gathering a great deal of scattered data, which it then gives meaning to. It includes our external senses of sight, sound, smell, touch, and taste and our 'body's internal awareness' as well. The felt sense can be a softer way of approaching intense feelings, as it represents a complete gestalt. This is especially helpful in working with trauma where our memories, perceptions, or sensations may be too intense. When sensations are too intense to manage, imagery will often come first.

Imagery and Intuition

Imagery is the language of the mind and body and it is the way in which the body consciousness communicates to our conscious mind, which then discerns the meaning of the imagery we find with the aid of our intuition. As we relax and open to the imagery within us, we touch into our intuitive mind. When working with imagery we allow the symptom to speak to us directly, we follow the imagery associated with a problem, sensation or emotion we are trying to understand by allowing images to form in our mind's eye that are connected to our problems or symptoms. As we do this, insights can come to us. Working with imagery in this way is like Freud's technique of free association. Imagery becomes a way our unconscious can communicate with us and this is why working with imagery can be so powerful.

Imagery is our direct link to our subconscious and is one of our best allies in our path to healing. Although we tend to think a lot about the events in our lives and the relationships and disharmonies that sometimes exist, thinking alone will not necessarily resolve our problems. I have found that imagery can help us find the wholeness we seek.

Accessing Imagery

In Transforming Embodiment we start each session by relaxing, focusing our attention inward and letting go of any preconceived ideas or beliefs we may have about the situation, symptom, or problem we are inquiring about. Holding our attention lightly and staying relaxed allows images to surface. As we inquire within, we need to let any images arise freely, without judgment. In this receptive state of understanding, insights, and new clarity can be found. Jeanne Achterberg refers to this kind of imagery as "receptive imagery."[210] She expands on this idea saying:

> The gist of the therapy involved relaxing, imaging the part of the body, and then letting the exercise work instead of trying to force a change (using 'passive volition'). These are the ingredients of all healing techniques that use the imagination to heal.[211]

Perhaps we feel a tight knot in our abdomen. When asked its color, in our mind's eye the knot might appear to be a deep purple. This color may bring up emotional memories connected to this color and following those memories can lead us to why our abdomen is tight. The color can also be broken down into its component parts of red, blue, and black and each of these colors can be explored for any memories or emotions that are associated with them. We can then look for where, when and under what circumstances we first felt these feelings or emotions. The possibilities are as limitless as the imagination. We can inquire about the sound, size, shape, or animals associated with any physical, mental, or emotional tension. We can even ask the image to give voice to any messages our mind-body wishes to share with us. This description only scratches the surface of how imagery can inform and teach us about our symptoms, deep emotions, or problems. Similar ideas and techniques can be found in Psychosynthesis.

Relaxation and letting go appear to be the keys to accessing imagery. Our memories also need this same kind of environment in order for them to surface. "Memories do not break free upon being attacked by a jack hammer. They float up as we 'think sideways'. If a person relaxes and lets the mind drift, the memories are far more likely to come in."[212] Memories, traumatic emotional experiences, deep emotions and beliefs all can be accessed when we are in a relaxed state, and with curiosity and detachment we can examine these emotions, memories and beliefs by bringing them into consciousness and initiating a process of possible transformation. Jack Kornfield, in an interview with Daniel Rothberg takes us still further:

> Often, in a person's experience, there will come a constellation of fear, inner attachment, and difficulty that on one level is related to personal history, to trauma in childhood or in this life; this constellation

arises together with emotions, beliefs, and a bodily stored contraction, the 'body of fear'. As the person enters this complex or knot with awareness, interest and compassion and opens to it, then it begins to dissolve, as it is seen, understood and allowed. The constellation is naturally transformed in this process into spiritual energy or spiritual perspective.[213]

Symbols

Symbols are a part of imagery and are another way that the body and psyche can communicate with us. They can be found within our body or chakras. For example, a dove is often considered a symbol of peace, but it can have countless meanings, depending on the individual. In Transforming Embodiment, the client determines the meaning of symbols and imagery and the practitioner only assists in this interpretation process. There is no set interpretation for any given symbol or image. Symbols are understood within the context of each person's experience and intuition.

Symbols and imagery are a means of communicating with the subconscious mind. Symbols circumvent the conscious mind, which is busy perpetually analyzing one's actions and responses, so that a deeper form of communication can take place. Symbols are a form of intuitive communication that the subconscious mind and the wise inner Self might use to communicate with each of us. As we hold an image of a symbol in our mind's eye, and free our minds of thoughts and ideas, intuitive communication begins, allowing us to see the meaning of symbols as we leap beyond our discursive thinking. In this way insights surface and can reveal the inner meaning of symbols.

By contemplating symbols, we are able to identify with them and understand their meaning, how they affect us, and what they represent. By identifying and merging with our experience, in this way, new learning and information is attained.

Imagery and Past Life Memory

When working with imagery and memories from other lifetimes we often identify with the experience we are perceiving in two ways, by direct experience or through detached awareness. In the first we feel the experience very directly, and in the latter it is viewed as if we were watching a movie..."in nearly all cases with claim of memory of a previous life, the subject identifies himself with the images of the claimed memory."[214] and that "...the percipient seems to blend with this other person so that it then seemed to the percipient that he was reliving a previous life directly."[215] This perception of past life experiences is what I call reliving. Knowing is instantaneous and we are certain the experience is real and true. We feel it in our minds and bodies as a resonance and some have shared with me that they feel it in their bones. Others experience their memories at a distance.[216] This is what I call experiencing with detached awareness. In this case, events are viewed as if they are our own but in a remote way. In whatever way we are experiencing these memories and events, whether relived or seen at a distance, we are left with the distinct feeling that we have personally experienced these past lives. Both ways of remembering are important for discovering the origins of our problems.

Working with imagery and memory requires us to merge with our experience while maintaining a part of our consciousness free of the merged association. Ninety-nine percent of the personality is merged with the experience, thus enabling the other one percent to make changes. If we fall into the experience totally, we cannot effect change. This is similar to how shamans work in the Hawai'ian tradition.

Symptoms, physical tensions, and sensations within the body carry past life imagery as well as beliefs and emotions. Our body's experiences, for example, can direct us to the roots of our symptoms and emotional pain. Imagery is used to help us commune with our body experience and questions are utilized to discover the meaning of the images and memories. Our rational intelligence is paired with our intuitive sense as we search for answers and meaning.

Our fears and symptoms can find their origins in past life memories and our fears, tensions and symptoms can help us find the original moment where our fear or pain began. By asking simple revealing questions, like "Where was the first time I encountered this feeling?" "When did I first feel this emotion, and in what context?" or "What was happening to me when I first felt this symptom?" Imagery and memories then form in our minds to answer these questions and the origins of our current problems become a bit clearer for us. We begin to understand what events and situations caused our fear or pain, and we understand why they have stayed with us. With a curious and spacious mind we can discern the beliefs that hold our fears and symptoms in place, and grasp how current symptoms or emotions can be informed by, or linked to, events in both our current and past lives.

Jeanne Achterberg cites Oyle's[217] therapeutic work with a patient called Lillian, who was diagnosed with nonspecific vaginitis and urethritis, chronic cystitis and pelvic inflammation, with no known cause. Lillian found relief for her symptoms in a past life experience. The following description shows how imagery from another lifetime can impact current problems and how it changed Lillian's symptoms.

> ...one night when Lillian was practicing her imagery at home, a coyote named Wildwood flashed into her mind. He advised her to stay by his side, and watch what was about to happen, and told her that what she saw would be related to the fire in her body. She then sensed herself sitting by a campfire, in the midst of a hostile tribe of Indians who held her captive. She experienced the horror of being brutally gang-raped and murdered. 'At the instant of my death...I woke up and was in my body in my room, only the pain was completely gone and hasn't returned since.'[218]

Oyle's patient chose to attribute her experience to a past life, even though she'd never believed in reincarnation before.

I have seen this kind of healing occur—clients who have never considered reincarnation have found solutions to current problems and symptoms within other lifetimes. Jordan, who we met earlier, was surprised by his multiple past lives that he shared with his ex-wife from this lifetime. Alia, who we will meet, had always thought that her stomach problems had originated when she had surgery as an infant. Little did she know that the origins of her symptoms went far beyond this lifetime.

Concerns about False Memory

In the past decade, false memories have generated a lot of controversy in the field of psychology. Memory is seen as an amalgam of events, feelings and images, so what we must look for is sensory-based information or internal body sensations, to determine the "reality" of any given memory. The reality or truth of our memories may not be as important as was once thought, because the body is reacting to the memory as if it were true.[219] So, the important thing is to work with the body's response. Peter Levine. who specialized in working with trauma, feels that it is important to follow the felt sense and the body's reactions even if the "truth" of the experience is in question. The symptoms that comprise the core of the traumatic reaction are the surest way to know that trauma has occurred—if you can recognize how they feel. "I can say with no hesitation whatsoever that *whether Margaret's story was completely accurate or completely 'fabricated' doesn't matter at all in terms of healing her traumatic symptom.*"[220]

Even if a memory is imagined, if there is sensory-based information, i.e., symptoms accompanying the memory, then it is real for the participant.

It is not important if the memory is true or false; if the body reacts and has a felt sense of an incident, then trauma is present. The emotional imprint must be treated as if it were real and released from the individual's nervous system and energy body. Levine's assertions coincide with those of Lenore Terr, who believes that memories are present if signs and symptoms accompany the memory.

In nearly all the cases I have witnessed, clients do believe the experiences they are remembering are actual memories. Their own impressions and feelings about their experiences give them this perception. It is true that memories can be implanted, so it is vital that we ask questions in an open manner, without expectations. Memories will gently flow to the surface then, like dolphins coming up for air. It is also essential that our minds be empty and clear. When we are working on our own, we must be calm, centered, and free of expectations or doubts. This allows the intuition to flow. When our questions are broad and as open ended as possible, memories will be unearthed as we follow our intuition. The mind must be stabilized, though, and we need to be able to distinguish the difference between the voice of our ego and the voice of our wisdom Self.

It is important to understand that the message behind a memory or the meaning of a memory is of far more importance than the truth or fiction regarding the memory. Memories can be metaphors and it is imperative that they are dealt with regardless of their status since they are the body and psyche's means of communicating to each of us. This may sound controversial, but whatever the body believes is its truth. We must respect that and work to resolve whatever symptoms and emotions arise.

Traumatic memories from other lifetimes appear to be governed by similar parameters as traumatic memories in this lifetime, with similarities and parallels. Dr. Lenore Terr, a psychiatrist working with childhood trauma, describes traumatic memory as having certain attributes, such as returning perceptions, behavioral reenactments, and trauma-specific fears. This is similar to what Peter Levine also observed in his work with trauma.

I have found that clients remembering and re-experiencing traumatic memories from this life and other lifetimes have similar experiences. Recurring visions of events, habits of behavior, fears, and phobias can accompany traumatic memories of past lives as well. Sara was never comfortable with sex and, when she recalled a memory from another lifetime where she was sexually brutalized, she was able to understand this fear and reaction. Josette never liked heights, so when she remembered being thrown off a cliff, the severe injuries, and slow death that followed her fear somehow made sense to her. When she released the imprinted memory from her body and visualized the wounds healing, her fear of heights lessened. It became a caution instead of a phobia that immobilized her. Whether the memories are from this life or from another lifetime, they have an impact on us, since these experiences organize our behaviors, fears, relationships, and responses.

Signs and symptoms such as phobias, fears, extreme reactions, and behaviors are associated with traumatic and repressed memory. This is what singles out these experiences. False memories are not accompanied by these types of patterns. This appears to be true of past life memories as well. Patterns, behaviors, and symptoms are cues that something unresolved is present. Stevenson found that signs and symptoms also accompany other life memories. "I believe that one solution to the question of survival lies in the observance of patterns within one personality or organism which were not or could not have been inherited or acquired in the present life of the personality."[221]

When working with memories from other lifetimes or our present, physical sensations give us the understanding that we are on track. If signs and symptoms are not observed or present, we may be in what might be considered a false memory. Memories without signs and symptoms are just a story.

If a person encounters emotions, feelings, energy vibrations, people, places and moods similar to those of the original memory, retrieval of that memory can occur. Like this author, Levine believes that a general emotional state, cue,[222] or trigger is necessary for traumatic or repressed memories to move from the unconscious into consciousness. Memories are prompted to the surface when these cues are triggered, allowing old feelings and emotions to reemerge.

Sara was living with a sexually addicted man who wanted sex every day, when memories of past violations and abuse began to haunt her.[223] These memories were triggered by current life events that were similar to what she had experienced in her past life. However, now unlike in her past, she felt safe enough to review these memories, even though they were scary and painful. When we feel supported and safe memories have a better chance of emerging. And when secure, we are empowered to pursue the origins of our problems and difficulties. When memories surface we are often driven to find out why these memories are so powerful and how they are linked to our present day.

Once a buried memory begins to emerge it cannot be stopped. The process of remembering often has an independent momentum. It appears that the images and memories want to tumble out of our psyche, and there is no stopping this action. This may happen gradually, or in some cases it can happen quite rapidly. If the process is gradual, the filling in of details can continue for weeks as the client works with the memories and events both consciously and unconsciously. This gives the client the opportunity to work with the arising feelings at their own pace without re-traumatization.

Chapter Eight

Embodied, Cellular, Genetic and Systemic Memory Defined

Where do these memories come from that are seemingly buried within our unconscious and subconscious? I have determined that they reside within the very fabric of our being: in our cells, organs, bones, tissues, muscles, blood, skin, i.e., in every system within our body. They lie dormant within us imprinted and etched there by virtue of our intense emotional or traumatic experiences. I firmly believe that memories, which are too intense for the mind to comprehend fall into the body and are embedded there. Memory of this kind is embodied memory, which can be cellular or systemic in nature.

Embodied memory is the record of our relationship to everything: our emotions, thoughts, memories, and energy systems. It encapsulates the body's capacity to remember every event, emotion, thought, or experience we have ever encountered that holds a charge or intense emotion. Embodied memory is a part of what I call the body of experience and is similar to what others like Daniels, call cellular memory; Paul Pearsall identifies this as systemic memory. These forms of memory are different from genetic memory, which consists of the ancestral memories of our forbearers.

Dr. Paul Pearsall, who wrote the *Heart's Code*, regards memory as being systemic and suggests that systemic memory flows freely within the body as "L" energy. Dr. Candace Pert, former researcher for the National Institute of Health and author, of *Molecules of Emotion* has discovered that neuropeptides, tiny chains of amino acids, are pervasive within the body and mind. Dr. Pert says these neuropeptides are molecules of emotion that float freely with our systems, much like what Pearsall describes as L energy. In Dr. Pert's recent lectures she has expressed a willingness to believe that our cells have a form of memory and that the body is an outward manifestation of the mind.

Embodied Memory and Belief

Understanding our memories, emotions and the beliefs accompanying them are the keys to achieving lasting healing. The memory and emotions of an event, or trauma and the beliefs that solidify within consciousness, create our worldview. Thus the belief as well as the memories and emotions, must be treated. The understanding that memories, emotions, and beliefs are not just within the territory of the mind is critical.

Memory In Our Bones

All three are stored within the body. Our body consciousness stores our deep emotional reactions, our memories of experiences, and traumas, as collages and imagery, until we are equipped to face, trace and transform these experiences. The practices of Transforming Embodiment enable and empower us to find both the origins of trauma and the beliefs that ensnare us into maintaining our trauma. By uncovering trauma, deep emotions, and beliefs from the body, we can heal the place where the trauma first occurred. In doing this, we change our experiences and create a new reality for ourselves. We do this to heal the deep emotions that cause our suffering. We must treat the origins of our pain and beliefs that form as a result of our traumatic experiences lest they continue to plague us.

Embodied Memory

In working with embodied memory, imagery, and our senses, body tensions and feeling are our way into the body of experience. Through imagery and sensory-based experiences we can remember and rediscover old feelings, emotional states, physical wounds and even deaths from other lifetimes. Imagery and sensation unlock the doors to these memories, which emerge at any pace; often the process can be intense. The emotional pain and mental anguish of our past experiences are very real and there is a fine line here, because we do not want to re-traumatize ourselves. This is why it is necessary to cultivate a quiet meditative awareness that is both present and detached before attempting to work with traumatic or past life memories. The investigation of symptoms needs to be undertaken when one has truly stabilized one's mind.[224] Many times I have remembered traumas and death experiences; in each case, as I was remembering these previous lifetimes and situations, I was certain that my memories were of real events. My body and mind felt these experiences not as a story but as something remembered from my past.

Out of these past life experiences, I have come to believe that consciousness and thus, memory, have the potential, especially in traumatic events and death experiences, to continue forward. Could it be possible that traumatic events and death memories might be carried forward if, as Buddhism says, the mindstream continues after death?

Stevenson's research confirms my personal and clinical research. "If rebirth does occur, then we would expect information about a previous life to present as memories and ought to be surprised if it is presented otherwise."[225] and "the percipients [in his studies] have always experienced the images as memories of something they have lived through."[226] Even individuals doubting their experience candidly reported that the images came in the form of memories "like images of past experiences of the 'present' life."[227] He also says that the majority of his subjects felt there was continuity between their past and present personalities and that the relationship was akin to how one would experience memories from one's childhood as an adult. My clients have shared the perceptions that Dr. Stevenson's percipients describe.

Memories are systemic and held within the body as imagery, feelings, pain, and beliefs. These memories can be found by exploring muscle tensions, pain, and by going inward to the cells, and systems within the body. All the vital systems and organs of the body, as well as the subtle energy systems of the chakras, aura and energy meridians, can retain memories, which are most often unconscious and may lead to the repeated action in our lives that causes us pain and suffering. By the careful review of the body, its energy systems and memories, one can find deep healing. By working directly with the body's imagery, memories, and sensory experiences, we can transform the origins of our trauma and suffering, and remove these patterns, vibrations, and memories from our consciousness once and for all.

9

THE POWER OF BELIEFS—THEIR GRIP ON OUR REALITY

> For the Kahunas, belief is the fundamental basis for experience of any reality. The idea is that our experience is conditioned by what we believe, and we can only experience what we do believe is possible at some level of consciousness. The more firmly we believe something, the more profoundly it affects our experience.
>
> Serge King [228]

A belief is any idea that we accept as true. Beliefs influence our mental, emotional, and physical behavior. This is why beliefs can be so powerful in our lives, because they shape our perceptions and give rise to our emotions.[229] Feelings and emotions are energetic responses that occur when a belief is stimulated; our emotions are by-products of our beliefs. Beliefs are the basis for all experience and they structure our reality, giving rise to our emotions and symptoms alike. It's as simple as that. Because beliefs are such a centralizing force in organizing our reality, the shamans of Hawai'i have come up with some great definitions that I would like to share.

In Huna[230] there are three different kinds of beliefs: assumptions or *paulele,* attitudes or *kuana,* and opinions or *mana'o.* An assumption is a state of belief where there are no doubts whatsoever. Paulele translates as 'confidence' or 'complete faith' Assumptions often crystallize in consciousness and are not easily changed. Attitudes or kuana are beliefs that are picked up during one's lifetime. They become habitual. We may have doubts from time to time about our attitudes, but they influence our actions and reactions towards life. They are like liquid beliefs that are more easily changed than assumptions. Last we have opinions, or mana'o, which "influence behavior as long as we hold them,"[231] However they are easily changed when we gain new information. All of these contribute in some way to the formation and solidification of belief systems.

There is a sub set within attitudes called kuana,[232] which is a state in which attitudes are seriously questioned. Strong doubts have emerged about the attitudes in question because our experience no longer supports them. This is the state of mind most clients are in when I see them. Several attitudes are competing, causing states of confusion, anxiety, and psychological distress. Some conflicts have been in play so long, that physical symptoms have manifested.

Beliefs Shape Our World

Belief systems are complex, interwoven structures of perception, memories, ideas, feelings, and emotions that have coalesced into systemic and habitual ways of thinking and acting. Belief systems are multi-layered and multi faceted and often unconscious sets of ideas, habits and behaviors that create and organize how we experience our reality. Beliefs, based on familiarity alone, limit our current experience, by repeating unwanted actions or responses in all areas of our lives. Our emotions and symptoms are a direct result of our beliefs or thinking, according to Hawai'ian shamans.

Further, our beliefs and the emotions and perceptions they generate are not limited to those from this lifetime alone. We are deeply impacted by beliefs and experiences from other lifetimes and these events can shape our reality in the present as a result. Stanislav Grof calls these unique systems COEX systems.

Grof explains,

> ...memories of emotional and physical experiences are stored in the psyche not as isolated bits and pieces but in the form of complex constellations which I call COEX *systems*[233] (for "systems of condensed experience") Each COEX system consists of emotionally charged memories from different periods in our lives; the common denominator that brings them together is that they share the same emotional quality or physical sensation. Each COEX system has a theme that characterizes it. They [COEX systems] can reach further into prenatal life and into the realm of transpersonal phenomena such as past life experiences,...[234]

COEX systems are complex organizations of belief systems, memories and emotional experiences, which are referred to as the body of experience[235] in Transforming Embodiment.

Belief systems structure how we think, feel, and perceive our world and our belief systems tend to solidify, if an experience is accompanied by great emotional force. Strong emotions and emotional outbursts impress the unconscious mind and can cause belief systems to form. Traumatic memories and experiences can also create a wide gambit of beliefs.

Language also contributes to the formation of belief systems. How many times when you have been sick have you said, "my chest, or head, or throat, or stomach is killing me." If healing is our goal, this is not a good statement to make, even if you feel it is true because our ku, or subconscious mind, will take you at our word. "The power of language, the force of words shape the landscapes in our minds. The landscapes in our minds shape our environment."[236] Belief systems are often as intricate as Spanish lace or Irish knot work, with a central belief, giving rise to generations of other beliefs all of which create a very complex interwoven system.

Our emotional responses and even our symptoms can be deeply connected to our beliefs. If we are told something repeatedly either by our own mind or by others, this too can form into a belief system. If, as a child, we were told repeatedly that we were special and these words were emphasized with hugs, our belief about ourselves would include that we were special. If, in contrast, an adult told us that we were bad in a booming voice, this too could solidify into a belief system.

Belief systems can be overt and known, or unconscious. A simple example of an overt belief might be: "I feel better when I take vitamins." The interesting thing about belief systems is that they unwittingly send messages to one's unconscious. So, if we make the statement, I feel better when I take vitamins and miss doing so, then this opens the door to not feeling well if it is a belief that we strongly hold. Another example of how our language can affect how we feel is the statement that "so and so is a pain in the neck," so each time we see this person our neck may throb or tighten and become painful. The body consciousness is quite literal and takes much of what we say to heart. This is especially true if strong emotions accompany our thoughts. These examples are simplistic, but they illustrate how the unconscious can grab onto our thoughts and words and those of others and subsequently affect our reality. The power of the spoken word has a direct effect on our unconscious, which takes what we say quite literally.

Our thoughts impress our ku or body consciousness which does not distinguish between thoughts about others or ourselves. There is a simple muscle test[237] that you can do and it goes like this: think of something you like about yourself, hold this thought strongly in your mind, really marshal all your resources and think only about this thing you like about yourself, then hold your arm out and have someone gently push down on your arm. What happens?[238] Then think of something you don't like about your world and test again. What happens this time? This exercise shows you how the body consciousness does not differentiate. All experience, both positive and negative, is taken to be about the self.

Unconscious belief systems affect us all and they help perpetuate unwanted thoughts, limiting behaviors, and repetitive patterns in our lives. If we are able to uncover these unconscious beliefs, however, we have the opportunity to change our habits and patterning. When faced with a problem, people have two basic options: the first, to respond instinctively based on past experience; or secondly, to find creative alternatives. Finding these creative alternatives can be a painful process;

but the growth that results after changing our recurring patterns can be deeply rejuvenating.

Affirmations and Unconscious Thoughts

Affirmations are a positive example of a thought form. Affirmations, are consciously repeated messages created by a person to attract new possibilities into her life. The problem with the wholesale, and sometimes unsuccessful, use of affirmations is that the underlying "negative" beliefs we hold are seldom addressed. If these underlying negative patterns are not acknowledged, they can become stumbling blocks. If an affirmation goes against a more deeply, unconsciously held belief, conflicts arise as the consciousness tries to resolve these contradictory ideas. A person's consciousness, with two sets of opposing thoughts or beliefs operating simultaneously, causes confusion, distress, and even illness. If the conflict is not attended to, the affirmation is diluted or negated.

Unconscious thoughts and thought forms create the same difficulties for people as do unconscious belief systems. The common denominator between belief systems, thoughts, and thought forms is that they are born from repetitive patterns of thought and powerful emotions. We are all too familiar with the mental ramblings and ideas that repeat themselves in our heads. Thought forms are shaped by thoughts that are emotionally charged. When emotional and persistent ramblings are perpetuated over time, they become thought forms and can begin to affect our experience. When thought forms congeal, they can generate enough force to attract or detract, whatever may be the focus of the thought.

Our thoughts are like vibrations that send out impressions, energy, and feelings into our world. Have you ever walked into a room where two people have been arguing? Do you remember how it felt? Perhaps the room felt like you could cut the air with a knife, it was so thick with emotion. Or, in contrast, a room or hall filled with compassion and love. I have experienced this, when powerful enlightened teachers are teaching and speaking. Places vibrate with energy and they naturally pick up the energies of people who have been there. I remember as a child traveling to Gettysburg and the Little Big Horn, and a cold eeriness pervaded both these places.

Neuroscience has noted that molecules and atoms vibrate at different rates. I believe that our thoughts are energy, and that our thoughts and feelings vibrate and reverberate too. Recent prayer studies have found that when groups of people pray for someone who is sick, healing speeds up. Their thoughts or prayers vibrate and expand beyond their minds and immediate environment, like ripples on a still pond, to the person they are focusing on. As research expands, thoughts may be proven to be more non-local than we have ever imagined.

Unconscious beliefs and thoughts are generally inaccessible unless we are able to slow down our thinking enough to grasp them. Meditation is a good tool for slowing down the thought process. Thoughts and belief systems can be observed as the flow of our thoughts, feelings, and emotions slow down. With practice, we can cultivate the "watcher" or "inner witness" awareness within our mind. The ability to simultaneously observe and participate in a stream of thoughts becomes possible when the watcher is created. By cultivating this mindful awareness,[239] our mental process naturally slows down and we are able to grasp our thoughts, feelings, and reactions much more clearly. Meditation gives us the opportunity to examine our mental and emotional creations, by inquiring into and transforming our habitual beliefs, their emotions and thoughts, we can change our minds and bodies.

The body of experience carries all our beliefs, feelings, memories, and experiences from this lifetime and previous lifetimes and encompasses what occurs in the mind, body, psyche, and the energy fields of the body[240] since we first took breath. By creating an inner environment of open curiosity, we can delve into this rich landscape within ourselves for purification, release, healing, and growth. The examination, exploration, and eventual transformation of our beliefs is the goal of this work.

Using Inner Wisdom to Understand Embodied Beliefs, Emotions and Symptoms

The body of experience naturally includes the innate wisdom or sense of knowing that lies within each of us. This wisdom is present within us from the moment of incarnation. This wisdom aspect is known by many names: higher Self, essential Self, spiritual Self, or one's inner wisdom or spirit. Tibetan teacher Sogyal Rinpoche refers to it as one's wise guide. Body wisdom is another form of inner knowing that corresponds to the body's ability to know how to heal itself.

The aim in Transforming Embodiment is to establish a relationship with and a connection to our inner wisdom. It is this aspect of Self that helps guide the healing and investigative process. "What the hypnotists noticed even in the late 1800s, is that there was often a part of the personality that really knew what the whole personality needed in order to heal. I think it is similar to what contemporary hypnosis researcher Ernest Hilgard calls the 'hidden observer' "[241] Jack Kornfield shares his thoughts with Rothberg: "I've come to trust deeply the psyche itself in its knowing how and when to open."[242]

This aware and observing Self helps us find the original experiences that contribute to problems and symptoms. It is this aspect of the Self that perceives how we can heal ourselves, it is from this Self that inner knowledge and intuition springs forth, to inspire and deepen our understanding of our world and ourselves.

How Beliefs and Emotions Affect Our Health and Well Being

How we think about any problem determines how we experience it. This can affect our health, relationships, and inner peace. Beliefs create how we experience our world and give rise to our emotions, reactions, symptoms, and environment.

> An emotion arises when the activation of a belief or belief complex is stimulated by an internal or external event (a thought can be considered an event in this context). This discharges a current of energy through the physical system which acts as a carrier for the content of the belief.[243]

Conflicting assumptions and attitudes create ineffective beliefs and conflicted beliefs lead to confusion, illness and distortion within our energy fields. Our conflicting ideas are thought to be the source of all illness in kahuna teachings. Belief complexes guide the flow of energy, or mana. If the flow of energy is distorted by either our thinking or emotions, muscle tension develops, which then can lead to stress,[244] pain, and illness. Relaxation is one way to disperse emotional energy, since relaxing allows the energy from the thought pattern to be released. Emotions also induce muscle tension and can affect our organs, muscles, and cells. Dr. Candace Pert believes that all illness has a psychosomatic component based on the fact that emotional molecules run through every system within our body. The kahunas appeared to have had this figured out long ago. Our mind, and its beliefs, thoughts, and ideas, have a direct relationship to our body's symptoms, well-being, and our emotions, as reactions and responses to our thought are equally important.

The kahunas believe that if we recognize a root belief system we can change it. As we bring feelings and thoughts into full consciousness, we can experience them and release them. In the Hawai'ian healing tradition, kahunas pay more attention to where a disease manifests than to what kind of disease is evident. Different areas in our body are associated with different challenges or issues in huna. It is believed that conflicts in competence and communication manifest in the head, shoulders, arms, and hands. Conflicts of affection, responsibility and self worth manifest in the region between the solar plexus and the neck, while conflicts of security and authority manifest between the solar plexus and upper thighs Conflicts regarding support and progress manifest in the legs and feet. This is similar to how the different chakras hold certain energy patterns and psychological issues.

How Imagery and Intuition Communicate

Imagery is the language of the mind and body. Imagery is the primary way in which the body, mind, and psyche communicate with the conscious mind regarding the origins of our symptoms.[245] Imagery uses all of the senses to communicate the information stored within the subconscious and unconscious mind. "It [imagery] is the communication mechanism between perception, emotion and bodily change."[246]

When the body of experience and our connected wisdom are tapped, layers of images, memories, feelings, sensations, and the subsequent beliefs associated with present problems are revealed. With a quiet and focused mind, we are able to follow our body's sensations, tensions, emotions, and feelings, revealing even deeper layers of experience.

As we become more curious about the construction of our memories, feelings and belief systems, we can return to events from the present, from childhood or past lifetimes. The events that form belief systems can then be re-experienced and examined with new clarity. The emotions and feelings from the original situations can be felt by the body and mind but in a detached way this time. This detached awareness and perception enables us to remember and relive experiences without becoming overwhelmed by the experience, which allows us to explore and express layers of emotions in a safe manner and discern the beliefs that structure our reality.

All of our experience is carried within our body and mind, so we just have to journey within to find the answers. One way to begin this process is by working with the imagery. In this way, we can build congruency within our minds and bodies and gain a deeper understanding of what our inner wisdom wishes to convey to us.

Working with Imagery

Begin by taking a few deep breaths and allow your self to come fully into the moment. With your mind's eye and imagination I want you to visualize a lotus flower. See its shape begin to emerge, see its petals, blossom, leaves, and stem, notice the depth of its color, the shading and texture in the petals and leaves. Notice its fragrance. Visualize this lotus with as many details as you possibly can (pause). Now, widen your field of vision and notice the environment that the lotus is in as well. It may appear to be in a vase, outdoors or just floating in front of you? Just note the environment and see any new details about this lotus. (Pause). Then imagine that you can deepen or lighten the color of the lotus at will. Make it darker, then lighter, and see if you can restore it to its original color. Once again, notice anything new. If you want to add dewdrops or a ladybug, let yourself visualize these changes as well. Play with the image a bit. Imagine a flame rising from the center of the lotus and see the roots of the lotus extend down into the mud. Imagine that you are like the lotus and imagine the flame connects you to spirit and that the roots of the lotus connect you to the earth. Breathe in this synergy and allow yourself to be a bridge between heaven, or spirit, and the earth. Then when you are ready allow the image to dissolve from your field of vision.

This exercise is used to develop your visualization skills and your ability to focus. You may practice it as often as you like. As you become confident in the exercise you may also wish to explore the lotus at a

Chapter Nine

sensory level. While visualizing it, you can also experience the feel of the petals, leaves, stem, and blossom. Explore its scent as well. See what emotions or memories the lotus evokes.

Visualization as an expansion of memory works as an instantaneous touchstone that gives you the opportunity to travel back in time to older memories and feelings. Imagery is a way in which the subconscious communicates. I have found that if you change the imagery of an older memory, you can change how you experience the present. This exercise gives you the foundations for exploring your inner world later. Your inner world, as reflected in the imagery and the memories within you is a treasure trove of information and healing right at your fingertips.

10

THE HEART ESSENCE OF TRANSFORMING EMBODIMENT

> We see in the last decade a spirituality growing in which the ego is neither killed nor indulged, but embraced with a mercy and awareness that integrates the whole. Paralleling this expanding spirituality, we recognize a new psychology arising which does not limit the inheritance of being human to just the conditioned and easily recognizable and readily categorized.
>
> Stephen and Ondrea Levine [247]

Transforming Embodiment has five steps. The first step is to develop a quiet meditative mind that is self-observing, aware, and curious. After cultivating this mind state, which is open, relaxed and free of any daily cares contact with our innate inner wisdom can then occur. From the stillness of relaxation and rapport, communication with our intuitive Self naturally develops. Fostering this mental and emotional attitude creates a space to do inner work. This is the first step.

The second step is to use our discerning mind to identify and ask specific questions, in order to elicit information and understanding from our intuitive Self about the obstacles in our lives. Questions act like beacons of light, that illuminate and direct our attention to the stored memories, images, symbols and unconscious experiences, which remain unresolved. Questions help us to find the origins of any state or situation that is troubling us. We use the question to focus our attention, in a precise way, and then we allow our intuitions to guide us.

This leads us to the third step of remembering, as we go back to the moments, events, and memories where our symptoms, emotional patterns, and misunderstandings in relationship first began. Again, our intuitive Mind guides the process as we discover the origins of our current life triggers and challenges. As we open our minds and hearts to long forgotten memories, we may re-experience old feelings that have unwittingly shaped our reactions in the present. This can at times be a painful process, but it is one that is ripe with insight and rewards. Connections between our past and present are made and new understandings blossom.

We then move on to fourth step, the release phase, where we employ a wide variety of visualization and psychic practices to transform the memories and emotions held deep within our psyche and body. Reorganization is the fifth step which accompanies the release phase, as we see the way our emotions, memories, and beliefs have created our experience in the present. We realize what beliefs have controlled and limited us, from our past experiences, and how these beliefs have influenced us. As we integrate these lost aspects of ourselves and release past wounds and histories, we are able to establish new beliefs to replace our outdated ones. Again, certain energetic and psychic techniques are used to remove any residual energy or old beliefs that were once held.

We explore our mind, body, and chakras to locate the origins of our challenges and obstacles in this lifetime, and in so doing we often find deep memories from our ancient past. Consciousness continues and so do our potent and highly charged emotional experiences.

Traumatic events, emotions, beliefs, and behaviors continue beyond physical death. These experiences remain unconscious and lie dormant within our minds, and are preserved within our bodies until they are resolved. People, places, objects, and our emotions that are similar to those we have felt in the past can trigger these memories.

Madison, a long time client, walked into a store one day that carried African art and cultural items. She enjoyed the shop very much and felt at home she said, but she also felt very unsettled and shaky as tribal music played in the background. In session, we were able to find a group of lifetimes, some of which were centered in Africa, that related to symptoms and conditions she had experienced her entire life. As we resolved these critical memories, her symptoms disappeared and she felt renewed vigor and aliveness come back into her life.

Memories and events we have endured survive, and can spontaneously surface as fragmented images, montages, and body feelings or sensations; strong emotions often accompany this deep imagery. Present life situations that are similar to those experienced in our past or past lives can also bring these memories to consciousness again. With the practices of Transforming Embodiment these memories, their emotions, and beliefs can be investigated and transformed so that deep change and healing can occur.

Transforming Embodiment also helps us find and understand the emotions, sensations, and beliefs held within our bodies that drive repetitive patterns and reactions occurring in our everyday lives. Imagery is the language of the body and images often surface as we explore how patterns and memory are embodied. Past life events and memories are also encountered as we explore our inner world, and these events feel quite real to us. "...Our experience at a particular moment—whatever it is—is the reality of that moment."[248] This is a basic tenet in Transforming Embodiment: whatever we are experiencing simply *is* our reality in that particular moment. Experiences of previous life events are taken quite literally, and by being in the moment, by being completely present and unconditionally accepting of our experience, healing can take place.

Discovering where our painful emotions and symptoms began gives us the opportunity to uproot the original seeds of our suffering. Origins can be traced back to past lives, prenatal events, childhood experiences, or memories from any encounter we have witnessed or partaken in. There may be more than one event that has produced our current emotions, experiences, our mental and physical response reactions, and symptoms in the present. In healing origins we need to traverse and explore these memories and the emotions and beliefs that accompany them. By remembering, releasing and integrating these core components, held within our psyche, present life challenges can be transformed at a basic level.

Jordan's Story

This following case is taken directly from a session with Jordan and will illustrate the five steps of the practices of Transforming Embodiment.

Over a period of a few years, Jordan had taken a series of classes with me. Problems and issues about relationships often surfaced for him as he explored his chakras and body. Communication issues, resentment, anger and distrust were central themes for him. He felt his anger, resentment, and distrust were his primary problems and he had worked in men's groups and individual therapy before seeing me on these issues. So, when Jordan came to see me privately, he had very clear goals.

He wanted to resolve any issues with both his ex-wife and daughter before his daughter's upcoming wedding. He said his interactions with both women had been painful and strained for years. He believed they constantly judged him and this made him angry and judgmental in return. He explained that he felt that his ex-wife, Jody, had alienated his children from him since their divorce many years ago. Jordan declared that he wanted to release any negative feelings he had for his ex-wife and to finally understand why their relationship had always been so difficult. Our session began with Jordan making the following statement:

> "I want to look at this relationship and understand it. Each time I connect to my inner self and ask, can I forgive Jody? I hear no, not until I let more love into my heart. I know that I have to release my judgments and assumptions about Jody, but this is really tough to do because of our history together. I also need to let go of the anger I feel about being judged by her and my daughter. I want to increase my sense of compassion for both of them but that's been very hard to do."

Chapter Ten

While Jordan spoke, a scene flashed before my closed eyes. I saw a man and a woman on an ancient barge traveling along a river. I knew at once that the man was being manipulated by this woman and that she thought she was better than those around her. I suspected that these scenes were of Jordan and his ex-wife, Jody, but I released these images from my mind and came back to the present moment.

Our session began with Jordan doing his grounding and protection and connecting exercises he'd learned in class. Jordan's eyes closed as he focused inward. Earlier in the day I had done these visualizations too, so as Jordan was completing them, I breathed with him for a moment and connected[249] with his higher consciousness. I let the energy from Source flow into the room as I created a "space" where Jordan and I could work that was calm, still and connected to the earth.

This environment is imbued with stillness, vastness, and spaciousness. The practitioner infuses the environment with these same qualities by holding or embodying these states of stillness and spaciousness within herself. In this environment, the client is literally given the space to slow down his thoughts and emotions so he can go inside himself, connect with his inner Self, and explore his inner world.

After a few minutes, I asked Jordan to take a deep breath and release any tensions from his body, mind, and emotions so he may come fully into the moment. Since he was familiar with this process, I began right away and asked, "Can you locate the first time you felt the judgment you described earlier?" I waited and "held the space" while he moved into his inner experience. Jordan's eyes lightly closed and they rolled back into his head, revealing the whites of his eyes. His eyes and eyelids moved like a dreamer's eyes during REM sleep. I breathed with Jordan and asked him what he saw.

Jordan shared the following:

> "I'm on a barge on a wide river, fanning a woman. Her eyes and hair are dark. She's Egyptian. I'm wearing a loincloth and sandals. She looks at me with disdain, as though I am irrelevant, not her equal, but there is something more. I feel that she manipulates me a lot. It's like I'm her slave. I have a feeling, too, that this woman is my ex-wife Jody, or a part of her somehow."

I asked him to go back in as he held the question, what else do you feel and notice in your mind. His eyes remained closed as he continued,

> "She scorns and teases me in front of the others, but in private she is attracted to me. (Time passes). We have a child together, but she can't be close to me, and the child is used in some kind of scheme. I'm so angry and bitter at the end of this life."

I asked, "Is this the first place you felt this way?" Jordan says, "Yes."

I have a distinct impression that there were other times where Jody and Jordan had interacted. This belief spontaneously enters my consciousness from Source. I asked Jordan, "Can you find any other events that need to be remembered, that may relate to you and Jody?"

With closed eyes Jordan began to "see" again, his eyes and eyelids flickered, and much time passed. I notice changed in Jordan's expression and body, as if he were reacting to the scenes before him. I sensed that he was experiencing a rapid succession of events.

When I noticed calm come across his face again, I asked him, "What have you been seeing and feeling?"

Jordan states:

> "We have killed each other many times. We have both been men in many past lives. I have killed her and she has killed me, over and over again, until I realize that the anger and killing between us is of no use. I am sick of fighting."

Jordan's face is marked with pain and his voice conveys a futility that is uncommon for him. There is a pervasive sense of weariness as he speaks. I continue, "Is there anything else?" He closes his eyes and goes within again.

His face is calmer and I notice he's smiling. I continue to breathe with him and "hold the space."

"What are you noticing Jordan?"

> "I am a wood cutter in a great forest and Jody is my wife. We are very happy together. We have a simple and happy life."

Chapter Ten

Jordan sounded so surprised and I noticed the tension in his chest softened, the rigidity in his shoulders fell away, and he released the tension in his arms as well. The image that he had let go of his swords popped into my mind. Jordan's eyes opened and there was clarity in his eyes that I had not seen before. He looked like he understood something new. I explained to him that this last lifetime is crucial.

A voice speaks through me to Jordan, "This past lifetime gives you the opportunity to understand that love and compassion have been a part of your relationship, a part of the vibration that you have shared. This is critically important, because the love and compassion are a part of your history. They danced in your hearts in this sweet life you once shared, and they are available for you to remember and draw on even now."

Jordan looked very relaxed and nodded his head. He shared with me that he never imagined that he and Jody were happy together and said it was hard to remember ever having that feeling in this current life with her. He said he understood why they had such a difficult time together and felt that he had let go of the need to battle with her now.

> "I am amazed at the love we held for each other in that life, that feeling just radiates through my body as I sit here. We actually loved each other (he pauses as he takes this fact in) very deeply and had a long life with each other that was so happy. We spent our days and nights together in such joy. That's amazing to me, such bliss and simplicity, not all the drama and subterfuge that we have had in this lifetime. This feels very good."

Jordan's experience illustrates how he literally felt and participated in his memories. His story also details how memories from multiple lifetimes organized his current experience. It shows how, by reliving these memories, Jordan gained a new and expanded awareness and perspective about his relationships. Jordan realized deep in his body that there had been love and happiness between Jody and him. This gave him the opportunity he needed to heal old wounds that stood between them. In later sessions we tackled his relationship with his daughter.

By working with the original causes of current problems, patterns are uprooted and one often becomes painfully aware of the futility of one's repetitive actions, as Jordan did. This moment of realization is one of the richest junctures within Transforming Embodiment, when old, outmoded behaviors are cast off and transformed, making room for new possibilities. With this shift of consciousness, understanding as in Jordan's case naturally follows.

Deep emotions both painful and joyous are often felt when re-experiencing events from the recent past or other lifetimes. These emotions can lead us into the process of remembering or they give us a greater understanding of the cause-effect relationships that surround us in our daily lives. A new and larger context regarding our problems surfaces when we explore our emotions and experiences in this way. Difficult relationships, symptoms, and psychological aspects of personality are understood with new clarity as our patterning emerges and we can see how particular behaviors, emotional reactions and beliefs began. This is the power of working with origins.

By understanding origins the limitations that have shaped our life experiences in this and in other lives can be seen and identified. Change can manifest in the present as the links and interconnections between our emotions, beliefs, memories, and other life experiences are brought into awareness. As these interconnections are illuminated, the process of release and reorganization can begin. Interacting with memories and potent emotions from other lifetimes is both powerful and transformative because an underlying continuity between life and death is perceived as we recognize the timeless nature of our being and as a result, the finite definition of death is often reconsidered.

Who Benefits from Transforming Embodiment and Who Does Not

Many people who come to see me have been on a healing path for some time. Their experiences vary, some have been in traditional therapy, attended men's groups, and others have been involved with: meditation, bodywork, massage, and workshops. Most are individuals that have reflected upon their lives, habits, and relationships in some way.

Reactionary states and interactions with other people often bring clients into my office. As an example, June came to see me after an angry encounter with a tenant. She felt her anger had been excessive and blown way out of proportion in light of the situation. She also was upset with herself that she had gotten so mad. It was this intense reaction that June wanted to understand so her communication with her tenant could be improved. She also wanted to see if she and her tenant had any "past lives" together, since her feelings were so strong.

This is the case with many people I see. Clients come in to work with fears and anxieties, to understand and resolve situations that baffle them, and to explore somatic symptoms. They also come in because they are experiencing strong emotional reactions, or traumatic imagery and memories that are frightening to them. Most clients have very definite goals.

Alia wanted to understand the chronic pain in her stomach. The rest of her life was going well; she was doing work she loved and was happily married. She felt, however, that the pain and discomfort in her stomach was linked to an unknown fear that she had felt since she was a child. As Alia relaxed and was able to shift her attention to her stomach, I asked her if she could become one with the pain. As she did she told me that she saw herself in a wooden coffin, buried alive. She re-experienced the terror and panic of that moment. She wept and understood that she had had cancer in her belly and that she had been buried while still in a coma. The terror of that death had lodged in her stomach. As she took in this new information, she said her stomach began to relax and the pain eased. By diving into the symptom within her body, her body shared with her the origin of her pain. By reliving the trauma with awareness, Alia was able to release the shock of that death.

Another example of when Transforming Embodiment is helpful is when a person has experienced a long-standing difficulty or way of thinking in relationship to another person. This kind of relationship difficulty plagued Jordan. Whenever he thought of his ex-wife, the same reactions occupied his mind. They even colored his interactions with his daughter. By delving into his and his ex-wife's relationship to their origins, Jordan was able to understand and detach from his reactionary states and participate in his daughter's wedding, without the usual tensions.

Jordan had done extensive counseling about his family of origin and his own nuclear family in both men's groups and in therapy. Many clients who come to see me have been working on their issues in traditional therapies and various therapeutic settings, such as counseling or bodywork, for some time, and many are intimately aware of their patterns, but few have found the deepest keys to affect release and reorganization of their habitual reactions and symptoms. TE is not for the weak of heart. The work requires awareness, courage, willingness, and a readiness to delve into the deepest recesses of the Self to find answers and healing.

Another client, Amelia, was two months pregnant and experiencing fear that her baby might not be healthy. In session, we followed her fear and found that it originated in her childhood. She remembered a friend's younger sister, Janey, and shared that she wanted to protect her baby in the same way she had wanted to protect this little girl. As we worked with her memories, she recognized how being different was an issue for her and that her family had not accepted her in the same way that the children in her neighborhood had not accepted Janey. Her fear continued to loosen as she also remembered how she had teased Janey at times, so the other children wouldn't tease her for being Janey's friend. She forgave herself, and in turn asked for forgiveness from Janey. As she understood the origins of her fears, her body and mind found a sense of peace and she began to relax. She had a smooth pregnancy and seven months later she gave birth to a fine, healthy baby. Amelia's memories were from this lifetime alone, but they were just as potent as those clients experience in other lives.

Sometimes clients experience the spontaneous arising of feelings and images from other lifetimes. This was the case when I first met Sara, who came in to see me because she was experiencing "memories" of another time. She was fraught with confusion and the feeling of being in two times at once, and she was worried she was going crazy. These spontaneous memories moved her into an accelerated state of *time-shifting*, and were triggered by a present-day boyfriend who she was trying to leave, and another man. Visual images and scenes from this other lifetime arose incessantly as her mind tried to understand the images and emotions she was seeing and feeling. The memories were violent and troubled her a great deal. She felt completely overwhelmed by the emotions and feelings that these images and memories evoked. Over and over she saw images of a dark forest and scenes of herself being captured and toyed with sexually, and tormented by her husband's men at arms for being unfaithful. She discovered who the people from these scenes were and how her present was mirroring her past, and thus was able to remove and release the fear and dread she had felt. In the end, she successfully and joyfully left her relationship to live on her own.

The practices of Transforming Embodiment can be useful for those who have experienced spontaneous memories from other lifetimes. Facilitation by a practitioner who has experienced these same phenomena is invaluable and can help us connect back to the present moment. Otherwise, we may be misunderstood and traumatized further.

This leads us to who would not benefit from this work. It is my belief that anyone without a strong sense of self, or healthy ego strength, would not be advised to undertake a therapy like Transforming Embodiment. I have also found that people who have difficulty settling their minds and trusting their inner resources and intuition do not do well. This may be because a quiet, attentive mind is needed, as well as the ability to stay present when difficult or scary memories or emotions arise.

A deep wish to resolve and understand personal and spiritual issues, as well as symptoms, memories, extreme reactions, intense emotions and relationship troubles bring clients to this work. It is important for clients to understand that they are basically healthy, and often self-aware. Many have worked on themselves, on their bodies, their emotions, their family and relationship issues in a variety of healing modalities for years. Most importantly, those who see me have a strong motivation to change and this may be why the work is so effective.

Relating Transforming Embodiment to Modern Psychology

Transforming Embodiment is a multi-dimensional, verbal, spiritual, and psychological therapy. It is also a broad-spectrum psycho-spiritual process that works with the energy centers within the body to heal the core issues held within our psyche and soma. The practices of Transforming Embodiment evoke and use the psychic, transpersonal, and somatic information and memories within us to help us find new levels of healing and empowerment in our lives.

Transforming Embodiment finds its foundations in both psychology and within the contemplative traditions of spirituality. It shares similar assumptions that Janet, Breuer and Freud held in the late 1800s, namely that problems result from particular traumas and if these traumatic origins are investigated, an emotional and symptomatic release can occur.

Freud is quoted as saying,

> What we have to do is to apply Breuer's method–or one which is essentially the same–so as to lead the patient's attention back from his symptom to the scene in which and through which the symptom arose; and, having thus located the scene, we remove the symptom by bringing about, during the reproduction of the traumatic scene, a subsequent correction of the psychical course of events which took place at the time.[250], [251],[252]

This idea is built upon in Transforming Embodiment as we look at trauma and habitual behaviors and patterns that might be considered neurotic, but not pathological.

Transforming Embodiment similarly seeks the original experiences that may be traumatic, and which effect emotional, mental, and physical health, once they are worked through. In discovering these origins, hidden belief systems that drive repetitive patterns and current behaviors are unearthed and revealed; and the deeper meanings for these persistent patterns are found. The deeper meaning within or behind held emotions, patterns and belief systems that create current reactions are examined so that the persistent repetitive behaviors in our lives can be changed at their source. New beliefs and structures are then integrated into the psyche in the later phases of the work.

Jung's work with symbolic imagery is another area where Transforming Embodiment connects with certain elements of psychology. Jung found that the unconscious often communicates through symbols and imagery and he understood that imagery was a part of intuition. In Transforming Embodiment, experiences from other lives, infancy, childhood, and a person's current past are often relayed to the conscious mind through imagery, symbols, and metaphors. In this way, the unconscious is able to communicate with the conscious mind.

Dreams are another way in which this communication takes place. Dreams often reflect clients' emotions and beliefs that have remained unconscious. By looking at our dreams, we can find out how we are feeling and thinking about an issue, event, or problem. Dreams, for many, serve the intuitive function and rather than seeing, feeling or sensing intuitive flashes come in the guise of dreams. Informative dreams can share valuable clues from our unconscious as well as help us solve current problems we are facing.

The inner realm of the unconscious works in deep and profound ways through imagery. The unconscious communicates via imagery and symbols, and Transforming Embodiment teaches us how to find, interpret and if necessary transform these images by connecting directly to our inner experience. In this work, we literally access the imagery accompanying body tensions, feelings and emotions.

According to Ira Progoff..."it is essential that we grasp the implications of the fundamental insight that the human personality unfolds by means of imagery."[253] He continues, citing Sir Herbert Read from "Icon and Idea" lectures, 1955; "The source of man's conceptions of reality is not the intellect but the nonrational depths of the psyche; for it is there that symbols are made."[254] Thus, in working with clients or on ourselves it is imperative to access the imagery within the psyche. In this way, the origins, emotions, and belief systems that form thought and actions can be located. Imagery in the form of memories, scenes from childhood or even other lives, are extraordinary resources for each of us as we endeavor to resolve old wounds, symptoms, emotions, behaviors and beliefs.

In working with reincarnational material, as Transforming Embodiment does, other life experiences can be interpreted as metaphorical journeys, revealing information that is symbolic and acceptable to the conscious mind. This format might give the client the needed distance to investigate deeply ingrained patterns. Experiences from another lifetime and another personality may indeed help people work more deeply on a problem. The problem of the ego's need to defend itself can be alleviated, because one seems to be looking at another person, not oneself.

Cognitive psychology seeks to modify a patient's feelings and behaviors by modifying her conscious thoughts. According to Hunt Albert Ellis, the father of cognitive therapy, says, "You largely feel the way you think and you can change your thinking and thereby change your feelings."[255] Transforming Embodiment is similar to cognitive psychology in that it reviews and changes our belief systems regarding our problems. Links are made between our beliefs and feelings. However, in Transforming Embodiment we need to delve deeper into our experiences; to understand not only the beliefs, feelings, emotions and behaviors, but to understand the unconscious processes behind our behaviors, actions, emotions and experiences. We look for the original belief systems as well as the array of emotions and memories associated with them. We find out how these emotional experiences are being repeated in the present, and a deeper understanding of the motivating forces behind them is brought to light. This process can take us into some very deep layers of ourselves, far beyond the parameters of current cognitive psychology.

Depth Psychology and Modern Man by Ira Progoff, and *Psychosynthesis* by Roberto Assagioli, both employ imagery, and acknowledge an intuitive or transpersonal power within the self. Transforming Embodiment shares with depth psychology and psychosynthesis this belief in an intuitive or transpersonal Self, and uses imagery to evoke the depths of the Self.

Depth Psychology works to reveal the core or to evoke the depths of experience within the personality by searching for the active factors beneath the surface of behaviors. It recognizes the importance of seeking the depths of personal experience to reveal how the personality may best grow. "The depths contain what is implicit in the psyche, what is potential there, what is working in the background of individual development towards fulfillment by means of growth."[256] Transforming Embodiment also seeks to reveal the depths of individual experience. It is here, within the depths, that symbol and imagery manifest to aid us in understanding our Selves. Symbols and imagery serve as guideposts into the innermost regions of our psyche, and they reveal the inherent truths and conflicts we are experiencing. Imagery is the fertile soil of

Chapter Ten

our inner landscape that has the ability to teach and instruct us about ourselves.

Progoff acknowledges the psyche as a process. "Above all else, the psyche is, like protoplasm, a process."[257] Transforming Embodiment shares this idea; therapy and healing are seen as a process in TE, a process that is organic in nature and that follows its own unique path at times. It can be both linear and circular and sometimes may even spiral, taking us to new levels of healing previously unvisited. Progoff states further that, "It is by the flow of imagery out of the depths of the organic psyche that ever–new meanings are made available for man's life experience."[258] This is how meaning is found; by exploring the depths of our psyche we are able to retrieve unknown aspects of the Self and discover the meaning of conflicts, perplexing patterns, our deep emotions and the issues in our lives.

Progoff believes that the psyche gives us both imagery and meaning, and says, "Images are the raw material out of which meanings are made."[259] In Transforming Embodiment, images, and felt sensations are often two primary ways in which we can contact our psyche's raw material. Meaning is found when we feel certain body sensations and tensions and then explore what is being held within those feelings. Images often are found when we encounter the tensions and emotions within our body and psyche; it is these images that can be retraced, integrated, or removed as needed.

Further, Transforming Embodiment shares the belief with psychosynthesis that "...We have already been given everything we need; our task is to assemble and use it in an appropriate way."[260] Psychosynthesis also moves to evoke experience and create growth by working directly with experience. In this way, Transforming Embodiment and psychosynthesis are similar. The body, its experiences, emotions, memories, feelings, sensations, thoughts, beliefs and ideas, including memories of past lives, are all within us. These are accessible and can be directly engaged creating both growth and healing.

Progoff says "...the wholeness of human personality with its fullness of spiritual and creative capacities lies hidden in the *depths* of the incomplete human being, silently waiting for its opportunity to emerge."[261] The idea that the individual has at her core a deep inner wisdom that seeks fulfillment and a voice is central to Transforming

Embodiment. In Transforming Embodiment, men and women are seen as creative and spiritual beings with the capacity to find and realize their own healing if given the opportunity. Transforming Embodiment seeks to give spirit a voice, and to open intuitive lines of communication between symptoms and imagery. In this way, the depths of the personality and individual healing become known.

Psychosynthesis takes the idea of holism a step further and acknowledges the superconscious or the transpersonal Self. Assagioli and Jung were pioneers in recognizing that spirituality is a genuine and authentic force within the psyche. Ferrucci writes that the transpersonal Self is at the core of the superconscious and is seen as "a *timeless essence,*" and "a living entity which is perceived as unchangeable, silent, pure being."[262] This concept of the transpersonal Self is similar to the perception of aumakua in Hawai'ian, or the "wise inner guide" as described by Sogyal Rinpoche. This aspect is experienced and cultivated in Transforming Embodiment. Acknowledging the transpersonal Self is perhaps the most important interconnection between Transforming Embodiment and psychosynthesis.

Transforming Embodiment also bears a keen resemblance to psychosynthesis in that both carry a desire for wholeness[263] by way of an organic process[264] that empowers the client, and recognizes the client's inner wisdom. Silence and the accompanying potential of spaciousness give the client room to inwardly explore transpersonal states in a holistic and organic way.[265]

"[Psychosynthesis] aims to evoke wholeness and the dawn of a new and wider frame of reference in the human psyche."[266] This wider perspective and new view where we can activate our inner resources and realize our true Self is fundamental in Transforming Embodiment. It is within this process that empowerment is found and our full potential is realized.

Huna and Modern Psychology

In Huna, the spiritual teachings of Hawai'i, one's beliefs about events are of special interest. Memories are important, as are emotions, but they are seen as manifestations of a basic underlying belief system that organized one's reactions and responses, based on memory. Recurring thoughts, daydreams, persistent emotions, and the content of speech are all means for tracing beliefs. "Beliefs are the basis of all experience, say the kahunas."[267] Freud worked through chronologically associated memories in order to reach the nucleus of a problem or pathology. In Huna, the belief system itself would be examined thoroughly and changed if necessary. Unlike most psychosomatic treatment where a change in behavior is sought, Huna seeks to change our beliefs, the roots of how we think and those beliefs that have shaped our world. Transforming Embodiment combines these two approaches and works with memories, emotions, body sensations, chakras, and energy to trace the stored experiences held within the cells, bones, muscles, the body's energy system, and mind.

Transforming Embodiment therapy is eclectic in both its view and approach. Its deepest roots emerged out of channeled material and transpersonal experiences; it was also influenced by shamanic and spiritual practices both ancient and new. These all have been essential in the creation of the practices and therapy of Transforming Embodiment. Though inspired by Buddhist, Taoist and Hawai'ian healing and meditation traditions, and bodywork, this therapy follows no particular school. It works within a much broader sphere, within spaciousness itself, with the goal of developing individual potential and Self-realization by exploring our psychology, symptoms and emotional patterns from the realms of spirit, body and mind. Upon investigation, like-minded psychological traditions have been found that are compatible with Transforming Embodiment, but TE has proven to be a unique marriage of spiritual traditions, somatic psychology, channeled information and transpersonal psychology.

The Benefits of Meditation Practice

Meditation allows us to contact our mind directly. It gives us the opportunity to cultivate a relationship to our inner wisdom, and to develop mindful attention. Meditation also teaches us to settle our minds, release our emotional agitation and persistent mental thoughts, and this enhances our success when undertaking therapy or diving into our inner world. Meditation also expands our natural intuitive gifts and stabilizes them.

Meditation slows down our thoughts, so we can begin to watch the constant flux of ideas, feelings, and emotions as they ebb and flow within our minds. This observation of our mind in all of its diversity awakens the inner witness. This witness-awareness is needed when doing deep work. If the inner witness is in place, then we can replay events without being overwhelmed by our fears. This is tremendously important when reviewing highly charged emotional experiences and memories. The self-observation of our mind states, which is gained during meditation or quiet reflection, can be extended to any inner work we do.

By engaging in meditation we can begin learning about the workings of the mind. Meditation can teach us very directly how the mind operates, reacts, responds, and defends itself. With focused awareness we can investigate the conditions of our mind, body and spirit. As we sit in meditation, or any reflective or contemplative state, we start to relax. Relaxation naturally opens our hearts, as our thoughts and emotions drift away, like clouds on the wind. Equanimity opens into spaciousness as our minds open like flowers, and acceptance and non-judgment grow.

Meditation encourages us to study our minds and develop an understanding and compassion toward an assortment of fears and emotional states.[268] Compassion and a gentle acceptance for whatever arises or occurs in our life, naturally increases when we meditate. Contemplative reflection[269] of this kind instills the ability to simply observe things as they are without the usual attachments. This is of great benefit as we endeavor to understand ourselves.

A basic acceptance and friendliness toward life helps us review problems without judgment and self-condemnation, which strengthens our sense of self from a psychological viewpoint. A non-judging mind observes things as they are and does not berate us for past actions. Forgiveness is a natural extension of this basic acceptance and friendliness that we can gain from practicing meditation.

Meditation helps us stay present with whatever comes up in ourselves. For instance, after a long period of sitting meditation my legs often feel like they are on fire or made of lead, but by not judging my experience, aversion does not cause me to jump from my seat. Non-judgment helps us observe intense events, fosters healing, and gives us a fuller expression of ourselves.

Chapter Ten

With gentle acceptance and love we can open to any experience and know that whatever we are experiencing will be okay. This is very critical to understand when we are doing deep inner work; meditation can provide us with the needed skills to dive deeply and resurface again safely. The ego is not accustomed to this kind of acceptance; we usually like to avoid or disassociate from negative experiences or emotions, but by befriending all conditions we can see through them and understand their origins. We learn to watch our thoughts and feelings, instead of constantly identifying with them; in this way, detachment from the incessant play of our minds grows. This helps us break the cycle, as we stop identifying with our habits and beliefs and are no longer absorbed by them. This ability to be self-observing and non-attached is vital when engaging in intuitive, creative therapy or inner exploration.

Over time, meditation gives rise to the realization that we are not our thoughts. As we investigate who is thinking this thought, we recognize that there is no true and perceivable "I." Our dualistic perception and subject object relationships forever changes as a result.

Meditation teaches us how to be focused, present, aware, open, accepting, non-judgmental, compassionate, and loving.

> Meditation does not have the aim of solving problems or making us feel better; rather it, provides a space in which we can let ourselves be, just as we are and thus discover our basic nature (beyond all our stories and problems).[270]

When we attend to and are present in the moment, we can sense our mind directly and this is why meditation or quiet reflection is so helpful, because it allows us to just be, so we can slow down and see the truth within us.

Part Five: The Process

11

CREATING AN ENVIRONMENT FOR TRANSFORMATIVE CHANGE: DEVELOPING THE INTUITION

> True intuition is a stable and reliable function of the higher levels of consciousness & awareness from which a wide range of information is accessible. The intellect and emotion flow together and become integrated, permitting a new kind of knowing, a kind of knowing which both depends on and promotes self-realization.
>
> Swami Rama, Rudoph Ballentine & Swami Ajaya [271]

Body, mind, and spirit are inseparable and it is through inner work that we can come to know these unique and intelligent aspects of ourselves. Balanced intuitive inquiry bridges the mind and body and invites spirit in. Transforming Embodiment as a dynamic, verbal, body-informed transpersonal therapy engages the intuition and spirit while focusing inward to find solutions to every-day problems and long term concerns.

It is within these inner realms that we will discover more about ourselves; the nature of consciousness and healing will expand into unknown territories, as we dive deeper into the mystery and sit by the fires of our own inner knowing. Spirit will be our guide and our intuition will be a source of inspiration and understanding.

Connecting to Source

When I am working on myself or with clients I always connect to Source. The requirements to create a still and quiescent state are simple: the body must be relaxed and at ease, the emotions must be calmed and any cares and concerns from our day need to be released. This will take some time and practice, as well as concentration, awareness, and focus; as the mind and emotions settle and inner stillness grows, a sense of peace and clarity naturally arises, giving us the ability to merge with Source or connect to the vast energy beyond our individual self.

The energy of Source creates a unique environment to work within. This energy interacts with the environment through our contact with it; we will know this energy because of the stillness and quiescence that permeates the space we are in and our being. Holding this space with our mind and body stabilizes the environment and keeps our mind quiet and non-reactive.

When connecting with Source, the boundaries between body and mind begin to melt, consciousness expands into spaciousness and there is a distinct feeling of merging into something larger and vaster than our Self, with this, a personalized sense of self falls away. The feeling is one of expanding outward, while remaining open, settled and connected. It is in this space that we can experience insight, inspiration, and instant knowing. When this spaciousness is created within our being, information can be translated from formlessness into form.

My earliest experiences of this occurred when I was singing. One day, while singing an aria with my teacher and accompanist, the voice sang me; I became one with the voice, as it flowed through me there was no difference between what I was doing and myself. It become effortless effort, what Taoist's call *wu wei*. This experience can happen to all of us when we let go, when our minds are uncluttered with self-consciousness, and we are fully immersed in what we are doing. A feeling of emptiness comes out of this experience as we become a conduit for something larger than our individual identity. Emptiness here means that the ego-driven self is submerged, forgotten or unimportant in that moment. This is when Spirit is able to communicate with us directly.

A client of Carl Jung said the following in regard to this: "By keeping quiet, repressing nothing, remaining attentive and by accepting reality, taking things as they are and not as I wanted them to be--by doing all this, unusual knowledge has come to me and unusual powers as well, such as I never could have imagined."[272] It is from this attentive state of awareness or attention that we can access deep understandings about the nature of relationships, symptoms, belief systems, and life patterns.

Connected Knowing—Balancing the Intuition and the Intellect

Intuition or inner knowing is innate. It is a natural ability possessed by everyone. It is not a mystical talent held by a select few. Intuition functions much like our other senses, and is deeply connected to a pervasive universal energy.

This wisdom is accessible to everyone if an environment setting or space for the experience is created. Using the preliminary practices can help create such a space. Any activity that quiets our mind and allows our thoughts to settle can also help us get in touch with our inner Self, and our individual wisdom energy. As we learn to quiet our mind and slow down our mental process, our intuition can take root and grow. By settling and quieting our mind, intuitive ways of perceiving the world are awakened and the intuitive experience itself is stabilized.

Intuitive ways of seeing and knowing are enhanced when we quiet our mind, and begin to ask questions. Questions invite the intellect into the healing process, so the intellect and intuitive mind may function as one. The intellect works in tandem with our intuition. Using questions guides the intuitive process and gives our intuition form and direction. The questions open the door and focus the mind, so the inner Self can communicate with us. Trust, patience, and releasing self-doubt are central to the success of intuitive communication, as is discernment.

Patience and Discernment

Patience helps us discover our inner voice. Listening requires patience and openness, and a Beginner's Mind. Being able to discern the difference between the voice of the ego and our innate inner wisdom [273] requires that we cultivate a quiet, open, patient, non judgmental and curious state of expanded focus, so information and knowledge from within can be revealed. As we engage our inner wisdom in dialogue and conversation, a relationship develops that can guide our healing process to deeper levels.

This aspect of inner wisdom is connected to a universal energy, the force that pervades all life and experience. This energy is deeply connected to primordial energies and is the point from which all existence and experience arises, in an ultimate sense. In a relative or manifest sense, inner wisdom is the force within each of us, that is all-knowing, and that links us to this vast universal energy.[274]

When we learn to tap into this wisdom, and the energy that accompanies it, we can merge into and out of this energy to gain insight and answers. We move away from the idea of being helpless victims, who need to be told what to do, when we listen to our inner voice and are able to distinguish it from our ego's voice. I believe that each of us, as embodied spirit, knows precisely what to do to find healing. We just need to create the necessary lines of communication, so this access to our innate inner knowing can take place. Discernment is the key, so we are not misled by our ego's need to control and stifle our inner wisdom with the will of the ego. Ego can be infinitely subtle as we traverse deeper and deeper levels of healing, so it is essential that we be able to differentiate between the voice of our ego and our spiritual Self. Remember that the spiritual Self is motivated towards unity, and will never tell us where to go or what to do in an autocratic way. It may direct us, but harmony and respect are the watchwords. The Hawai'ians say that the only time our aumakua will tell us what to do is if it is a life-threatening situation.

Answers Lie within Us

The answers to our deepest questions lie within us. Our job is to discover the right question that we are seeking an answer for and to ask it with a calm and open heart and a curious mind. Questions act like keys that open the doors to information, energy, memories, and emotions that reside within us. The question is an activating force that focuses our intentions and energy, and this question animates the whole process. Without the question, we can flounder and get lost in infinite possibilities. I have seen how the right question can cause a cascade of insights to unfurl, insights which inform us about our journey in this life, and lead us to knowing how we can best heal ourselves. So, it is essential that we allow ourselves to ask probing questions, because it is the question that reveals the truth within our being. The question begins a search for answers that often spring into our minds, when a space is created where the question can be asked and examined. Answers float to the surface of our consciousness when we ask questions. It is the nature of the dialogue between our unconscious, conscious and higher mind.

The question also connects to our life and purpose. Over the years, I have discovered that we come into this life with three major questions: a central, secondary, and tertiary question. These questions often shape how our lives unfold, and each question shapes time, meaning that each question is addressed at different phases within our lives. These questions often will be related and may build upon each other in profound ways. The events in our life can be understood when we understand what question is operating in our lives at any given moment. I have noticed that there is a thematic quality to these three questions once they have been revealed. They weave in and out of our lives but each one is focused on at a different time in our lives. I have found that the primary question is central to our early life from 15–30 years of age; the secondary question flows into our awareness and focus from 30–45 and the tertiary question is sparked after age 45. All three questions are interacting within us at all times, though our focus may be on each separate question at different times of our lives. Please realize that these numbers are only guideposts and are not set in stone. Each of us will have our own unique timing and experience.

Developing Intuitive Awareness
Our intuition is a natural gift we all possess. Like developing a quiet intuitive mind that rests in deep stillness, the essence of the practices of Transforming Embodiment rest with the growth and enhancement

of the intuition. My training and inner experiences have taught me ways to develop the intuition. The steps are simple, and yet they require patience, stamina, and courage as we face the endless stream of thoughts that our minds produce.

Our first task is to quiet our minds, and to cultivate a Beginner's Mind. This mind is open and free with no expectations and carries with it a distinct experience of not knowing, quiescence, and curiosity. In cultivating these aspects of mind our guiding light is our breath. Breathing deep into our belly or lower energy center encourages the mind to settle. Breathing develops our sense of presence and a mind that does not judge.

Spaciousness can arise when our minds become quiet. Like the sky, our minds become spacious, and with spaciousness, like a flower that opens to the sun our minds naturally will unfold. Not knowing and non-judgment flourish in this spaciousness.

Neutrality is key as we learn that energy is just energy, no more, no less; neutral in its nature and essence. It is only our thoughts that create distinctions of negative and positive. Avoidance or attraction gives rise to duality and judgment. These reactions limit our ability to experience spacious not-knowing, which is a requirement for deep intuitive work.

While negative forces and energies may be alive in the world, who are we to judge their true reality? These energies may be happening for a larger reason, one our limited day-to-day consciousness cannot conceive.[275] When judged from a universal level, both positive and negative reactions arise from our beliefs, assumptions, and judgments. The idea of evil comes out of our belief in it. Cause-effect relationships are at play, so neutrality and equanimity are needed to help us see things as they are, rather than to see them through the veil of judgment. This is important to realize when nurturing intuition.

Creating boundaries and self-definition includes having a strong sense of where we begin and end energetically. It is important to maintain self-definition, so that as we merge into spaciousness, we don't become diffuse and ineffective. In addition, having this distinct sense of boundaries creates mental and emotional stability. Having boundaries creates an open and free environment for our energy and intuition to work within us. Boundaries also allow us to distinguish

Chapter Eleven

between which feelings and emotions are ours, and which are not. Boundaries separate us, in a good way, from the mental and emotional energies of others. Boundaries help us discover who we are, and talents and gifts we possess. Balance and self-definition are the positive results of having good boundaries.

The ability to participate in our experience with a detached, self-observing awareness is needed in order to become an active force in our own healing process. If we merge one hundred percent of our awareness with our experience, we can no longer transform our experiences, emotions, or beliefs. It is critical that we learn to see, feel, and sense our experience from the inside out. Inner observation and a detached inner observer are mandatory because it is this part of us that watches our memories and story unfold and it is through this inner observer that we initiate change. Without it, our mental and emotional states would remain static. There is a delicate balance between our observer and participatory awareness. We must not be too detached or emeshed in our experiences or we will not be able to affect change.

Trust in your intuition develops as you stabilize your mind, energy, and emotions; feeling our emotions and experiences is necessary in order for memories to surface. Trust is essential, set aside any doubts, and trust your first impressions, feelings, memories, or emotions, once you have asked a question. Trust the first thing that pops into your mind, before the thinking mind becomes engaged and this will connect you with your intuitive mind.

If we stay open and trusting, reliable information will emerge from our inner wisdom self. If we are carried away on a stream of thoughts, our ego may take over and we will need to restabalize our mind. Go back to the breathing and start again.

Equanimity is a mind-state where all things remain neutral. There is no perception of good or bad, energy just flows or doesn't flow, no judgment arises when the mind perceives with equanimity. This mind state gives us a fresh immediate perception of our reality. When this balance is achieved, a reliable intuition blossoms.

When cultivating the intuition it is wise to create a space to work within. This space can be created when we focus our attention on our breath. We can also make the statement that we wish to create a space that is free from any and all interference, be it known or unknown to us. This "protection" is necessary, because there are forces outside of us that can create interference. Waves of energy and emotions from others form electromagnetic impulses and even microwaves and computers can affect our personal energy field. Protection gives us boundaries and creates a space in which to do psychic or intuitive work.

These are basics for cultivating and developing the intuition. While these steps may seem simple, they can be challenging. Being connected to our inner wisdom is our strongest ally and foundation when undertaking deep healing. Our intuition becomes a constant source of support and guidance when we are connected to our inner Self and our mind is settled, still and clear as a mountain lake. Clarity and new insight will naturally arise when we are tranquil and open. Cultivate this mind state, and the intuition will grow firm and strong.

12

FINDING OUR STORY—LOOKING FOR EMBODIED MEMORY

> Mind retains memories, images and thoughts related to the past and casts them into the present, interpreting the present in light of the past, it evokes emotions that in turn reflect back to mind, generating further distortions and leading ever more surely into painful states of mind.
>
> Tarthang Tulku [276]

Transforming Embodiment helps us uncover unconscious imagery, beliefs, thought forms, and memories. These aspects are parts of our personal puzzle that can help us understand our actions, psychology, and symptoms. By bringing our unconscious thoughts, beliefs, memories, and the imagery associated with each of these into consciousness, our puzzle will take shape. As we put the different pieces of our puzzle together, a larger picture emerges and with this new understandings we see how repetitive patterns and actions are perpetuated and how they create pain.[277]

Our powerful emotions, memories and traumatic events can keep us stuck; if we do not break the cycle we will remain in it until the original pattern or energy is detected. A desire for wholeness, or homeostatsis, exists within each of us, and our body's wisdom combined with the wisdom of our spiritual self is accessible to each of us. This is the part of ourselves that drives us to complete the puzzle and to see the meaning within the events in our lives. Our inner wisdom opens us to the knowledge living within ourselves. As our relationship to our inner wisdom grows, we can discover the best way to heal ourselves. The body and intuition communicate with us via imagery and this can be invaluable when we are trying to understand a problem or symptom. "Because of their intimate contact with the physical body, images appear to express a body wisdom; an understanding of both status and prognosis of health."[278] Images not only give us an understanding of our health but also extend to and give us a deep understanding of our spiritual and emotional lives as well.

To begin this process we must listen to our bodies and our intuition. We must open our hearts to all possibilities and create space for answers to come to us. We are like sculptors and detectives all at once, and as we remove each layer, more of the origins of our problems are revealed. Each question asked is like the sculptor's chisel, peeling away layers upon layers of imagery, memory, emotion, and belief. Questions lead us to the answers that lie within us, to ancient histories and stories that when recovered can bring closure and release.

Questions allow for the heart of a problem to be revealed to us. Each question directs our attention deeper, revealing previously unknown pieces of our psycho-spiritual puzzle. The question guides this journey and allows us to inwardly explore, by chiseling away the layers of our conditional ways of seeing problems and experiences. This act of questioning and following our intuitive process by using our intellect can show us the very origins of why we experience our life as we do. As the chisel gradually reveals a stone's inner nature, our questions can reveal our inner radiance.

The questioning process lets us explore unknown territories within ourselves and helps evoke the memories and imagery deep within us.

Insights, Imagery and Interconnections

Images can be of events from the present or the past. There are often

Chapter Twelve

striking and direct correlations between past events and how we are experiencing or viewing problems in the present.

June came to see me for a reading.[279] She explained that she had had a very angry encounter with a tenant and was shocked at the violence of her reaction. After renting her home to this tenant, she said the woman had decided to back out on their agreements and was angrily demanding all of her money back. June and her husband had rented their main house and were living in the guest house to help pay their mortgage, so a great deal was at stake for them financially. June had even left a few precious things in her home for the tenants to use.

June wanted to know why this encounter was so volatile. As she voiced this question I saw how she and her tenant might have been involved in the past. Images of two women struggling for food in a dirty European city street centuries before emerged. The city was experiencing some kind of epidemic and famine, and I had a distinct impression that this was a life or death struggle. I sensed that June had died, soon after this struggle, from illness and hunger. I felt this could be a part of why her encounter with her tenant had been so extreme.

June began to cry as I told her of her struggle over food, and she said this felt accurate. I only shared this small bit of information with her, and asked her to connect to her feelings. As she connected with the anger that she felt in this life, she saw a violent struggle, one in which she was strangling another woman. She felt this woman in the past was her current tenant, and said they dressed alike. As June sat in stillness, she said that she had wanted to kill this woman over the food in the street but had been overpowered by the woman and lost the food. Her memory was both visual and visceral. Upon reflection, she said she would have been willing to share the food if she had had the chance to do so. I mentioned that this was similar to her willingness to leave some valuable things in her home for the tenant to use.

As we processed this experience, June saw that she and her tenant had struggled over food in the past and now it was a struggle over money. Each experience triggered survival issues. June noted that she felt her financial survival was threatened, as she and her husband needed the income from the rental to pay their mortgage. When the woman backed out of her financial agreements, it sparked a similar violent response as in her past.

As June emerged from her experience, she realized why her reaction, as well as the other woman's, had been so extreme. She saw how, when the tenant backed out of her financial agreements, the struggle began anew. Not only were financial issues sparked for them both, but also it became a life and death struggle. Realizing these connections during the reading, June was able to disengage, and began to release and integrate her experience. June realized how this experience influenced her relationship to money and contributed to her general patterns of scarcity.

June discovered the following beliefs: I have to fight to survive and life is a struggle. I never have enough of what I need, and though survival is possible, there is no comfort in life.

Seeing this interconnectedness between present and past experiences helped June understand and release her anger.

Using questions, following the process, and watching events and scenes unfold allowed June to re-experience the pain and bear witness to events she had been powerless to change in the past. She understood that she did not have to live by those old beliefs any longer and that she was not a victim anymore. This restructuring of her beliefs and the release of pent up emotions from the past changed the dynamic of the relationship with her tenant.

Seeing patterns and relationships is important because it shapes the process and helps us piece together seemingly divergent bits of information. Intuitive insights give us a map that guides this work and with them we create a new narrative. Seeing the interconnections between our past and present helps us develop new strategies for tackling old and persistent problems.

Listening and Language

Listening to how we talk about a problem, and the language we choose to describe it can be very informative. Listening to how we speak and think can help us understand how we construct our reality. Remember, body consciousness takes what we say at face value, very literally, so listening carefully to our words can give us access to the beliefs we hold, and patterns may emerge.

Thoughts and language can reveal the common themes that recur in our lives. Our personal story and the beliefs and emotions we cherish can help us understand why symptoms, relationships struggles and emotional pain persist. Listening helps bring us to new levels of understanding.

The Art of the Question

The questioning phase begins with a series of inquiries, questions, and statements used to evoke imagery and memories. Questions illuminate the who, what, where, when and how of our experiences. As answers are found, more specific and detailed questions are used to elicit more information and to fill out the narrative surrounding our experiences and memories. Our spiritual or intuitive Self and Source guide the entire questioning process. Questions gather deep levels of information from our unconscious and a variety of questions are asked in order to evoke memories and experiences from within.

Questions help us focus and open the doorways into our inner world. Questions open our minds to what is beneath the surface. One client described the experience as follows,

"When you ask me a question, it feels as if a veil is pulled away, and I enter another space where things are revealed to me about my inner life and past experiences. Questions create a mental space that's very open. This lets me enter into this other reality in a gentle way and gives me the choice to follow my experience or not, which helps with any fears I may have, and encourages me to go deeper, even if it's scary. Your questions help me focus and give me a bit of a push that says it's okay to go there."

Questions and this responsorial approach allow us to stay in control of the process, where we need to go, and how safe we feel about going there. Questions also have various functions. When we are checking in with ourselves or a client, questions are used to gather information. They can help us decide the direction we want to take, as well as focusing our attention, so we can discern the information held within our body, subtle mind and psyche. Questions have the added benefit of shifting our attention from our outer world to our inner experience, so we may search for the emotions, memories, and beliefs held within our body and subconscious. Our questions can take us deeper into our past experiences and they help keep the process moving.

Since the space of our body of experience is quite vast and timeless, a focusing point is needed. Questions are focusing points, like beacons of light from a lighthouse. They illuminate our way within the process and direct our attention. We just follow the light, as it were. Or think of this vast inner space as a university library. If we have a specific subject category, like Italian renaissance art that we are looking for, we can go directly to the correct file. However, without a specific subject in mind, we could wander the stacks for hours and find nothing. Questions help narrow our focus and direct our attention to the answers that lie within us.

Here are a few guidelines or requests and examples of questions: First, feel your body and your body's energies and notice if there are any tensions within your body. Now, what is drawing your attention the most? Follow the sensations and feelings in your body and let yourself go to the first place, memory, or experience connected to these body sensations.

Follow your strongest feelings and let yourself move to the memories that can help you understand your problem. Questions and statements that can aid you in searching for the origins of a problem might include: Where was the first time I ever felt this particular feeling or emotion? Where am I and who is there with me? What is going on around me? Why am I in this situation, and what has brought me to this point? These kinds of questions and directions can help you discover the origin of difficulties you are experiencing in the present.

I have found that a mix of statements and questions like these helps you experience and participate in memories as they arise. These kinds of questions and statements connect you to your body and your timeless self. By being in the moment, time passes away and other lifetimes can flow into your awareness. One client referred to this experience as entering into a timeless reality, where all time could be revealed.

Many different layers of experiences and memories can animate a single problem. So it is important to follow the process as it unfolds, and let yourself move from one experience or memory to the next. In this way, your history or story can take shape.

Keep your questions as open ended as possible, with no expectations. This will provide you with a space and focus at the same time, and can help you discern, see, and experience patterns, memories, events,

Chapter Twelve

and cause-effect relationships. Use your intuition and your intellect and old problems can be understood from different points of view. Insights might be missed if you limit yourself by not remaining open and aware. Just thinking about a problem has a tendency to bring you out of your experience, so use both your rational and intuitive mind and information and answers will come to you. The key is to have the spirit of inquiry and curiosity run through your inner explorations so you can directly experience your memories, feelings, and emotions.

Experiencing and reliving difficult relationships or traumatic events can be very frightening. Please respect your defenses and fears when doing this kind of inner work. Most people simply cannot jump into deeply troubling or traumatic events. So, it is imperative that you stay attuned and connected. Be delicate with yourself and yet persistent. Follow your process and imagery. If it appears that you are getting lost in your story, losing focus, or moving away from origins, an open-ended but specific question can help get you back on track. You might ask: Where have I felt this feeling these emotions before, where have I experienced this problem? Then, let your mind and body relax and move deeper into the experiences, memories, or emotions you are feeling.

More than one set of images or events may emerge during the remembering process. You may choose to explore the imagery that is less frightening first. However, if this is taken too far, you can get lost in the unwinding story and avoid the other imagery altogether. If this occurs you try to bring your focus back to the imagery that was more challenging if it seems appropriate. You need to check in and see if you are splitting off and avoiding the imagery that may scare you or if you have come to a point, where you are at session threshold. Sometimes you just need to take a break and regroup. This is fine, go lightly and be gentle with yourself, you will know when you can persist and when you need to finish something.

As Jordan worked to find the origins of his difficulties with his ex-wife, he saw and re-experienced many different lifetimes that they had shared. With each lifetime, more details were found. The history they shared became known to him and the present began to make more sense to him. By following his experience, he moved from one lifetime to the next and discovered the healing that was available for both of them.

Give yourself a large field to work within, so the mind, with its fears and reactions, is given the space it requires. Openness helps you review and remember your pain and move through it. Constriction of your energy, body, and emotions may appear to keep your pain at bay but it actually keeps it with you. Respect your boundaries and limits but also become familiar with your mind and its reactions, so you can move beyond your habitual responses. "The most skillful teachings may often be those which melt one open, rather than somehow pry open the door, which later only slams shut."[280]

As the process of remembering deepens, you may move through a number of other lifetimes. Each lifetime stresses a specific aspect of how a problem, symptom, or belief is held in place, and shows you the many ways a problem has been experienced, sometimes even from opposing points of view. Asking questions guides your process and takes you deeper, so memories and events can be brought to light and you can see how your past affects us in the present. Questions might include: Where am I, what is going on and why am I in this situation?

These types of questions give you access to hidden gems within your experience, beyond your usual patterns of thinking and behaving. During Jordan's first session, he came upon a lifetime that he had shared with his ex-wife where they had been happy. They had shared a simple, contented life together and were at peace with each other. This memory came to Jordan after he had recovered numerous lifetimes where they had done grave harm to each other. Two simple questions, "Is there anything else I need to know, and what more does my aumakua want me to understand about this relationship?" opened the door to this memory of peace between them and this, more than anything else, changed Jordan at his core.

These questions helped Jordan discover pivotal points about his relationships and deep emotions. The recovery of this memory and its integration entirely changed the dynamic of his relationship with his ex-wife and allowed him to also heal his relationship with his daughter. The gems within the body, mind, and unconscious in the form of ancient memories can help us change long-standing patterns within our lives. These memories open up new ways of thinking and new levels of healing and usher us into the integration phase.

Chapter Twelve

To summarize, questions allow you to gather information and to define your goals as we begin this process. Within the remembering phase questions evoke memories and emotions and give you a place to start your inward journey. They help you see the interconnections in your lives and in using them you gain a greater understanding of how problems and patterns are intertwined.

In the integration phase, questions are used to develop connections. Question you might use include "what connects my experiences from my past to my the present situation; what similar themes flow from my past into my present day life and what beliefs do I still hold from these ancient experiences that limit me?" These questions help you see the connections between your past and present and enable you to recognize any cause-effect relationships that might exist. The very construction of your beliefs and the reasoning behind your actions in the present can be understood when connections between past events and present symptoms or difficulties is discovered. This gives you a context for your experiences and a starting point for making change. You can see the broader implications of your habitual actions and reactions, while perceiving the larger picture. Life becomes full of possibilities, opportunities for change appear, and new options naturally arise as you reshape your past, present and future.

13

FINDING ORIGINS: WORKING WITH EMBODIED MEMORY

> Therapeutic work has shown that many emotional disorders have their roots in past life experiences rather than in the present life, and the symptoms resulting from these disorders disappear or are alleviated after the person is allowed to relive the past experience that underlies it.
>
> — Stanislav Grof[281]

Remembering is an act that is mostly a cognitive and verbal process. Reliving, on the other hand, almost guarantees that we will see, feel, hear, smell, and even taste our past experiences. These two aspects are often interwoven. Reliving is one part of the remembering process, which begins as we see and unearth or remember events from our past. Traumatic events can be accessed safely, when we recollect the past by remembering, because we maintain control while still remaining open. As the remembering process continues, we begin to relive the events, emotions and memories from our past and discover the beliefs that we maintain because of our past experiences.

The origins of present difficulties and symptoms are revealed as we remember, relive, and complete processes left undone at their roots. If the original causes of difficulties are found, we can actively change our inner experience and effectively transform problems and symptoms at what appears to be a cellular level. Exploring emotional and traumatic memories and events is essential, so we can understand and release the beliefs that limit us. The release of ancient beliefs and the creation of new ones are necessary for a complete clearing and transformation to occur.

While remembering and reliving past experiences, many things can occur. A cascade of memories can tumble into our consciousness, revealing layers of our reality we had previously been unaware of. This cascade of memories is often sequential, moving backwards in time from the present or most recent memories, to those of our distant past. Often we will remember the least traumatic events first before experiencing more dramatic memories. The progressive movement from the present backwards gives us a buffer of sorts and can provide an easing into origins, however the process can be reversed as was the case with Jordan. He discovered his earliest memories right away and moved forward in time. This can be more intense because we are moving rapidly to the source of present conflicts.

At this point, the process can take on a life of its own, as momentum builds and moves us from one life to the next. Origins and the complex belief systems that fuel current difficulties come into view. These discoveries lead to deeper understandings of how and why repetitive emotional patterns of behavior and belief have continued. Origins are important to uncover because they provide an understanding and context for our current problems.

In Jordan's case, his remembrance and reliving of a happy lifetime with his ex-wife was of great importance. The earlier manipulative and painful experiences and memories gave Jordan a background to understand their conflicts, but the memory of happiness is what truly changed him. This recollection of love let him see and understand that love and gentleness had once existed between he and his ex-wife. It was this shared love and the remembrance of this love that changed

Jordan so deeply. This experience enabled him to change his most basic beliefs and assumptions about his ex-wife.

Uncovering origins is not the only goal in this work. Resolution of limiting beliefs and the emotions that accompany them is of paramount importance because as we see with Jordan the key to healing can unexpectedly be found elsewhere. The origins of his distrust came out of his life in Egypt, but the healing he sought came out of his lifetime as a woodsman with his ex-wife.

"What other experiences, lifetimes or events are connected to my present problems, how are they interrelated, and is there anything more that I need to know or understand at this time" are questions we can use to deepen our inquiry. These types of questions can help us uncover invaluable parts of a larger story that goes beyond origins. Insights can then bring to light the heart a problem as well as its beliefs. Sometimes the answers and connections that we find have been inconceivable from our present perspective and this may shock us, but it is these points that deeply change our experience and perception of our problems. This is what occurred for Jordan, in remembering a happy lifetime with his ex-wife.

Focused attention and curiosity will guide us to the most pertinent material as it applies to our present day situations. If our attention is scattered, the information will appear to us in a disorganized way and lead us only into confusion. We will tend to go off on tangents and bounce from one experience to another like channel surfing if the attention is not honed. This is why quieting and settling the mind is so essential. With focus and an intention of healing a problem for good, amazing insights will come to us. Even seemingly small details can have great effects, so expect the unexpected, and keep the mind spacious because when working with original causes or origins and the phenomenon of previous lives we never know what gems will be unveiled.

Within this phase of the process, we may actually re-experience memories from our ancient past as if we were there again. This goes beyond the cognitive experience of remembering. Feeling and directly participating in past events in the present characterize reliving. As with Lynn, emotions and physical sensations from our past experiences may be revisited and we may feel these events are taking place in the present moment.

While sensations and feelings are being rediscovered, we need to stay centered and grounded so we can safely immerse ourselves in our memories and emotions as they arise. Paying attention to our breathing, any body tensions, or muscular constrictions as well as to our mind's reaction to the images we may be seeing is important. If this becomes too uncomfortable focus back on the breath for a few moments, if necessary open your eyes and shift your attention to the present, however remember that sometimes there are insights just beyond the discomfort.[282]

During one of Jordan's experiences, he felt he was hanging on a wheel of some kind, tied to it at his ankles and wrists. This was quite uncomfortable but I asked him if he could stay with the experience for a few moments beyond his initial description. He maintained his presence and when I saw him begin to struggle with the physical sensations and feelings, I told him to imagine someone coming to his aid who could untie him and ease him back to the ground. By remaining in the experience, Jordan was able to contact his original feelings from the incident. He said he felt it was okay to suffer this punishment and by doing so, he said he was able to release a lingering sense of guilt he had carried.

As in this example, pain can help us if it is accompanied by a change in view. If a change of view does not occur, pain is not a constructive tool for change; it is a form of abuse.

In *Yoga and Psychotherapy*, Swami Rama, Ballentine, and Swami Ajaya speak at length on pain and growth, saying, "Shedding the old and moving into the new is a transition that necessarily includes some pain."[283] Furthermore, "Anxiety, fear and equanimity lie along a continuum. As attachment is decreased, one's ability to observe increases, he feels a more manageable fear. With further detachment one can respond even more constructively, limited by neither anxiety or fear."[284] I have found that pain can be a profound ally in the healing process. Pain can give us focus, and with focus the roots of our pain can be observed and examined. Through this kind of examination, we can release painful events, memories, and experiences that have previously been unconscious.

> A traumatic story can be retold a hundred times, with the teller trying to work through the pain and reaction, but not until this experience is truly felt in the present moment can there be true healing and freedom from the negative pattern.[285]

Past experiences can be revisited again and again, but until these experiences and traumas are relived with conscious awareness, healing and change may not occur.

For Jordan, the reliving of the torturous event described above allowed him to observe with detachment his situation and to feel his emotions simultaneously. By doing this, he realized that there was a feeling of appropriateness to the "torture." He said it was somehow normal and anticipated. By staying with the situation in this detached way, he was able to move through the original discomfort, and in so doing he became curious about his feelings and reactions. Instead of his usual anger, he began to feel compassion for his ex-wife, as he saw that she too was entrapped and unhappy. He saw sadness in her that he had not known in this lifetime, and it was this experience that took him beyond his normal conditioning and patterns of thinking and response to her. His pain had allowed him to release deeper layers of anger and frustration. Here the pain served a purpose and was of use because it let behavioral patterns be modified and reorganized.

When recovering and reliving memories from previous lives, there are some unique mental shifts that can occur. They are *acceleration*, time-shifting, and *flipping*. Acceleration is a phenomenon where we experience a heightened sense of movement, as time appears to speeds up. During acceleration a rapid firing of memories, images and events comes into our consciousness and we can experience multiple layers of images and memories from a series of different lifetimes or moments from our past. These images or events can come as a rapid sequence of impressions as our memories flash before us very quickly. Acceleration also occurs during time-shifting. In time-shifting we move back and forth between past experiences and the present very rapidly.

We can lose our sense of being anchored in the present time during these accelerated experiences, and as a result, become confused as to temporal location. This can be frightening, so it is of utmost importance to do the preliminary practices and develop intuition and meditative awareness before attempting to work with time.

Time-shifting is a phenomenon where we feel we are moving from one lifetime to another very rapidly. Time becomes very fluid, as we jump from one experience to the next. At first, this can feel very disjointed but as we grow more adept at following these movements, the randomness of the experience gives way to order. Time-shifting can also be felt as movement within one lifetime. Sara had this second experience: as she closed her eyes, past experiences came alive, bits and pieces of scenes and memories surfaced. First, she saw a stone castle and felt the dampness and cold of that place, then memories of being chased down, caught and probed assailed her, at which point an earlier memory of an assignation and a young man came into her consciousness. Then a dark knight, furious and vengeful, who was her husband, shook her and she felt herself trying to escape until finally she was overtaken with deep sadness and resignation. These events appeared random but as the story was filled in, they began to make sense to Sara. Randomness often will give rise to organization.

For me, the experience of acceleration and time-shifting move me very quickly from one lifetime to another, especially if I am asking to see and release a problem in its entirety. Jordan experienced time-shifting in this way as he moved from one lifetime to the next, in working through his relationship struggles with his ex-wife.

Flipping is a part of the experience of acceleration and time-shifting. Here we feel as though we are literally flipping back and forth between different times. This experience can create confusion as our sense of self, sense of space and time becomes disoriented. What arises from all these experiences is confusion; yet, this confusion helps the overall process. Confusion allows embedded belief systems, emotions, and personal patterns to be disassembled. This disorganization, I have found, is necessary for reorganization and healing to take place. Confusion and disorientation can give us an opportunity to identity and change limiting outdated emotional, mental, and physical patterns and the residual energies from "past" lifetimes. Confusion states are a way of knowing that our deep issues have been reached.

Similar senses of confusion can occur when we work at an *edge*. An edge is a place that is at the limits of our experience. At an edge, a person can become confused and usually does not know what to do. The information at an edge is new, frightening or unacceptable on some level[286] Edges, like confusion and disorientation, can be places where relearning occurs. Working with our confusion, or edges, can help us attain new understandings.

Reliving and participating in memories is the most direct way to release and transform our reactions to present problems. By reliving past traumas and experiences, we are able to release the shock and other emotions and mental formations built from these past experiences. As these original responses change, our present is changed.

Detached participation and the ability to both observe, while simultaneously experiencing the situation at hand, encourages transformational change. In Huna, this participatory but detached experience is referred to as maintaining the "one percent shaman." In this mind-state ninety-nine percent of our awareness is participating in an experience while the other one percent is free to make change. Without this one percent awareness constructive changes cannot be made. If we lose our sense of detachment, we can become overwhelmed or get stuck in our story and memories that we are trying to release. It is essential to develop our inner observer, so we will not fall into these states.

Reliving an experience is different from flashbacks. Reliving brings with it a sense of bearing witness to the events we are experiencing. Our inner observer acts as a witness to the events as they unfold in our mind's eye. In this way, trauma is not reinforced but is actively worked with to create new ways of relating our past experiences. We are empowered as we bring current skills, knowledge and abilities to our former self, in order to better cope with situations and events from our past; this is much like inner child work where we bring our adult self to assist our inner child in order to heal and care for that younger self.

We need to learn to consciously observe and participate in our experiences. When Jordan experienced feelings of being tortured, he was in touch with both his emotions and the physical discomfort in his body. This experience of being both the observer and participant is similar to what we find in meditation, when we discover that we are not our mind and thoughts. Meditation teaches us to observe and participate in our experience simultaneously. Awakened and expanded states of consciousness are fostered in this way.

The development of mental and emotional stability is paramount because it is necessary to be present and mindful when remembering and re-experiencing memories, emotions and events from our past either from this lifetime or from others. Merging into the spaciousness of meditative or universal mind can help us come into the moment and this presence or energy encourages the discursive mind to settle. As the spaciousness of the Energy is encountered, a quieting of the mind naturally occurs.

It is not always easy to stay present when we encounter painful or confusing moments from our past and we may wish to mentally run away from these traumatic experiences, however, it is the act of staying in the moment with full awareness, that ultimately transforms our experiences and their effects.

A delicate balance is needed here and the ability to watch our mind and its experience, almost like a movie, can be helpful so we don't get lost in or overwhelmed by what we are seeing and remembering. If we do get lost in the story we can re-traumatize ourselves, so, self-monitoring is essential and it is imperative that we seek help before any re-traumatization occurs. A skilled practitioner may be needed here more than at any other time in this work.

A variety of experiences can take place at this time. We may experience previously unconscious memories from our childhood, previous lives, infancy, or even family memories. All evoked or remembered experiences are worked with in similar ways. Here are a few examples.

Amelia came to see me after finding out she was pregnant at age thirty-five. She felt the normal anxieties of new mothers-to-be, but as she talked, this anxiety grew and revealed a deeper fear of having a child with Down's Syndrome. I realized that this fear could have arisen from a then-held cultural and medical belief, that women over the age of thirty-five have an increased risk of having children born with birth defects.

Amelia's session began with the preliminary practices. I asked her to see any physical tensions in her body melt away like snow when it is warmed by the sun, and to release any emotional tensions and to let go

Chapter Thirteen

of any mental cares or concerns from her day, so she could come fully into the present.

As her attention shifted inward I asked her to follow her breathing for a few moments, letting each breath relax her and bring her into the moment more deeply. When I noticed she was relaxed, I asked her if she was ready to look at the fear she had described earlier. She was ready so I asked her to imagine and feel her fear and the accompanying anxiety she felt and to hold them very gently in her mind, as if they were a small bird in her hands; and to simultaneously notice any areas in her body where the fear might be.

I explained that her fear might appear as tensions, images, or perceivable feelings in her body and asked if anything stood out. She at once felt something at her sternum; her attention was drawn to that area. She saw a tight ball of string and within this ball there was a jumble of childhood memories. I asked her to remove this ball from her chest and put it outside her body. She set it on an imaginary table in front of her.

By removing the image from her body she was able to examine this ball of memories more carefully. One set of memories was of a friend's sister, Janey, who had Down's Syndrome. Amelia remembered that she had been very protective of Janey and that she was always concerned for Janey's welfare. She didn't want Janey to be hurt by anyone and she felt very connected to her somehow. I asked if she could separate herself from Janey; she did so but said it was hard to do.

I asked Amelia if she had ever seen Janey teased or ridiculed by the other children. She said she had, but that Janey's family and home were very protective and loving. With this understanding, and having noted Amelia's difficulty in separating from Janey earlier, I asked if Amelia had been teased or ridiculed as a child. Her voice changed as she told me she had been teased a lot. There was a tinge of sadness in her voice as she spoke.

I suspected the ridicule that Amelia wanted to protect Janey from in the past had been directed at her. Like Janey, she had been the different one, by her family's standards. Her eyes opened wide as I verbalized this thought. She said this was true and described how she had moved far away from her family, as soon as she was able, and that they had never understood her choices and often criticized her. As a result she always felt like an outsider and unlike her sibling she left the state and town where she was born.

This sadness led us back to her heart and sternum. This time she saw a black veil, it was snapped like heavy canvas over the area where the ball of memories had been. I asked if she wanted to remove this veil. She said, yes and added that she no longer wanted to protect herself in this old way. Amelia took the veil off and out of her sternum. As she finished doing this, her sternum and chest became like gold, very precious, vast, and sacred like a cathedral. She reveled in and took this new experience in for a few minutes.

I asked if anything needed to be done with the ball and she shared that it had unraveled and that the black veil had turned into a flat coaster like those used to protect tabletops, and that the coaster had turned into a Frisbee and flown away.

Amelia said that protecting her heart in this old way was not necessary any longer. "I'm safe and can allow myself to feel this new strength of undefensiveness. I've been trying to achieve this undefensiveness, that I now feel in my heart, for some time in my relationship with my husband and within myself." This new vulnerability was a very important change for Amelia, which allowed her to feel a deeper level of safety, self-acceptance, and intimacy.

Amelia carried away this new feeling in her heart that she had long been working to achieve. Her anxiety and fear dissolved, and seven and a half months later she delivered a healthy baby boy.

This example illustrates how forgotten childhood memories can be worked with and how current fears and outgrown defensive patterns can be resolved and released by working with the memories and emotions stored within our consciousness and body. It also demonstrates how imagery and feelings are linked; by working with the imagery within our body we can find healing.

This next example illustrates how Sara processed and released memories from a previous lifetime. Sara came to see me when spontaneous "memories" and images from another time began to plague her. These images were very upsetting and Sara felt they were linked to her current boyfriend and her feeling of being trapped in her relationship.

Chapter Thirteen

She explained that her partner, Ed, was obsessed with sex. He often persuaded her to have sex when she did not want to and hurt her unknowingly in the process. The image she had recalled was of being tortured by a man she felt was Ed. This scene replayed over and over in her mind and it was this experience that brought her in to see me.

Sara was confused and scattered when she came in to see me, and felt she was in two different time periods at once. This whole experience left her feeling out of balance and she was afraid that she might be going crazy.

Sara described a series of very disturbing images that had been coming to her in waking states. The imagery repeated the same theme of sexual torture. She mentioned she had not enjoyed sex much in her life, but it had never been painful for her until she met Ed. She explained that even from the first, their lovemaking had been excruciatingly painful.

She was very tense as she related these details, so I asked her to take a deep breath and try to release any tension she was feeling in her body. I also let her know that she was not going crazy. I proposed that perhaps she was remembering something from the distant past. I mentioned that there might be a possible healing for her within these images. She agreed and calmed as I offered her these possibilities. I asked her to continue to breathe and to watch her breath as she inhaled and exhaled. I joined in and breathed with her for a few minutes. She calmed still further.

She said she very much wanted to understand what was going on and said she was ready to go back into the images she had described earlier. I asked her to take another deep breath and let her attention float back to these old images, to see if she could find out why these images were surfacing. She moved into the memories and again remembered being tied down and tortured.

As she sat with this image, she began to tell me the following story. "Ed was a lord and a wealthy man who owned land. He had servants and a cold dark castle." As Sara said this she began to shiver. I gave her a blanket and asked if there was anything else. Her eyes were closed, but she continued to see as rapid eye movements danced under her lidded eyes as if she were dreaming.

She said, "I did my duty in marrying Ed but I didn't love him. I took long walks on the land to ease my loneliness. While on a walk I met a man on horseback. We met repeatedly and I fell in love with him." She said that when they met they would frolic and that she got pregnant as a result.[287]

I asked her what took place next. She said as her pregnancy advanced and she could no longer hide it, she left. She grew agitated at this point. I asked her to focus on her breathing again and to take a few deep breaths and allow her body to relax, adding that she could let go of the pain for the moment and just relax.

As she did this I asked if she could continue. She said yes, and told me that she had the baby alone and that Ed had sent men out to capture her and bring her back. The father of the baby, she realized, was gone and she felt he had been pursued as well.

When the men found her they sexually tortured her. They tied her down and poked her insides with something, she recalled. They took her baby and her back to the castle. After being taken back to the castle she said, "I lived like a zombie, half alive, alone, cold and afraid." She began to cry and said, "I was never happy again."

She shared that all of this made sense somehow and that she now had a context for the images that had been so insistent. She said these memories had originally arisen when she was walking, and while she was in the bath. "The time and scenes changed but the essence and energy remained the same." She knew she had to get out of her relationship with Ed, but she felt it would take some time.

At her next session, we worked with another set of images that related to her first experience. These images had occurred spontaneously while she was shopping with a friend for a mountain bike. At the store, she met Sam, a bike salesman, who she instantly recognized as her lover from the past life memory she had recently recalled. She became "nervous as hell" she said and left the store. She did buy a bike later from Sam but not that day. She wanted, on some level, to get together with Sam but when they did get together for coffee, Sara told Sam, "This is not right," and left. She was still with Ed at the time and trying to work things out. She felt guilty for wanting to leave him, which she desperately wanted to understand.

Chapter Thirteen

The following event helped to close the circle between them, Sara said, and allowed her to finally move on. Just as she was going to leave Ed, he got her pregnant. "He wanted me to have the baby and even said, you have it, and I'll take care of it." Sara said his response was so similar to the "past" lifetime it was spooky. She knew she could never do this or have this child. She scheduled an abortion, and left the relationship.

Sara was truly amazed that Ed had wanted her to have the baby and that he said he would take care of it. She said this incident was so like the past it gave her a chill. In the past, her husband had raised her child as his own, possessing it as he did her, as a belonging. This sense of possession still pervaded her relationship with Ed in the present until she left him.

This case is unique because Sara experienced many constellations of memories on her own. After the first occurrence these memories seemed to accelerate, taking the situation toward its eventual conclusion. We worked together throughout this time with each session going a little deeper, until in the end, as she said, things came full circle.

The sense of amazement and synchronicity described above is what I call the "ah-ha" experience. This experience can occur a number of times and tells us that the origins of a dilemma are being found. The "ah-ha" experience is a defining moment. It is a point when events from both the past and present come together, sparking a moment of revelation and wonder in us. Interconnections are seen, acknowledged, and digested all at once. This experience can occur when we work with other life memories, prenatal, infant and childhood material, or body memories.

This "ah-ha" experience would be like a child playing with dominos. After standing each domino up successively in a long row, the simple touch of a finger brings on a cascade. This cascading effect, including the interconnectedness as each domino hits the next, is like an "ah-ha" experience.

Amazing awakenings take place in these moments. It is at this time that the implications of our behaviors, and of how these behaviors create events in our lives are seen. These experiences can be startling, exhilarating, and illuminating all at once.

I would like to share one such moment from my own experience. It occurred while I was having bodywork that focused on my abdomen. This area of my body had been an area of weakness and recurring tension. I chalked this up to the fact that I had had surgery to this area as an infant.

There had been much fear concerning this surgery on the part of my doctors, nurses, family, and friends. I had worked with these fears and the memories I had of the surgery through bodywork and by using the practices I've outlines. So, when Susan asked if she could work on my scar I said, "Of course."

As Susan worked on me, new images began to pour into my mind. The first image was of thousands of women in pain from illness, childbirth, and malnutrition. Then a woman with cancer throughout her belly area stood out. As I felt this experience, I realized the woman was me. The tension increased until it became an excruciating pain that seemed to inhabit my whole body. My belly felt on fire. Susan continued to work on me, gently following my process.

As the pain peaked, another set of images came into my mind. I saw myself unconscious, but not dead, and buried alive. I saw myself regain consciousness and struggle to claw my way out, but I failed. I lapsed again into unconsciousness and finally died.

As the imagery and the accompanying emotions of fear, panic, and pain subsided, a moment of great calm fell over me. Out of this calmness came an understanding of how these events were connected to a whole constellation of behaviors and beliefs. In a single flash, a whole lifetime of behaviors began to make sense. This was a classic "ah-ha" experience.

Since that time the chronic tension in my belly has decreased, as has my need to fight and struggle. This experience allowed me to see my deeper relationship to struggling. It literally linked my struggle to survive in the present to a possible past; it was a defining moment. While there may be many layers that can animate chronic problems, the "ah-ha" experience allows us to see possible interconnections and even the origins of current problems and symptoms.

The Shadow

The shadow within our unconscious may be encountered when

remembering and reliving events and memories from our past. The shadow[288] carries unwanted, unexpressed, and disowned positive and negative parts of the personality that we have abandoned because they are unacceptable.

> Today, shadow refers to that part of the unconscious psyche that is nearest to consciousness, even though it is not completely accepted by it. Because it is contrary to our chosen conscious attitude, the shadow personality is denied expression in life and coalesces into a relatively separate personality in the unconscious, where it is isolated from exposure and discovery.[289]

While the shadow may appear to be negative, it is not. It carries with it the possibility of healing the most wounded aspects of the self. Accepting this aspect of the self requires tolerance, acceptance, and most of all, love and kindness toward the self. "If a client can stay with and unfold his negative feelings, they will eventually yield or point to some more positive, wholesome direction underneath them."[290] If we can embrace the unconscious aspects of our personality that we perceive as negative, gifts can be found.

Both the positive and negative aspects of our personality come into play in the healing process. Each aspect must be acknowledged and worked with. In our work together, Jordan saw numerous occasions where he was killed by his ex-wife and where he had killed her. This murderous side was a part of each of their shadow selves, which could not be expressed in society or even acknowledged consciously by Jordan. Nonetheless, this aspect rules him and was a literal part of his past when he reviewed it.

Jordan was familiar with his shadow. He had worked diligently to manage his anger, frustration, and pain. However, it was not until Jordan saw these shared past lives in vivid detail, that he became willing to give up the old patterns of behavior. His shadow instructed him. It showed him the "false glory," as he called it, of his actions. The shadow also revealed that both he and his ex-wife created their interactions. So in this work, the shadow is invited in.

The shadow is given the space to have a voice, to be revealed and hopefully understood.

This example also shows how roles can reverse from one lifetime to the next. Jordan and his ex-wife routinely exchanged roles from one lifetime to the next; in one life, he would kill her and in the next she would kill him. They perpetuated the dance of violence, anger, and resentment by engaging in repetitive behaviors that carried over from one lifetime to the next.

These repetitive patterns of behavior could be very much like what Freud described early in his work as repetition compulsion. Repetitive compulsion is described as "tendencies to repeat self-defeating or painful acts. Freud believed that repetitive compulsion came from the instinct to destroy."[291] Repetition compulsion is a complex wherein a person needs to repeat certain patterns that are habitual as a way of defending and keeping their ego intact.[292]

The shadow can help us find the origins of our problems, as Jordan discovered. By inviting the shadow to be a part of our process we are able to acknowledge, retrieve and integrate the many aspects of self into our consciousness. Erich Neumann writes,

> The self lies hidden in the shadow; he is the keeper of the gate, the guardian of the threshold. The way to the self lies through him; behind the dark aspect that he represents there stands the aspect of wholeness, and only by making friends with the shadow do we gain the friendship of the self.[293]

It is love and acceptance that opens the door to greater knowledge of the self and healing. This is why the shadow is engaged.

Working with Trauma

In searching for origins we may uncover death memories traumatic memories, and highly charged emotional experiences. These traumatic events from the past are repressed yet accessible. Traumatic memories of sexual abuse either in this lifetime or from issues from other lives can be addressed using the practices of Transforming Embodiment.

Chapter Thirteen

Practitioners and lay people alike must work very gently with traumatic memories as they can be shocking, and volatile and ignite deep emotions. Often, the clients that I have seen have had bits of memory surface before they see me. Some have just learned that they may have been abused, while others have known of their likely abuse for some time. Whatever the circumstances, the remembering, removal, and release phases of this work can be very helpful in working with abuse.

As with any client interaction, practitioners need to find their own methods, remembering that clients who have experienced sexual abuse with family members are particularly conflicted. Supporting a deep feeling of safety and confidentiality are of utmost importance. Rapport building and the holding of space, in an open and compassionate way convey a sense of safety that many may not have ever experienced before. I am hesitant to reveal these stories but in an effort to understand how to work with abuse using Transforming Embodiment they are included. When possible, each person has been asked permission to use her story.

Elise[294] came to see me because she had been experiencing bits and pieces of memories that gave her the impression she had been sexually abused as a child. She also experienced signs or behaviors that related to sexual abuse. She longed to understand some disturbing images and feelings she had been having for some time. After doing the preliminary practices I asked Elsie to feel her body and see if there were any areas where she felt tension, constriction, or temperature changes, and to go to the area in her body that felt the most stressed when she recalled the images and feelings she had spoken of earlier. She was drawn to and merged with the tension in her jaw and face, and soon images and feelings, began to surface. She remembered and saw scenes from her childhood, where her mother and her mother's friends abused her, she said. She grew very emotional, and experienced a mixture of grief, humiliation, and anger. We gently examined each of these emotions briefly, acknowledging and touching them with loving-kindness. I mentioned that she would need to seek help either in a group or privately when she got home. I asked if she wanted to work with any of these feelings now. She said she wanted to explore the rage she felt inside.

We explored what she felt she needed to do to release this anger, and take back the part of herself that she had lost. Right away she said she wanted to hurt her mother like she had been hurt. She wanted to strangle her, she said. Honoring this, I offered her my arm, which she grabbed with incredible force. She wept as she did this, crying, why did you do this to me? I dialogued with her as her mother to deepen and evoke her buried feelings. Through this process, she said, a variety of feelings and emotions kept surging up in her culminating when she forcefully and from a place of power said, no, to the abuse and to her abusers.

We talked about her feelings and emotions, and I reiterated that she needed to work with them more in a therapeutic setting when she got home. I assured her that her feelings were quite natural. She was surprised at her ability to be so strong and also that she had felt such a great need to harm her mother. She said she felt conflicted about this before she grabbed hold of my arm, but as she got into expressing her anger and pain, she felt better and was not as concerned that she might hurt me. As the session closed, she said she felt she had recovered a part of herself—her strength that had been gone for a long time. This aspect of recovering a part of oneself is common within indigenous shamanic traditions.[295] Elise wrote to me later to let me know she was in a woman's incest survivor group and was seeing a counselor.

This is only a brief example of what might occur when working with abuse without preconceived ideas. This single session shows how working directly with the body and its memories gave Elise the opportunity to regain her ability to defend herself and finally say "No" to the abuses she had suffered.

In working with trauma we may focus on your chakras, physical or energy body to remove images and experiences of abuse directly from our organs, tissues, and chakras. The practices described herein help us create a space, so our intuition can grow and we can learn to trust ourselves and discover for ourselves what we most need to do to find healing. Empowerment and healing go hand and hand as we create our own healing. There is no set form to follow; only guidelines are given. It is in our hands to develop our intuition and follow our aumakua and Source so we can become an active partner in our own healing journey.

14

MAKING, EMBODYING AND SUSTAINING CHANGE

Effective eradication of psychological problems does not come through alleviation of the emotional and psychosomatic symptoms involved but through their temporary intensification, full experience and conscious integration.

Stanislav Grof[296]

We can remember an event repeatedly but until the original shock of the event is remembered, relived and integrated, the event will not be released from our consciousness and deep healing does not necessarily take place. It is not enough to just remember the trauma, we need to discover the circumstances surrounding our traumatic experiences and release them from our mind and body, as well as reorganize any outdated beliefs we might still hold. When we have accomplished this we will find that our life will take on added dimension, as we understand our problems with fresh eyes and insight and pieces of our life will finally come together and make sense for us in ways previously unknown to us.

There are many different ways to effect release. Bringing past traumas and events from the unconscious into conscious awareness is one way of releasing. Release also occurs when we sense how a problem is held within our mind and body through imagery and understand the underlying beliefs that animate our feelings, memories, and experiences. The removal, examination, and understanding of these images generate release. The removal of colors, emotions, feelings, and memories in the form of imagery from our chakras and physical body is a direct way of working with our problems. Examples will be given to illustrate these techniques. The technique of *decording,* or the literal removal of attachments from the body, will also be explained.

In the release phase of this process, our intuitive Self guides us and shares strategies for the releasing, removing, and detaching of memories that have been embodied and held within our consciousness. Insights from our intuitive Self are vitally important and this Self knows how best to release the held patterns and memories that are alive within us.

Amelia's case illustrates how imagery, in this case a ball of string, contained a variety of memories. As Amelia visually unraveled the ball of string that held her memories, she remembered old friends, family patterns, and relived old feelings and emotions. Release for Amelia took place on a number of levels. It occurred as memories emerged from her unconscious, as she felt the emotions anew and as she worked with the accompanying imagery. Later as she removed the images associated with her current feelings of anxiety, another release took place.

In some cases, just remembering or bringing to consciousness information and experiences can be enough to create a release and this moving of material from the unconscious to the conscious mind can bring about profound insights. These insights can deepen further we explore this material.

Remembering and reliving forgotten memories can be enough to release habitual patterns, fears, deep emotions and beliefs, and even change physical symptoms. However, the emotions and feelings accompanying our memories need to be examined and integrated, in order to maintain any kind of lasting change.

Reliving events provides an opportunity to deepen a release. This, however, should not be a goal. Goals tend to create agendas; so our only goal is to connect with our inner wisdom and follow our experience in a safe space that allows us to explore our individual inner history.

Each person is different; some of us will literally relive our experiences to release them. Be ready for this, it is a potent part of this work and can be intense. Reliving gives us the opportunity to replay old emotions, feelings, and memories with current skills and abilities intact. During this phase, we observe our own reactions and experience their impact simultaneously. By doing this these imprinted memories can be changed. This idea of being in an experience and being able to change or transform it is at the heart of Hawai'ian shamanic work.

As an example from my own life, years ago, a small kitten I had been tube feeding died in my hands. As I tried to resuscitate him and failed, a flood of images and feelings burst into my consciousness and a memory began to coalesce. I say memory because the grief I felt and remembered, along with the agony and pain of walking into my baby son's room and finding him dead, were as strong as any memory from my present life. This memory helped me to understand my excruciating grief as I helplessly watched this little kitten die. This experience illuminated a whole system of beliefs and deep emotions I had about having a baby. Recovering and reliving this event helped me to release the pain and unconscious fears and beliefs associated with having children and helped me make clearer decisions.

Reliving highly charged emotional events is one way of letting go. It allows for emotions and the structures of beliefs to be revealed, and reckoned with, so new beliefs can be established that no longer reflect the limitations from our past.

Release is also achieved when we remove images and memories from our bodies. To do this we use our imagination, paired with our intuition. In active imagination we first intuit how a problem is imprinted within our body; we ask our wisdom Self the best way to remove the imprints, then we visualize ourselves removing the intuited imagery literally from the body, chakras, or aura. Images are laid out in front us, so we can examine them, and memories associated with them, from a distance. This separation creates the detachment necessary for careful review. This technique can be especially helpful when working with highly charged emotional issues. Imagery that had been removed is also surrounded in clear light, so the habitual imprints do not enter back into our body.

Decoding is another technique used to release memories, emotions and beliefs. In this technique, we ask to see if there are any ties or attachments between ourselves and the people connected with us or our current problem. Decoding is used to separate and unwind karmic ties, deeply entangled relationships, our most ingrained emotional and behavioral patterns and beliefs, and any convoluted energy patterns that may exist. We can decord from people, places, and events.

Sara was having personal and professional difficulties in a number of relationships and was upset and confused. As she quieted her mind and connected with her spiritual Self , I asked her to visualize each person she was having problems with one at a time, to see if any cords existed between them that hampered their relationship. As she imagined each person individually, she noticed a variety of cords. Each was different in kind, size, and color. These variations informed her about the intensity and depth of the connections she felt with each person. Sara noted that some connections were intense and unpleasant while others were enjoyable.

When Sara asked her inner wisdom how to divest herself of these unwanted energies she was guided to cut, unravel and release these dysfunctional and unpleasant connections with each person concerned in specific and fitting ways. Afterwards she said she felt lighter and a remarkable sense of well-being came over her, replacing her former confusion with clarity and peace.

It is important to understand the emotions, feelings, and beliefs that are shaping our life experiences before a release can take place. This understanding can be quite simple. When Ian remembered an ancient injury and the circumstances surrounding that injury the piercing pain in his back receded. Sara's difficulties subsided as she untangled the ties between herself and people at work and with her ex-boyfriend. While situations may be complex in the present, their origins do not have to share this complexity. The opposite is often true.

It is important to bring whatever abilities we possess into this work. Creativity is a large part of transformation healing and the more open, non-judging and creative we can be, the better. Ian was just such a case for me; I had to use skills I never dreamed could be applied. He came to see me after he had been unable to relieve the pain in his back, which he felt might be an old injury from another lifetime. He then asked if I could sing to his back in the same way he played flute to open meditation practice. This action on my part and his open willingness to explore his pain allowed us to find the origins of his suffering. He also discovered the answers to why certain patterns existed in his life and, as each pattern was worked with, the physical pain subsided more and more. If the process had stopped with just the revelation of where this injury had taken place; before meaning could be made, the pain may have persisted.

Using active imagination, Ian took the spear out of his back that he had seen and I then rewove the area psychically. The technique of *reweaving* is a visualization technique that is very much like repairing a hole in a knit sweater or darning a sock. I perceived the spear wound, and then imagined that I rewove the area, so there was no longer a puncture wound or hole present. We can do this kind of visualization for ourselves and expand upon it. We might include the use of healing herbs to staunch wounds and to help render the energy body whole. Surgery can cause the energy body to be torn, or rend holes in the aura and this is another time the technique of reweaving is useful.

Integration Phase

"Nothing is meaningful as long as we perceive only separate fragments. But as soon as the fragments come together into a synthesis, a new entity emerges, whose nature we could not have foreseen by considering the fragments alone."[297]

The integration phase is where we start making sense of what we have been re-experiencing and seeing. It is a time of discovery as we actively make connections between our past and our present and reorganize our thinking about our problems, emotions, and beliefs. Existing connections between past lives and the present are integrated at this time and the meaning of these events is digested and understood.

Integrating pulls together the various retrieved experiences and correlates them to our present day situation. Here is where we connect the dots and perceive the cause-effect relationships between present challenges, emotions, and symptoms in a synchronistic way. After identifying old wounds, behavior patterns, outdated emotions and beliefs, we recognize how these past experiences fuel our current dilemmas.

Insights from "ah-ha" moments can emerge again, accompanied by the cascading and reorganizing effects that happened during the remembering phase. However, this time we can delve deeper into the origins of our beliefs and emotions and find meaning in our past experiences, which we may have missed before. Here is where we can rework entire sets of memories, emotions, and beliefs and free ourselves from them.

During this time, direct connections to our past may be realized for the first time. Many of us may not have any experience with healing the present by recovering past life histories and imprinted memories, but these imprints affect us each and every day. Jordan was raised a Catholic with no background in reincarnation or rebirth, per se. After his experiences, was certain he had experienced a series of past lives that he had shared with his ex-wife and daughter.

Jordan was amazed how reliving these events from his distant past could so deeply change his present emotions. The repeated murderous incidents and role reversals led him to understand that he, too, had been responsible for their troubled relationship. He knew now that fighting was no longer an option, even if his ex-wife chose to fight; he would not. He would tell me later that when she snubbed him at their daughter's wedding, he only felt sorrow for her, instead of his usual rage and indignation. He believed his ability to resist being drawn into the drama came as a result of understanding and releasing the past life patterns between them and the imprints he had held within his body and mind.

These epiphanies led him to behave in new ways toward his daughter and ex-wife. As he integrated his experiences, he found he no longer needed to react in the old ways. He felt closer to his daughter and more compassionate toward his ex-wife, and was able to attend his daughter's wedding without incident.

What I observed and took part in was a reorganization of a whole set of emotional reactions he held about his ex-wife and daughter. He moved beyond his own limitations and no longer saw their relationships

Chapter Fourteen

in just one way. New possibilities emerged as he remembered the love between them; this love was a powerful healing force for him. By remembering the love and the experience of it they had shared, he was able to let that love into his consciousness and heart again. Love, instead of anger and hatred triumphed; with it his entire view of the situation was transformed in an instant. Love is a truly remarkable key that opens the doorway to new understandings and deep healing.

The integration of changes, like these described above, into our lives can be quite spontaneous in some cases, yet in others it may take deliberate effort and time to digest and readjust our ways of thinking and being. Lynn felt her symptoms lessened as time passed and former triggers affected her less and less. Then one day her symptoms, once experienced so dramatically, disappeared and the old triggers no longer caused her heart to race. It was at this moment that her integration was complete.

Epiphanies have marked Sara's healing journey and taken her into uncharted areas of her psyche, bringing her deeper and lasting understandings about the new strengths she has gathered along the way. Like Lynn, it has taken Sara time to integrate and digest the origins of her relationship struggles, but through it all she has faced each challenge and is more authentic in her relationships, and less afraid. She has learned to trust her feelings, even if they differ from the men she is with and she is far less tolerant of emotional blackmail and abuse. These new beliefs and behaviors have become her guidelines when in relationship; she has developed her new patterns of relating and Sara feels much stronger as a result.

Amelia's fear subsided as soon as she keyed into the origins of her fear and anxiety. Her case illustrates the possibility of spontaneous release, change, and integration in one session.

Change can sometimes be easy to accomplish and at other times quite difficult. I believe how change occurs is based on how ingrained and deeply held the patterns are within the self. Deeply ingrained patterns tend to take more effort and time to change. With effort and attention even difficult habit patterns can be released and new ones established. Reaffirming these new patterns or ways of being, on a daily basis, helps stabilize new behaviors and beliefs. This is the final segment of the integration phase, when we are able to live our lives based on these new patterns of thought, belief and action each day, without the old reactive patterns taking over.

With all change, there may be times when we feel we are sliding back into old patterns and behaviors. I have noticed that if this occurs, a gentle reminder may be all that is necessary to see that we are reacting in the old way. Be disciplined and remember to use mindfulness, and self monitoring when necessary. If old patterns reassert themselves we may need to explore another layer that has opened up new experiences or other origins that need our attention. Sometimes healing our deep core issues is like a parfait with many layers, as one layer is released and integrated with time, another layer may percolate to the surface, giving us the chance to heal deeper levels than before.

The process is always evolving, leading us to healing possibilities that are broader and deeper than expected. A cycle of beginnings and endings can be seen, with each ending reaching out to a next beginning, and at each step, new learning is established.

Healing is pregnant with these beginnings and endings. Each ending naturally reaches out to a new beginning. As new learning is integrated, one process ends and another begins. Step by step layers are healed and with each cycle, healing deepens and moves us closer to the core of our Self and to the deepest healing that we took birth for.

Part Six: Time and Energy

INTERLUDE

WORKING DIMENSIONALLY: UNDERSTANDING THE WEAVE OF PARALLEL TIME, PAST LIVES AND KARMIC CONNECTIONS

> [To be reborn as an animal]—would mean some enormous deed in a human life which has closed the sensibilities. It could be something which involved some incredible shock, terror or a huge recoiling...Dogs and cats can be emanation bodies.
>
> Dr. Robert Thurman [298]

This case began over a decade ago. It is extremely complex and I have done my best to convey this complexity as simply as possible. Many cases are intricate constructions due to the interweaving of memory, belief, emotion, past life and present day experiences. The interconnections often are a maze that take both skill and time to unravel and sort out, but the rewards of doing so provide a healing that is deeper than any I have ever witnessed.

I hope this story or case will engage your mind and allow you to reflect on what you believe are the boundaries of time and space, as well as how your own consciousness chooses to interact with other consciousnesses and even with other species. It is also a case about parallel time. Parallel time is not much talked about in past life therapeutic circles, because it is hard for the mind to wrap around the idea that at each critical decision-making point in our lives, where we have focused attention and energy into both sides of a decision, the intensity of thought and feeling creates a second or parallel timeline, and these timelines do not just dissolve when a decision is made. They continue in their own unique way. We can draw on the skills, gifts, and awareness from these parallel times/lives; we also need to work with the emotional and traumatic events that may arise from these lifetimes/timelines.

As an example, before I began working as a mind-body counselor and channel, I sang classical and operatic music. For 13 years, I studied the old Italian art of bel canto, not just the repertoire but the science and sensation of vocal tone. It was an arduous study with a wonderful but demanding teacher. After so many years of toil and tears, learning to sing in this manner, I realized that I had learned what I had sought to understand and that performing was not my calling. I had been invited to study in England, but my path took me in another direction. However, the time line did not stop there. Because of the intensity of my study and the energy I put into that dream, that timeline maintained its integrity. In fact, in this life I have been able to tap into this other self or other part of my consciousness that is living as a singer in Europe. When I first started speaking in public, I used her skills in front of large audiences and tapped into her confidence, which is also a part of my own consciousness.

I know that this may sound like science fiction but the next case I hope will invite you to free your mind and think beyond the limits of time and even space. It may even touch your heart as you read of karmic connections of such depth and love, that suffering was endured to help those one had loved in ones past lives. It demonstrates how these ancient loving connections persist across time and even across species. So let us begin.

Kiren's Story—Memories Re-Awakened
I had been caring for a 3 week old lilac point Siamese kitten, whose

mother had been killed by dogs, for almost a week. We had a nursing queen next door at the time, and it was our hope that the mother cat would accept him and allow him to nurse. When this failed, I began the task of bottle-feeding him. He did not take to this, and continued to weaken. The vet gave him fluids and taught me to thread a tube into his stomach in order to feed him. He did not like this much, but he was so tiny it was the only option we had. I fed him like this for a few days.

Then on May 13th, as I was feeding him, I accidentally aspirated him. He had done all the things the vet said he would do, but I had placed the tube into his lungs not his stomach. As his tiny body struggled for air I did CPR on this little kitten. With tears streaming down my face, I palpated his chest and gently tried to get him to cough up the liquid, I blew air into his tiny mouth to no avail. My heart broke as I watched him die right in my hands. A horrid helplessness reverberated in my mind as a memory surfaced that shocked me to my core. I recalled the death of a baby boy, who was my son from another life; he had died of SIDS.[299] In cloudy detail, like fog rolling into the coast, forgotten images and memories coursed through my mind.

This experience continued as I tenderly prepared this sweet kitten for burial and carefully put him to rest under a lilac bush in the front yard. I realized that in a time parallel to this one, my first love Kam, and I had stayed together, and that we had had a baby boy named Kiren. Oddly, this was the name I had given the kitten. This name, like the memories now flowing, had just popped into my mind when I thought of what to name this kitten. I remembered and understood that day that I was the one who found my darling boy dead in his crib, lying on his belly as we were once told to do, and that his untimely death had broken both my heart and Kam's. I was desolate with grief and guilt and never regained joy in that life or timeline. This is the back story that leads us to our star, Koa and how this ancient and dear friend came into my life to resolve and heal the guilt and sorrow, from both parallel and past times that this kitten's loss had given birth to.

Synchronicities and Finding Koa

Exactly six months before Kiren's death my 18-year-old Siamese, Miyoshi, had died. Shortly before she passed, to my utter surprise I found myself at the animal shelter instead of Alphagraphics. Puzzled by this turn of events, but knowing somehow I was in the right place I walked into the shelter. After visiting the dogs and seeing the new puppies I went to see the cats and kittens and there I the found Kea, a 6-month old lynx-point Siamese kitten, who would help me heal from the loss of my dear companion, Miyoshi. His was a soul I was familiar with and we became fast friends. He would wake me with kisses on my cheek, instead of the usual yowl of food. He too would die, much to my horror, accidentally killed by a neighbor's car exactly three months after Miyoshi's death.

The director and I had become friends by now, and she knew of these losses, so when I called to tell her of Kiren's untimely and devastating exit she excitedly told me that a 6 week old healthy male lilac-point kitten was at the shelter and that I should come right down and get him. He was a beautiful, long-haired boy with silver gray points, like a touch of San Francisco fog dotting his nose, mask, and feet. My heart melted, I fell in love in that first moment, and she actually gave him to me at no charge. I named him Makoa Makana, which means, roughly, brave gift in Hawai'ian.

For seven years we lived in the high desert of New Mexico: Koa, me, my husband, our dog, Mana and our lynx-point Siamese girl, K'ala. Koa loved to play and leaping up tall cabinets and flying down our thirty-foot hallway with wild abandon. He was my boy and I delighted in him. He didn't like to be held much but he loved being carried like a baby and as he grew to a healthy twelve and a half pounds my husband became his official carrier.

Connecting to Parallel Time—My Healing Continues

During the years 1991—1997 I took classes in body-mind integrative therapy. It was in this setting that I unearthed still more of the memory and experienced the awful grief anew of my son's death, in a life parallel to this one. My body's sensation of blinding, overwhelming horror and grief as I walked into Kiren's room and saw him not breathing shook even the teacher as her hands worked to help me unravel the pain that surrounded this memory. The silent scream that emerged from my lips tore my heart asunder. It was a pain I will never forget, even though

Interlude

it has been removed from my muscles and cells. A trace of it will always be in my mind.

In the summer of 1997, as my doctor of oriental medicine, Kalani, and I were working together, the events of that death and the memories surrounding this parallel timeline crystallized still further. As Kalani placed the activator to my back, she gasped. She would tell me later, "My hand actually slipped through a vortex and was sucked into another dimension. This experience was so striking. I was physically in two dimensions at the same time. My feet were on the ground in one dimension, I could see them, but my hand was in another. I had the uncanny feeling that my hand was in some other time and place. I held on tight to the activator and clicked it. I withdrew my hand not knowing for sure if it (the activator) would come back. My hand had penetrated into another dimension through your (Elizabeth's) body. You had a body within your body. I reached for your wrist to take your pulses and found none. I asked you, Where are you?" You said, "I'm dead."

As I lay on the table I focused my attention inward. I saw the dead body of my other self from this parallel time. I watched my breath, in my present body and entered into a light meditative state. This life flashed before me, in perhaps the same sort of way that people describe their lives flashing before them when in grave danger or near death. In a rush of images and feelings I saw this other self's life. As I watched and listened, I understood that in this life parallel to my own, this self had been raised Catholic and had endured an even more difficult childhood and adolescence than my own in this lifetime. Events of my life were mirrored in hers: albeit hers were of with greater horror.

She had married her first love and given birth to joy, a boy she had loved more than her life. I learned they had almost 8 months together. The images moved on. I watched in horror as she found Kiren; in shock, she dialed the hospital and tried to resuscitate him; desperately wishing with every breath that she were a nurse. The feelings of helplessness and desperate confusion were enormous. Her son was dead. How would she tell her husband? Would he blame her, as she blamed herself? The doctors said he had died from sudden infant death syndrome. Her mind reeled.

Their families came, but she was inconsolable. The doctors gave her Valium to calm her. She nearly died a week later when she mixed Valium with alcohol. I watched as she was rushed to the hospital and her stomach was pumped. She told her husband that she didn't do this intentionally, but that she wanted to go to Kiren, to be with him, to take care of him so much. Weighed down by guilt, grief, sorrow and regret, she withdrew from her loving husband and died at the age of twenty-eight. Her heart had burst and just stopped. I felt that she had somehow willed her own death in order to be with her son.

I asked what was needed and the energy of the channel told me that this self needed to be cremated. Her family had buried her but her spirit was not free. I remember feeling her uneasiness. She wanted to be a part of the wind and sky, to have her body become flame and ash, and be free, finally free. This felt right somehow, so I began the careful visualization of tending and caring for this dead part of myself from this other dimension and time. Kalani held the energy as I worked. I saw this self rise out of my own body and she was there before me, holding her boy Kiren. I had been carrying this other self with all her dimensions of pain, without even knowing it. I took a gray smoky energy out of my body that had filled my pelvis, and the last vestige of this other self. As I did this, she breathed in this cloud-like smoke, accepting the remnants of her former life and self.

Understanding blossomed as I removed her from my being. I knew with utter certainty that she had, upon her death, merged with my own consciousness in this timeline. I released her, as well as the grief and sorrows from that life that mirrored my own. Anger melted as well. I finally understood the intensity of my reactions to certain events in my life and how this other timeline and self's emotions were wedded to my own. New clarity about my relationship with my first love Cam dawned. My near death illness at age twenty-eight in my current lifetime as Elizabeth took on new meaning. I recognized it was then that this other self had merged into my being.

She had died, but I had survived and so had her memories. Memories from her childhood and life moved through my mind like a movie and I understood how the merger of our two consciousnesses impacted some of my own reactions in this lifetime. I continued to remove imprints, memories, and emotions that were an overlay from her life to mine. I created in detail the cremation of her body, with all the rituals and prayers needed, and saw her husband and his family there. I felt her spirit relax as it was finally released. As her/our body burned, a deep peace settled into the room, so deep that Kalani noticed it immediately. I then imagined, a spiral of acupuncture needles. around my sacrum and up my spine. Kalani helped me integrate this experience and grounded me solidly in the present. I breathed deeply and felt the joy that accompanied this other self's release and the release of her pain as well as my own.

Koa's Journey and Our Walk through Hell to Healing

Late in 1997 we moved to Portland, Oregon, and the story takes a remarkable turn, with a simple event that would change all our lives. Fleas are a great problem in Oregon and Koa and K'ala both got them on the trip. The vets recommended a product and we administered the proper dose to all the animals. Each of them suffered from neurological imbalances but Koa was the most affected. His head began to tilt to the left and he seemed uncoordinated only minutes after we administered the medication. We took him to a holistic vet who said Koa was probably having a toxic reaction to the flea medication. Since his symptoms arose immediately after the application of the flea medication, this made sense to us.

They treated him and gave me some medicine to help detoxify his liver. For the next few months we took him to see a series of vets to determine why his head still tilted and why his balance was so wobbly at times. We didn't learn much; a few things were ruled out, but mostly there was a persistent disbelief by the traditional vets that the flea medication, Advantage, could do this sort of thing.

Then on November 30, 1998, Koa had a prolonged lapse; forgetting where he was, he peed on the floor of my office. This might seem incidental, but he was also losing weight and his hair was thinning, so we went back to the holistic vet and took another blood panel. They continued to be normal, but Koa was not his usual self. We found a Tellington-Touch practitioner and these sessions seemed to help him the most. In February of 1999, he could no longer jump up or down from his favorite seat, next to me on the couch, and by April he was only seven and a half pounds.

On the advice of the T-Touch practitioner we took Koa to yet another holistic vet outside of Portland in mid-April. She worked intuitively as well as traditionally. She examined him and said his vitality and will to live were quite low. During the exam she spoke with him. Koa asked for a remedy directly, she said. She cautioned me that she had never used this remedy and was uncertain of its outcome. She gave him a single dose of the homeopathic remedy *naja*, or king cobra venom.[300] His eye movements that had constantly shifted left and right for over a year improved immediately, and we were advised to take him home and wait.

The next night at 11 PM he began to have seizures and we thought he was dying right there in my arms. As Koa seized I began to sing Tibetan chants and I called upon the energy of the channel to help Koa and us. I put on the chants of Tibetan monks and sang and prayed like I had never done before. Koa's seized six times in an hour and then stopped. When he was seizing it looked as if he were doing battle with the great snake's energy. His head reared back and with mouth open he panted and clawed at something unseen before him. I thought of the king cobra that protected the Buddha while he sat under the *bodhi* tree and gave Koa this image, mind to mind, to let him know that the snake energy could also protect him.

When he finally settled, we all went to bed. Koa, wrapped in a soft towel, lay in my arms, on my chest with his head next to my heart. He would sleep or rest this way like a baby, every night for the next fifteen months. Two mornings later the energy of the channel gave Koa a gift of healing energy that was like no power I had ever seen or felt them share before. They sent pure light filled with such powerful compassion it was breathtaking, into and through the palms of my hands directly into his body. He improved after that day but went through thirty-six more seizures over the next 6 weeks. He was under the constant care of his T-Touch practitioner and his new vet. For the next six and a half months I never left him alone. We even hired people to come sit with him so I could get groceries.

During this time we talked to two animal communicators to learn more about how he was. One of these women, who worked more at a karmic level, mentioned in passing that Koa and I had been twin sisters. I laughed and said that when Koa was a kitten I had put his

Interlude

face next to mine and asked my husband, "Do we look alike?" He had laughed and said, "He's a cat, Elizabeth." I laughed too but her comment somehow rang true.

On June 10, 1999 I took Koa to another animal communicator and healer the vet had recommended. She sensed that morning that Koa was dying even before we arrived. His energy had been weak but I was surprised by her words. As we stroked him she helped me say good-bye. He had a small seizure as we talked quietly and I made peace and said that his dad would say his good-byes too. He almost died right there but rallied when I spoke of my husband. I held him in my lap and he was quiet and calm. We left and drove by the vet so she could say good-bye to Koa and then we went home.

For the next three days Koa lay quietly and there were moments when his breathing appeared to stop, only to rally again. I held vigil, as did my husband; we watched his every breath, we played the Tibetan chants that he loved so well and I began to read him the *Tibetan Book of the Dead* but, like a flame in my mind, Koa said, "No! Not that, I want to hear the one about no eyes no ears." I found a copy of the *Prajnaparamita*, (the Heart Sutra) and read it to him as I lay beside him on the floor. I told him that he was free to go but if he wanted to stay he could but he would have to eat, drink, pee and poop for himself. Our house was full of love and Koa then did the impossible, or so it seemed at the time. On the third day, he got to his feet and drank some water, and later he ate a little food. We held him and let him walk in turns and he peed on my office rug to my delight and would even poop a few days later.

Koa amazed everyone. His will was extraordinary. The T-Touch practitioners and his vets started calling him Lazarus kitty and they said my love had brought him through. The many practitioners and vets who had seen him in ER and regular visits and were all astonished by his recovery. They had never seen an animal come through so much. That summer we worked with a nationally known vet who specialized in toxic reactions to the nerve toxin in the flea medication. Koa wouldn't have a seizure again that year.

He still had to be held in my arms and on my chest in order to sleep, and for the next 6 months he only slept for about two hours at a time. I was up with him on and off all night long, like with a child, carrying him, taking him to his litter box, hand feeding him until he would find his food by himself and making sure he drank enough broth and water. He taught me devotion. The doctors said his digestive system was quite sluggish but we even found a Chinese herbal formula that helped his severe constipation, and he began to regain his strength.

He always stumped his vets, though, and after a while they would sigh and say they didn't know where to go with him. He had acupuncture, homeopathy, chiropractic care, as well as T-Touch, traditional blood work and neurological tests, but he loved Chinese herbs the best. He was like me in this. I thought it was funny, but then, he was supposedly my twin sister in another lifetime and somehow it made sense.

During the rest of his life when I would play various Tibetan chants Koa would just ease himself down and sit very still, as if he were taking each sacred syllable into his being. He came to love the *Mahakala* and the *Yamantaka* chants of the Gyuto monks the most. While the chants played, our other cat, because of the noise of the horns and the crashes of the cymbals, ran and hid; while Koa just sat like a little Buddha. When we traveled in the car, to yet another vet appointment that fall and winter, I would sing the OM MANI PADME HUM and he would immediately calm down during the ride. We spent thousands of dollars and I spent countless hours doing T-Touch with him. He loved it. Even today my fingers move in that circular rhythm when I pet my other animals or massage my husband's tired back.

Koa still needed a lot of attention, but we were now able to leave him for almost two and a half hours by the end of the year. By October he would sit in the sun and let his sister clean him and he walked around and ate and drank and even slept through the night. We felt blessed. Koa's health was much better in November, and the vet suggested he might recover completely. He still would react to things in exact opposition to the vet's expectation but did well on the Chinese herbs. Then, in December 1999, he seemed to plateau; his hair began to thin again over the next few months; in February/March of 2000, he stabilized. Once more he had baffled his current vet, a Chinese medical doctor and naturopath. The Chinese herbs helped him and he responded and seemed to like them so we continued with them. He also continued to get T-Touch and we settled into a routine of care that worked. We consulted a new homeopath in June and were given some new ideas. Everyone thought he was doing well.

Our World Changes

On July 21, 2000, when I was out shopping, Koa started to have a seizure. I came home and saw him lying on the throw rug and rushed over to him. I bundled him up and called his three vets, hoping one would return my call. He would seize for a brief time, mildly, then he would enter a resting state for a while before repeating the cycle. For hours I did emergency homeopathy on him as instructed by his doctors over the phone. Back and forth on the phone, I did everything they asked me to do. My mind reeled. We thought we were out of the woods. He had been doing so well for months — we just thought this was another set of seizures like those he had recovered from last year, but the remedies weren't helping him and his breathing became labored.

I called the local vet again and left an emergency message around 9:30 PM. We took Koa outside into the fresh night air hoping he would catch his breath. As he lay in my lap he struggled to get up. I would realize later that he wanted to pee and was trying to get down out of my lap. I never for a moment thought he was dying until he peed all over me. I was totally unprepared mentally. He had been doing better than ever the past few months. He had even pooped outdoors without falling over, which was quite a feat for Koa only ten days before. He hadn't had a seizure for fifty-one weeks. Why! Why now, my mind cried!

My husband brought me another towel and I dried Koa and wrapped him in it, then I laid him gently on the soft grass next to me to help him get grounded again. My husband watched him as I ran to change my soaked skirt. The vet called and told us to take him to the emergency vet. My husband went for his keys as I sat next to Koa on the lawn. Koa was still having trouble breathing and trembled slightly as I sat beside him on the grass. I moved to pick him up to hold him again but he just exhaled and stopped breathing. I called for my husband, who stood at the door ready to take us to the vet, but Koa was gone. That terrible anguished cry rose again in my chest—a silent then violent wail. He had been doing so much better...

NO! HOW COULD THIS BE HAPPENING? This had all happened in less than ten minutes.

Walking Between the Realms—Koa's Transformation

My husband held me and talked to Koa and said good-bye. I wept and was absolutely devastated. I held my boy for hours after he died, reading the bardo prayers to him and the heart sutra that he loved so much. Finally I put him in his carrying basket that was full of pillows and brought him into the bedroom. I missed his weight on my chest, as I lay there too tired to sleep when the most amazing thing happened: a freak thunder and lightening storm unexpectedly hit Portland. My husband woke up and we both sat in awe as the sky lit up and thunder crashed. It was just like New Mexico, where Koa was born. It was as if the thunder and lightening beings of northern New Mexico were greeting our sweet boy. It also came into my mind that when great teachers die there is often unusual weather that marks their passing.

The next day I made arrangements for Koa to be cremated. We took him to the vet and met the lady who would tend to the shell that once housed his noble spirit. We gave away his belongings, giving things to the vet who had been so faithful the night before and to the lady who would care for his remains. We gave her his traveling basket, so other animals could be carried comfortably even in death. For months we would donate items in his name. We said our good-byes, and knew Koa was in good and gentle hands.

I walked through that day like a ghost and began to fast. The next day we went to the beach, we listened to and sang Tibetan and Hawai'ian chants, and sent Koa prayers and instructions on how to merge with the great luminosity. As I was walking through the forest to the beach I sent images to my boy of the light as it shown through the trees and the feeling of joy and great beauty this scene bore. In response, a clear feeling of great bliss came to me directly from Koa. I saw him running and playing again and reveling joyously in his cat suit, healthy and robust.

On Monday I got his ashes and bravely transferred them into a silk pouch and put them into a koa wood box my husband and I received as a wedding gift. I also put some of his ashes in a Tibetan *vajra* amulet, which I wore over my heart until September. Koa spoke to me very clearly and was insistent about where he wanted the amulet placed. There was a small amount of residual ashes left, which I put over my crown chakra like a blessing. I ate little and continually sang and played mantras that first week. A Tibetan nun said the *phowa* practice for him and monks in India prayed to the Medicine Buddha on his behalf. Another Buddhist friend prayed to Tara and yet another sang Red Tara's death prayers for him. I did the prayers of the Buddha of compassion and Guru Rinpoche each day nonstop. We played his favorite chants that first week constantly, lit incense and burnt a seven day candle with Green Tara's image on it. Koa had more practice done for him than many people. He was a remarkable boy and one lucky dharma kitty. Kind messages poured in from all the people whose lives Koa had touched.

During the first two days after his death as I connected to Koa I saw him tumble into the bardo falling to his feet as kitties do. Each time he landed squarely on his feet and as he did he became golden, pure golden light. I saw this each time I checked on him. Each morning I read to him the bardo teaching and I continued to walk with him in the bardo, telling him to go to the luminous light that was his original nature. My husband also told him to go to the light each time he thought of him throughout his day.

Then early Sunday morning on the third day after his death at the time when he usually wanted to get up to eat or pee, he woke me. I saw my sweet boy kitty in his golden light body again, but this time he stood up fully erect, as he did in life when he pooped. He shrugged his shoulders and like a great cape his cat body fell away. He became a shining light body in human form once again right before my eyes. He walked directly into the luminosity of the realm of bliss on that third day.

Realizations: Links to Parallel and Past Lifetimes

That day I realized his role as a *bodhisattva* in my life and the healing he gave me by allowing me to be his mom in this deep way. My sister, my twin, had returned to me and given me the gift of healing. I was able to care for him deeply and completely. I did everything within my power to help him through and he had graciously stayed with me so I could heal from the guilt and loss of Kiren's death. Koa had come to me on the day I first remembered Kiren's death and I understood now that he had come to help me heal that wound. He became my devotion and taught me more about presence and practice than I ever could have imagined. He continues to be my joy, as he was my twin, and I know more than with any other person in my life that we will be together again. These insights came to me suddenly and unexpectedly, waking me out of my grief.

His progress was swift, and over the next four months whenever I would check on him in the bardo or the realm of spirit he would be sitting in meditation in human form, though without a body other than one of light. Then one day in December his form dissolved, and merged with the realm around him. I cried to see him go but was joyous for him too. One friend said when he passed that his spirit had just gotten too big for his body. It seems that she may have been right. I had told him to merge with the most luminous, radiant, and brilliant light, and he did that.

In the five months since Koa's death, insights about our deep connection have been revealed. When I sat in meditation or when awakening from sleep, our story clarified. In vignettes, the details were fleshed out and I learned that we had indeed been twin sisters. We had lived as nomads in Mongolia in centuries past, riding ponies and being quite devout, steeped in Buddhist teaching. His/her name had been Chalin and mine Tsolin. In that life, I had died of a venomous snakebite in my sleep and my sister had awoken to find me dead. Driven by grief she had killed the first snake she saw, which was contrary to her Buddhist beliefs, thinking this would ease her pain. It had not. Perhaps karma was being played out. Koa certainly passed through the fire during his long illness and I know that any previous karma has been cleansed and cleared for him.

What I believe in my innermost being and heart is that Koa came back to heal my heart and the pain and grief I had suffered when my son Kiren had died in a time parallel to this one. It seems beyond coincidence that he appeared in my life the same day as the memories of this other death. However, in allowing me to care for him and to do everything within my power for him, he let me heal the profound guilt and sadness from deep within my own heart. He knew I would care for him no matter what, and he came to me as one of the most brave and valiant beings I have ever met, a bodhisattva in the guise of a cat, coming back to heal my pain, no matter what the cost. I hope to honor him as my sweet boy and as my ancient twin, and to show the incredible complexity that two beings can weave together across time and space and how devotion and love can heal all wounds of body, mind, and spirit.

15

ETHICS AND ENERGY PSYCHOLOGY

The five precepts of nonharming[301] Are a vehicle for our happiness, A vehicle for our good fortune, A vehicle for liberation for all. May our virtue shine forth.

Jack Kornfield [302]

Building Rapport

By feeling the energies within ourselves, within a room, within a friend, or client, we are able to build rapport; the easiest way to do this is by being attentive to our breath. By breathing with others, and synchronizing our inhalations and exhalations to theirs, we are able to connect to that person, heart to heart. This technique can settle the energy, when a person is upset, without invading their space. Try it when you are in the company of someone who is agitated. Stephen and Ondrea Levine have used this form of breathing to comfort and be present with those near death. Breathing together is a non-invasive communication between two souls. By being attentive to our breath, we can adjust our own internal energy and allow our own mind and emotions to settle as well.

Energy awareness is a way of staying connected without overstepping personal boundaries. This keeps our interpersonal relationships clear and open and compassion flows more easily, when we are in rapport at an energetic level with another being.

Working with energy can be tricky, especially if the ego mind has expectations or is invested in a particular outcome, the intuition will often be misguided. This is why an empty mind, free from expectations, is so necessary, so our intuitions can operate at their optimal level, and we can discern the truths that lie within us. If the intuition is blocked by desire and expectations, then we will continue in the same cycle, instead of breaking out of it.

An open mind allows for love and unconditional acceptance to become available to us.[303] This love is available to all of us when our hearts are open and we remember to not displace our hopes and desires onto another, or even ourselves. The mind will follow our thoughts, so it is crucial to remain empty and hollow, like a bamboo flute, as the energy flows through us. To be conduits for the flow of this universal energy or mind, we need to have distinct boundaries. This is why the preliminary practices are so fundamental, because they allow us to relax, create connections to our inner knowing and develop the space in which to do inner work. Unfortunately, this is not always the case. Often expectations and desires get in the way of clarity. Our egos, instead of our hearts take over and this can lead us into trouble.

Often in doing energetic work we can experience what Stanislav Grof calls "spiritual emergency."[304] The question arises; how do we work with spiritual crisis and the overwhelm that can accompanies these states, as well as working with the resultant symptoms and difficulties after experiencing these phenomena? Grof believes, and I would agree, that it might be necessary for counselors and therapists to become skilled in these areas. "The use of the experiential techniques thus requires training that involves a personal experience of the states that they facilitate."[305]

If practitioners have encountered these states for themselves and been fired by these experiences, they can treat them with the compassion and understanding that is needed and deserved. I would suggest that if this is not possible, practitioners at least need to have studied these states in detail, so they can help people experiencing them.

Preventative measures can be taken so clients can explore the connections between current life conflicts and past lives without moving into crisis. Jordan was working on some family issues when he began to experience a memory of torture from another lifetime. As he was reliving this event, my focus was on his body cues, rapid eye movements, observable body tensions, and facial changes. I held the energy psychically, and followed his experience. I matched my breathing to his as I walked beside him while he walked between the worlds. Attention, close rapport and unobtrusive verbal contact with Jordan were precautionary safeguards used to prevent him from falling into a crisis state and being re-traumatized.

Each of us can bring ourselves into crisis states by manipulating our internal energies. Meditation, energetic and shamanic work, and certain forms of yoga create a quickening effect. We can get in way over our head when working with the energies of the chakras and body if we haven't created a stable ground and mind that is non-reactive. I caution even my advanced students, to go gently into their inner world and have found that a gentle approach is often best.

Finding Help—What to Consider

It is often assumed that Spirit never gives us more than we are ready to handle. This belief is a favorite of the New Age and like most beliefs needs to be examined. While on some level this belief may be true, I have seen too many people who have become overwhelmed by therapies or become casualties of the very processes they thought would help them to believe this assertion is completely true. As educated consumers we can become discerning and sophisticated, and ask some hard questions.

Do the techniques being used honor your personal autonomy, and subtle energies? Are they non-invasive? Is your process allowed to unfold and move on its own without intervention? Do you feel empowered by the work? Are you being heard and seen in the deepest sense? Is the environment open and safe and is the spirit of non-judgment and equanimity present? Is your inner essence nurtured and is the practitioner more of a guide than an authority? If these things are present, the face of therapy changes. The therapist, bodyworker, or counselor is no longer the expert, you are, and the mystery and the energy of Source guide the process.

When Things Go Wrong

Jennifer came to see me after taking an energy workshop with a well-known teacher and author. Soon after the workshop, Jennifer began to feel terribly confused and noticed that she was no longer able to concentrate. She was very upset. When she walked into my office I noticed quite a difference in her walk, posture, and speech. She felt out of sync, her body felt jittery as I stood beside her. Her chakras and overall energy were unusually chaotic, a dramatic change from when I had seen her before the workshop.

Jennifer confirmed that she had felt confused and overwhelmed since attending the workshop. She said she was ill at ease with the way her energy was flowing within her body. Her intense state of confusion was more than a case of just not knowing what to do. Her whole body and energy system appeared to be imploding and in spasm, and no new information could be allowed in. The energies in her body were so jumbled that the foundations she normally relied on were lost. Her connection to the earth and to her higher consciousness, which she ordinarily felt, was absent. She desperately wanted and needed to regain this sense of connection.

Together we found that many of the workshop's exercises were uncompleted and Jennifer was left in the middle of many different processes. The combination of the various exercises and their lack of completion sent her into a state of severe confusion, which was accompanied by a feeling of overwhelm. She was unable to organize the new information, and yet, by being in the middle of so many unfinished processes, she could not let them go either. The workshop exercises needed to be released or brought to completion so integration could occur.

Often within intensive workshops, little time is given to complete and integrate each phase of new learning that is taking place Jennifer had gotten lost in the process and later was so overwhelmed that she was unable to manage what was occurring within her own body and consciousness.

Chapter Fifteen

As a teacher, it is just this kind of experience that concerns me. Jennifer's experience suggests two things. First, that as teachers and therapists we need to be more responsible and attentive to our clients' and students' processes, especially when working with energy. Participants must not be left hanging in the middle of a process, or be left on their own to figure out a technique they are relatively unfamiliar with. Indeed, this may be where some teachers who address large groups fail unknowingly; by losing contact with their students, problems such as the one described above can arise. Problems often go unnoticed, and unaddressed, especially if the workshop is a short intensive training; the teacher may never know of the problem, since it is not until after the workshop that a student may experience problems or difficulties.

This example suggests that support systems need to be incorporated into workshop settings. Arnold and Amy Mindell, for instance, handle the problem of overwhelming emotional experiences in workshops by having counselors available to see students for nominal fees. They also set up support groups for people who may just need to ask a question, be held, reassured or voice a concern (Lava Rock Clinic, 1995).

However, even with these safeguards in place mishaps occur. At the close of a workshop with Arnie and Amy Mindell, a young man took all of us by surprise, yelling that he wished to kill everyone in the room, saying that if he had a gun he would have blown us all away. He threw tables and chairs and shocked us all. So even with the best intentions, safeguards can fail. This is why the preliminary practices can be so important, because they give you a means to ground, center and protect yourself from unexpected events and shock.

Part Seven: The Opportunity

16

WHERE WE GO FROM HERE

What we find as we listen to the songs of our rage or fear, loneliness or longing, is that they do not stay forever. Rage turns into sorrow; sorrow turns into tears; tears may fall for a long time, but then the sun comes out. A memory of old loss sings to us; our body shakes and relives the moment of loss; then the armoring around the loss gradually softens; and in the midst of the song of tremendous grieving, the pain of that loss finally finds release.

Jack Kornfield [306]

I never set out to create Transforming Embodiment, but as I taught and worked with clients I saw a new model for healing taking shape. This new model was built from the very roots of my own transpersonal experiences and reflects what I have seen clinically in my private practice. What I have witnessed has been remarkable—clients and students alike in various setting and circumstances have journeyed across temporal and spatial boundaries to resolve old wounds and situations and to create healing for themselves. Many have traveled across time to find healing. I learned as I did this process myself and with others, that each of us has the power to change ourselves and our experience of our world in profound ways. In retracing the origins of our pains, sorrows and woundedness, we can cross time and space and heal the very core of our being.

Again and again I have seen the power of memory: how it is held within our bodies and how this systemic and cellular memory is transferred from one body or consciousness to the next. I have marveled at how consciousness seamlessly continues, and most amazingly, as consciousness continues, so do the dilemmas from the past. Skills from the past are also available to us, but more often it is the problems from our past that confound us in our current lives.

My hope for this book, and the work it represents, is that this process will become a new complementary tool for healing. I believe that Transforming Embodiment takes the best parts of experiential psychology and transpersonal experiences, and marries them to spirituality to share with people another way to heal and release their suffering and pain.

This process also demonstrates how our consciousness has the ability to journey across time, so that all time and all experience can become available to us. I have seen this process help people heal, and offer it as a way to explain how our deepest held beliefs can regulate our lives and interactions. The practices of Transforming Embodiment help us release the memories that sustain our wounds, wounds we never would have imagined, but that the body holds nonetheless.

Transforming Embodiment honors spirit and the individual, the wisdom of the body and the power of our minds, and believes that these are our most important tools for healing now and in the future. Transforming Embodiment, as a new model, understands how healing is a spiritual journey, an energetic process and an odyssey that is not limited by the boundaries of time and space.

It seems to be a natural next step to combine the following cutting edge ideas: that the body has knowledge and wisdom, that spirit is always with us and can be of guidance and inform us at any time, that the mind is not limited to the brain, and consciousness as energy continues beyond death. These ideas form the foundation

Chapter Sixteen

for Transforming Embodiment and it is my belief that healing in the future will be informed from the basis of these new beliefs. As such, Transforming Embodiment is a cutting edge transformational tool for healing.

I have learned through exploration and clinical practice that healing goes beyond the limits of the current definition as we have known it. With these ideas in mind, may we all embark upon a healing journey.

ADDENDUM
NOTES TO PRACTITIONER'S

What I am speaking of here is not losing my boundaries, but letting myself experience what the other person's reality feels like. If I can hear another's words, not from a place of clinical distance, but as they touch me, then I can bring a fully alive, human presence to bear on the other's experience, which is much more likely to create an environment in which healing can occur.

John Welwood [307]

Transforming Embodiment is an interactive intuitive set of practices and questions that works best within a very open space that gives the client room to explore. Suzuki Roshi, a revered Zen master who brought Soto Zen to America, once said that if you want to tame the mind, give it a large corral.[308] Create an open environment within yourself and you will find that your clients willingly explore the nature of their mind, beliefs, and emotions more freely.

In preparing to work with clients I always contact Source, and this being an intuitive practice, I would encourage each of you to find this flow in whatever way works for you.

Connecting to the energy of Source creates a unique therapeutic environment. This energy interacts with the environment through our contact with it and touches the experience of our clients. This environment is characterized by stillness, vastness, and spaciousness. The practitioner invests the environment with these same attributes by holding or embodying these states of stillness and spaciousness within themselves. In this environment, clients are given the space to quiet their mind, connect with their inner world and spiritual Self, so they can ask questions, and explore their inner world to find answers and healing.

Stillness and quiescence permeates the space and my being when I am connected to Source. Holding this space stabilizes the environment and keeps the mind quiet and non-reactive in both you and in clients.

The requirements to create a still and quiescent state are simple. The body must be relaxed and at ease, the emotions must be calmed and your mental thoughts must be set aside or released from your mind. Spaciousness arises out of this quiet mind state and allows us to merge with this vastness beyond the self, that I call Source. Spaciousness encourages the mind and emotions to settle. As your inner stillness grows, a sense of peace and clarity naturally arises, giving you the ability to merge with Source.

As quiescence and spaciousness fill your being you can cultivate non-judgment and detachment. Non-judgment, in this case, is essentially the ability to sit with any state without personal judgment or reactions. For instance, if a practitioner is squeamish about volatile emotions, traumatic events, torture, or death, and is unable to stay present with detached but participatory awareness, a client may not feel safe enough to explore these areas. This stops the process. Even if clients are experiencing pain, being manipulative, or remembering vengeful or negative thoughts, it is necessary to stay non-judging and maintain equanimity when confronted with intense or unpleasant emotions. Cultivating this ability allows clients to feel safe, even when things appear frightening, because there is an attitude of loving acceptance present. Loving-kindness melts our fears and we gain confidence in ourselves and in turn feel confident with our process.

Preconceived ideas that you may have about what to do, what something may mean, need to be set aside. The use of labels to compartmentalize a client's experiences is also dropped. The session experience is taken as it is in the moment, and as the moment continues to unfold. Even the idea of being there to help the client is released. Basically, any ideas of how a session "should look" or proceed are relinquished. The mind must be open to explore the mystery and the sacredness of the moment.

Problems and even illnesses are seen as events in process, an ongoing adventure guided from within by the client's spiritual or inner Self. Any labeling of what a client is experiencing is discouraged. Labeling a client's experiences takes the process out of the moment and erodes the experiential ground.

Working with Universal Energy

Clients lead the therapeutic process, in the space provided by the practitioner, by enlisting the aid of their innate inner wisdom. I consider this aspect of wisdom to be connected to a universal energy that pervades all life and experience. This universal energy, that I call Source, is the beginning point where all existence and experience arises from an ultimate sense. In a relative or manifest sense, inner wisdom is the force within us that is all knowing, which links us to universal energy. This manifest aspect can also be thought of as your spiritual Self.

In Transforming Embodiment clients are active participants in their own healing process. In this work we move away from the idea of the helpless victim or the person who needs to be told what to do. In contrast, these practices foster a mutually helping relationship between practitioners, clients, and spirit. It is believed that the client, as one who embodies spirit, knows precisely what to do. It is just a matter of creating the needed lines of communication, so that access to their innate inner knowing occurs.

Making Connections and the Permission Process

The aumakua or spiritual Self is always available if called upon. Asking for this aspect to join in the healing process and for permission to work on a problem or difficulty a client is experiencing is the proper etiquette when working with others on an energetic level. In Transforming Embodiment you work with your spiritual Self, clients individual inner guidance systems, and Source and these connections are maintained throughout the session. The nonlocal nature of the mind gives us the ability to connect with each client's higher Self. It is important to have this direct unobstructed link as it ensures the integrity of the therapeutic space.

With a quiet mind, and inwardly focused attention, you connect with your spiritual Self, and reach out to your client's aumakua. Ask for permission, mind to mind, to work with your client's spiritual Self and invite this energy into the session. Connecting to this Self and gaining permission may come in the form of a simple "yes" that you may hear inside your mind or you may see a figure nod their head in a affirmative way. As the connection is made, a sense of knowingness arises, and a distinct calmness is felt. When contacting a client's spiritual Self I encounter a relaxed, assured, knowledgeable, guiding spirit, or caretaker of the self and there is a profound sense of being welcomed that accompanies this contact. Great love and kindness from the spiritual Self toward the client is palpable and there is a willingness to help and support the client in any way possible from their spiritual Self. These feelings can be augmented by images of welcoming figures.

Working with Resistance during Permission Process
If you encounter resistance while asking for permission you can negotiate with the ku or lono to address issues of fear, uncertainty or doubt. If you meet a client's ku, it is necessary to make this aspect feel safe, since the ku holds our memories of past emotions and trauma. The ku is very childlike, so treat it as you would a frightened or headstrong child, providing comfort, love, and firm tenderness and you can receive cooperation in return. By acknowledging the unconscious fears of the ku, a safe ground is created for the work and permission is usually granted. If the lono is encountered guide your client into deeper states of relaxation, so the conscious mind can let go. Let the lono know that it can rest for a while. This allows the conscious mind to achieve a sense of calm and the connection to aumakua can be achieved.

Roles
When practicing this therapy our primary role is to hold the space of the

session to create a therapeutic environment, as we observe and witness the client's process. Being a holder of space means that we create a safe container for each client. This includes making the connection to Source before the session, so the aspects of peace, clarity, spaciousness, love and unconditionality are brought to the space. Non-judgment allows clients to experience, perhaps for the first time, "negative" aspects of their own being, in a space of acceptance.

Attentiveness and "presentness" are necessary components that can aid you in observing and witnessing the client's process. Attentiveness is experienced as a sharpened perception and attention to the details and patterns presented. "Presentness" is defined as a mind that stays in the moment and does not wander.

In the background of your mind, you "hold the space" lightly and continually throughout the session. Presentness and this light holding of space would be akin to a figured baseline in contrapuntal music. The baseline continues throughout a piece of music or within session; while the content and the process would be like the melodic line that dances above the figured base. In a session, this presentness and the quality of holding space are the figured baseline, giving form, momentum, and rhythm to the process.

Working as a Shaman

In Transforming Embodiment the practitioner usually follows the client's process. However, as with any process, there are exceptions. There are times when it is appropriate for the practitioner to take over the process and work as a shaman. To work as a shaman means that the practitioner becomes an agent for the client and does the work for the client, when they are unable to work for themselves.

The incidence where this might be appropriate is when the client is in a state of confusion or overwhelmed. This type of confusion may occur as the process begins to accelerate or when the dissolving and disorganizing of old patterns is in progress. At this time there is often a feeling of emotional overwhelm as beliefs and emotions are being released and reorganized. It is appropriate for the practitioner to intervene and guide the process, and be wholly responsible for the process at this time.

Leading the process is always based on what the client is presenting, and as always, this is facilitated by continuing psychic rapport and a connection with the client's spiritual Self and Source. Sara came in one day crying and anxious and unable to concentrate, so I worked on her behalf until she could work for herself.

Sara's energy and body relaxed and her eyes became clearer as I untangled the energy in her chakras. As her internal tension eased, she worked in tandem with me, and then took over more of the process as the session progressed. By the end of the session she was able to work without my assistance. The client's process leads the session, even if it requires us to do things we might not normally do. In Sara's case, the process required that I change my usual role, to become a very active participant, working more as a shaman than a therapist.

Be Flexible

It is appropriate to intervene very directly if a client has been working with an issue for a long time and has come to an impasse. Early in this work (1986), Ian came to see me about pain in his lower back. He had repeatedly injured this area over the years, and it had flared up again. He was a strong meditator and had investigated his injuries in meditation, but was unsuccessful at finding out why he continued to injure himself in the same place again and again.

Ian asked for my direct assistance with this block, in both his understanding and body. As he lay on his stomach I began feeling the energy in his back and gently massaged his low back, then rather suddenly, I began to *sing his body*. *Singing the body* is a technique that focuses vowels on single pitches and in sequence, to vibrate the physical, emotional, and subtle bodies with sound. This singing is directed at the specific area of injury. This loosens up deeply held patterns within the body and mind and is especially effective and useful when treating long held problems.

As I sang his body, Ian's back began to soften. Images came to him, as the energies opened up and his back relaxed more. He spoke to me as I sang and told me that he had been wounded by a sword, thrust into his body at the same spot that he continually injured. The surroundings he said were ancient and not of this time. This memory helped Ian solve the mystery of his recurring back injuries.[309] By singing his body as I did and doing something out of the ordinary, Ian was able to discover and release this ancient wound.

On occasions such as this, where a client is experiencing an impasse, it is appropriate to enter into the process in this way. I have learned to trust the process, even if I am being asked to intervene or do something I have never done before. Trust your instincts and let your intuitive awareness guide your hands and actions.

A Few Cautionary Notes

While preserving good boundaries[310] is a given to most professional therapists and practitioners, clients have shared countless stories with me about having their boundaries overstepped. It is essential to maintain well-defined boundaries when working at an energetic level with clients or patients. Doing the preliminary practices of grounding and protection can help you sustain clarity and give you a way to create, with your mind and in your subtle body, distinctions between yourself and your clients. This separation is healthy and helps you discern what is happening with your clients and yourself. Here are some questions we can ask ourselves.

Can we listen to the words being spoken and observe body cues as well as partaking in the subtle energy of the person we are seeing? Can we maintain an open and safe space of non-judgment and equanimity, while also allowing for insight to flow and discernment to be at play? Can we nurture the client's inner essence and leave our roles as "authorities" or "experts" at the door? If we can do these things, the face of therapy changes. We are no longer the ones in charge— the mystery and the subtle energy of Source guides the process, as we become translators, as well as counselors.

Safeguards

Certain practices help create a safe clear space to work within as well as forming specific boundaries between clients and practitioners. One such technique I use when connecting to Source is to ask that the environment be free from any and all interference, whether known or unknown to me. This creates a distinct space to work within and assures that accuracy is achieved and maintained. Grounding, centering and visualizing a band of golden light just outside your aura creates firm psychic boundaries between yourself and clients, that separates us, at an energetic level, while maintaining rapport. There is a distinct feeling of protection and comfort that accompanies these visualizations; these techniques have proven themselves over time to be quite effective.

Burning white sage clears any residual energy within your office after sessions. This is called *smudging* in the Native American tradition; smudge is used to clear or cleanse a person, place, or thing of any negative energies. Various herbs and plants are used for different purposes. Sage and cedar are used for cleansing and clearing, while sweet grass is said to bring sweet spirits into your environment. I also sing the space[311] in order to open and balance the energies within my office or places where I teach.

We Are All Connected

Realize, if you can, that you are a part of an ongoing healing process, just like your client. Your energy while separate, acts upon the therapeutic container. This is why it's important to be as clear as possible about your own emotions and energies. Meditation practice can help you to be aware of your thoughts, feelings and emotions, so you do not confuse your inner material with that of your clients. Meditation fosters individuation and differentiation and helps us stay present with clients and not be debilitated or shocked by anything that may come up in a session. By being attentive and working with your mind in its many permutations, you can be more present nonjudgmental and compassionate with others. Whether you use meditation or some other means of therapy, bodywork or even exercise—finding a way to stay clear and open is essential. I have found that practitioner's, who have experienced and faced a wide range of states within themselves, will not be afraid of extreme states.

When in the state of being in the moment without preconceived ideas, we can join the client. By merging in this way we achieve the ability to follow our client's process at an intuitive level. Detached awareness allows you to create a healing environment, while also acting as a guide.

We need to stay connected to our client's experiences, while also maintaining detachment, especially if you are empathic. Detachment is essential or you can lose your objectivity and the ability to witness and mirror back to clients. Detachment creates and maintains the necessary boundaries between you and your clients, and vice versa.

A client's sense of detached awareness is a bit different from the practitioner's, as clients are often reliving painful events. By using observation they can disidentify with events they are experiencing, this distancing creates watcher awareness and this observing ability is essential. If clients access painful or disturbing events alone they might panic, unless the watcher is firmly in place within their minds. The awareness must remain detached, so they can continue to freely explore their body of experience. If the watcher is in place, then they can replay events without being overwhelmed by fear. This is very important. Practitioners need to help clients create this dual perspective of watching awareness.

Preconceptions: A Story

The importance of detachment from preconceived ideas was demonstrated to me one day when I was scheduled to see two business partners. Just before the appointment, I realized the woman coming in for this joint session was someone I had met in another setting and had found abrasive. When it came time for the appointment, only the man showed up, he mentioned that the woman realized she knew me and was unsure about coming. I assured him that I was impartial and mentioned that my having met her was not a factor. As I finished telling him this, the doorbell rang—the woman had come after all. We discussed her concerns and decided to proceed and had a lovely session. I was surprised at how pleasant she was and noticed that my previously held negative opinion of her had changed for the better. Detachment thus, includes the release of any preconceived notions that we may have in reference to a client or a client's story. In this way, the client's experience can unfold without the interference of the practitioner.

Seeing and Listening

I see patterns and relationships in a very clear and intuitive way. You too may have this intuitive ability; do not discount it, cultivate it instead. Whether insights come in the form of dreams or images that pop into your mind, they can be very informative. Seeing for me, is literally the experience of having images come directly into my mind, and underlying patterns that fuel emotions, actions, and symptoms are also discerned. The hidden framework of constructed beliefs, emotions, memories and the origins or original root causes for behaviors and reactions emerge as well. Seeing gives me the ability to discern patterns quite accurately.

This art of seeing is often accompanied by feelings of empathy, clairsentient impressions and clairaudient experiences or clear speech.[312] Clients' feelings are felt within my own being, as bodily tensions or emotions, and they guide me to areas of tension in my clients' bodies. Many body-workers have this skill and are highly attuned to feeling tension in this way, and it guides their hands. Empathy allows us to pick up the emotions clients are feeling. These intuitive experiences of insight convey penetrating and deeply personal insights and understanding about the clients I work with.

How does this work? When a client is describing a particular problem they are having, images come into my mind. These images give me information about how energies and emotions are held within the unconscious and the body. The underlying dynamics of relationships can also be seen and sensed. These images allow me to understand the possible origins or sources of problems in a general way. Often the images affirm a pattern I may already be noticing from listening to the client's story. As I listened to Jordan describe his problems with his ex-wife, I saw images of some very old interactions between them and understood how these past experiences were connected to their conflicts in the present. I saw images and sensed possible patterns that enabled me to understand what some of Jordan's beliefs might be regarding their relationship. It also helped me ask the right questions when needed.

The ability to hear the minute changes in a client's voice can be very informative. Cultivating the ability to hear these shifts in tone, color and inflection is of great benefit, especially when clients are working with past life memories. These changes in tone often reflect a former self that is being remembered. I recall one such shift when I was working with Jordan. As he was reliving an experience from another lifetime, the entire color, timbre, and quality of his voice changed dramatically. He became the shy monk he was describing. As he told me what was occurring in this past life, his voice became softer, rounder and carried with it a shyness that was not a characteristic of Jordan's usual character, demeanor or speaking voice.

The basic ways of seeing and listening that I have described above are my own ways of seeing and listening. Each practitioner who practices this work has to develop the skills involved in clear listening and clear sight. I have found that intuitive insight,[313] an open heart and an empty mind are invaluable. Cultivate them and you will find success.

The Steps: Guidelines along the Way
Finding the Story

To begin, the practitioner listens to the client's story. This helps to sort out a client's needs and confessions. Building rapport and being present at this time helps us discover what our clients want to accomplish, explore and what their concerns may be. Questions are used to gather information and can help clients focus on what they really want to work with at this time. Questions can be simple, such as, what has brought you in today? What is it that you would like to work with in this session? How do you feel about . . .? Where did you first notice or encounter this problem or symptom? How long have you been working with these issues? These kinds of questions allow the practitioner to get a picture of what a client is experiencing in the moment as well as some background and reference points.

Searching for Origins

Preconceived notions or ideas need to be set aside when searching for origins. If the practitioner leads the process the client is disempowered; this should be avoided. The only exception to this is when you work as a shaman, as I described earlier. The images and information received in the check-in phase are used only as guidelines giving the practitioner a sense of direction for each session, but don't be confined by what is said at this time.

When using these practices you need to become familiar with each client's pacing, and the speed at which they process. Observing visual cues, verbal remarks, and following your intuition can help you discover a client's pacing. If a client is getting stuck or overwhelmed, this has a distinct feel. The energy in the room, and around the client may feel like it is slowing down. This is a tangible experience and it can alert you to possible problems a client may be encountering. If this occurs you may align yourself with the client's energy and unobtrusively merge into their process.

To merge into a client's process, you need to settle your energies both internally and externally. I close my eyes and focus my attention inward. My breathing slows and I become one with my inner world, as my mind becomes still, I feel myself expand outward from this inner quiet to become one with the environment around me, which includes my client. As I do this I can sense my client's experience more directly.

Merging techniques like this give us the opportunity to perceive, and literally see, if a client is getting stuck or bogged down. If this happens you can ask a question to refocus the energy such as, what's happening, or what are you experiencing? These types of questions are characteristically a part of the remembering phase of this work, because this is where clients most often get stuck or bogged down. By using questions like these, clients are able to shift their attention and share what is happening for them, and then drop back into their experiences, and the process moves forward.

Questioning and Remembering Phase

The question is what animates the whole process. My role as a Transforming Embodiment practitioner is to ask questions, to "hold space" and to help connect the dots and clarify and discern the connections between the past and present for my clients.

Questions must not be leading; have your inquiries be as open-ended as possible, while providing space and focus for clients at the same time. Questions give clients the chance to discern, and experience patterns, memories, events, or cause-effect relationships for themselves, by using their intuition and intellect to see and experience old problems from new points of view. Questions evoke memories and provide us with insights we might have missed if we used only our intellect, as thinking has a tendency to bring us out of our experience. The key is to re-experience memories, feelings and emotions in a safe

Addendum

environment, where the skills of the client in the present can be brought to bear on their past experiences.

Experiencing and reliving difficult relationships or traumatic events can be very frightening for clients. The practitioner must respect each client's defenses and fears when doing this kind of inner work. Most people simply cannot jump into deeply troubling or traumatic events. So, it is imperative that each practitioner stay attuned and connected to each client. If it appears that a client is getting lost in their story, losing focus, or moving away from origins, an open-ended but specific question can get a client back on track. You might ask: where else have you felt or experienced this problem before, can you move deeper into this experience or into another experience that is important for you to understand?

Clients can have two sets of images that emerge during the remembering process and they may choose to explore the imagery that is less challenging first. If this is taken too far and you feel the client is avoiding the difficult imagery, you need to refocus your client's attention back to the imagery that was more challenging. This decision needs to take into account the level of session threshold that the client is experiencing. Sometimes clients just need to take a break and regroup, but if they get lost in their story this can be a sign that they are sidestepping the more challenging images.

Seeing patterns and relationships is crucial in directing the questioning process, especially if the process is missing the mark or skimming the surface. In Jordan's initial session, I perceived and saw a bitter relationship between Jordan and his ex-wife. Seeing this material helped me to know when Jordan was finding the origins of their conflicts. As he worked to find the origins of his troubling relationship, he saw and experienced several different lifetimes, unearthing many details, as he re-experienced the pain and confusion that bound him to his ex-wife. His willingness to re-experience his pain and disturbing emotions moved him to material that helped him understand his relationship and conflicting emotions and these experiences confirmed my original impressions of the relationship they shared.

Holding space and following clients gives them a large field to work within, and the mind, with its fears and reactions, is given the space it requires for exploring. In this way, clients' defenses are respected and worked with, which permits them to see beyond their habitual reactions.

As the process of remembering deepens, clients can move through these multiple layers of memory, and see how emotional patterns have continued. Each lifetime stresses a specific aspect of how a pattern or belief system is held in place. Each lifetime can also show the many ways a problem has been experienced, sometimes even from opposing points of view. Questions you could use during this phase might include "Where are you, what do you notice around you, what are you experiencing and why are you in this situation. Can you see what happened before this moment or what happens next?"

These types of questions give clients access to the hidden gems within their experience, beyond their usual patterns of thinking and behaving. For Jordan, he came upon a lifetime with his ex-wife where they had been happy. They had shared a simple, contented life together without conflict, and were at peace with each other. This memory came to Jordan after he had recovered numerous lifetimes where they had done great harm to one another, but this memory of contentment was the most important, it was the gem.

Two simple questions, "Is there anything else you need to know and what wishes to be revealed to you at this time that might help you understand this relationship?" opened the door to this memory of happiness and peace and would change Jordan at his core.

These questions helped Jordan discover pivotal points about his relationships and deep emotions. The imagery and memories within our body of experience help us change long-standing patterns within our lives. These memories also open the doorway to the integration phase.

To summarize, questions during check–in help practitioners gather information about their client's goals. Questions within the remembering phase are used to evoke memories and feelings and give clients the opportunity to explore their inner world. During the integration phase, questions help clients find the underlying connections between events from their past and their present and a greater understanding of how problems and patterns are intertwined is often revealed. Questions such as "Do you notice any similarities between your experiences in your past and your present situation or do you notice any similar feeling or emotions from the past you are describing and feelings you have in the present? Use questions that help your clients see the connections between their past and present and any cause-effect relationships that may exist.

Remembering and Reliving

When clients are reliving an experience, you need to pay close attention and stay in rapport and watch them carefully. Look for physical and visual cues clients may be displaying, as well as watching their body movements and overall energy patterns. These cues can be as simple as constricted muscles in the face and body, fluttering eyes, or rapid eye movements beneath closed eye lids, changes in breath, facial color, laughter, or changes in speech patterns or expression. With practice, you can also learn to see and discern energetic changes within the chakras and energy system.

Clients need to be assured of your presence, so that a sense of control of the process and safety within the process are maintained. This can take some time; be patient and assured that within this supportive environment clients can learn that it is safe to participate in memories from their past or past lives. Also remember that it is sometimes important to let clients stay in an uncomfortable experience as a way of gaining insight.

Working With Time: Some Cautions

Clients can lose their sense of being anchored in the present during accelerated experiences, (i.e., flipping and time shifting) and as a result, become confused as to their temporal location. This can be frightening to the client. It is the practitioner's duty to help the client back into the present and to re-anchor the client, should this experience become extreme.

The practitioner holds the space, bears witness to the process, and assists clients in staying present within their experience. This is not always easy for the client. The practitioner must help the client feel safe and cared for as this process unfolds.

If the client or student tries to do this alone, they may experience adverse reactions. If these reactions take over, clients may get lost in the content of their experience. This can send clients out of the experience of remembering and reliving and into trauma if they are not monitored. The practitioner is needed at this juncture more than at any other time in the work.

Releasing and Integration

During this phase of the work practitioners continue to use the spiritual Self to maintain contact with the client and to help guide the client's process, while clients use their spiritual Self to understand the best way to release held emotions and memories.

At this time you can comment on a client's experiences, offer new possibilities and help them see connections, and understand their problems and concerns with fresh eyes. Insights from "ah-ha" moments emerge again and the cascading effect from these moments can be reviewed in more detail to gain a deeper understanding of how certain beliefs motivate behaviors in relationships and within the body. The practitioner's objective observation of the client's process and patterns is of great help at this time.

The very construction of belief systems and the reasoning behind our beliefs can be understood by seeing the connections between past events and memories and present day symptoms and behaviors. This understanding gives us a context for our experiences and a starting point for making change.

In closing, meditation has taught me how to stay present with my clients in an open and loving way, and it continues to bring forth many creative techniques and visualizations to use with clients. I encourage each of you who use these practices to develop your intuitive and meditative mind in whatever way you see fit, because a spacious, open, non-judgmental mind is a creative mind. Using your intuitive mind and rational intelligence will help you see the broader implications of habitual actions and reactions, and enable you to perceive a larger picture, putting life into context in new ways. Life becomes full of possibilities, new options, and deep healing as a result.

GLOSSARY

Aka: the essence of matter, in Hawai'ian healing tradition. Aka is luminous and the vessel for *mana*. It has four aspects that are solid liquid gases, and plasma. Aka threads are similar to the cords we find when we are decoding experiences between ourselves and people or places.

Aumakua: One's Source Self, Spiritual essence and deep expression of Source, associated with the superconscious, all perceiving aspect of consciousness. Also refers to the ancestral spirits in Hawai'i.

Aura: The energy field around the body, which has seven layers.

Bardo: Literally means that which lies between. In Tibetan Buddhism the bardo refers to the intermediate state between this life and the next or between death and rebirth. Bardos are occurring continuously within our lives. Tibetan Buddhism believes that there are four bardos that are interlinked and continuous. They are (1) life (2) dying and death (3) after death (4) and rebirth.

Body of Experience: The sum of all experience either known or unknown that we have ever perceived. The body of experience is the imprint that we work from to function in our daily lives. It is this aspect of our consciousness that we contact, heal, and transform when needed in TE The body of experience carries all our beliefs feelings, memories, and experiences from this lifetime and previous lifetimes and encompasses what occurs in the mind, body, psyche, and the energy fields of the body.

Chakras: The energy centers or centers of consciousness. There are major and minor chakras within the body and the energy field of the body.

Decording: The psychic technique of removing the cords or threads that exist between people and places.

Emptiness: "a basic openness and non-separation that we experience when all small and fixed notions of our self are seen through or dissolved."[314]

Equanimity: The radical noninterference with the natural flow of the sensory components.[315] The non-judgmental acceptance of whatever arises in our lives and psyche.

Flipping: The experience of moving, sometimes quite quickly, from one lifetime experience to another. Usually, these experiences move from present time to a time in the past. Flipping is accompanied by acceleration and images move rapidly, like viewing time-lapse photography, and this can be confusing.

H'sien: Holy Mountain Immortals and a Taoist lineage.

Huna: Literally means 'the secret' in Hawai'ian, also the term for the spiritual and healing traditions of Hawai'i.

Kahuna: Literally means "one who knows the secret" in Hawai'ian. Also refers to the healing and spiritual practitioners or priests of Hawai'i.

Kanaloa: The companion spirit to aumakua and the co-creator with aumakua or the ideal human being.

Karma: Very simply, action and its results.

Ku: Subconscious mind, associated with memory, the body, habits and instincts.

Kundalini: The powerful psychic energy that lies at the base of the spine.

Learning Process: The gathering of information and data around a conflict, or new skill set.

Lono: The conscious mind, associated with the decision-making process. The aspect that directs, analyzes, and interprets information.

Mana: The energy of life. Power and life force.

Marika: The energy Elizabeth Burke trance channeled. Described as the combination of all high selves Elizabeth had ever been or would ever be.

Mindfulness: Continuous clear contact with the sensory components of experience.[316]

Nadis: The energy pathways or channels within the body.

Nonlocality: The idea that we are not limited by our body, mind, or perceptions. Nonlocality carries with it an expanded perception of natural interconnectedness. A central feature is a unity to all things and events.

Organic: Fluid, mobile and alive. An organic process is one in which one follows the body and sensory based information, not only the mind.

Origins: The source point or inception of problems from which imprints arise and become embodied in consciousness and the body.

Phowa: Tibetan practice of the transference of consciousness by realized spiritual practitioners at the moment of death.

Process: ongoing resolution of conflicts between the body, mind and spirit.

Psi: Psychic abilities including clairvoyance, clairaudience and clairsentience.

Reweaving: A visualization technique used to repair holes in the energy body or auric field.

Rigpa: Tibetan term for the primordial, pure awareness that is intelligent, radiant, and always awake.

Sem: Tibetan term for the ordinary, discursive, dualistic, thinking mind.

Session Threshold: The point at which you are at the limit of your capacity during any session of inner explorations bodywork or therapy.

Shaman: One who practices the art of healing and spirituality especially within indigenous cultures.

Source: The beginning point where all existence emerged out of or from.

Supramental Yoga: The yoga of Sri Aurobindo that he felt would be a guide in a willed mutation of the species—where death would not exist.

Tao: The Way or path, Tao is also considered the force of life or the way of nature.

Time Shifting: Time shifting is characterized by the melting away of the present, while an overlay of another time is impressed upon the mind. This experience is felt physically, mentally, emotionally, and psychically. Images, memories, and emotions from multiple lifetimes flood into your consciousness during time shifting. These experiences are often triggered by people we have known in the past or when feelings or emotions that are similar to those we have felt in the past come into consciousness again. When time shifting occurs, knowing is immediate and direct and there is often a feeling of the body knowing something before the mind can actually sort out what is being perceived. During moments of time shifting our experience is very direct and spontaneous because the mind is not engaged in its normal way. Time shifting loosens the bonds of our individual identity, so we can experience the multifaceted diversity of the Self. At first this type of experience is extremely confusing. When the confusion subsides, experiences of time shifting have a lasting effect upon us, because these experiences open our hearts and minds to the richness and history we carry within ourselves.

TE: Abbreviation for Transforming Embodiment.

Tulku: Reincarnated realized spiritual master in the Tibetan tradition.

BIBLIOGRAPHY

Achterberg, Jeanne. *Imagery and Healing: Shamanism and Modern Medicine.* Boston: Shambhala Publishing, 1985.

——— *Woman as Healer: A Panoramic Survey of the Healing Activities Of Woman From Prehistoric Times To The Present.* Boston: Shambhala Publishing, 1990.

American Psychological Association. *Ethical Principles of Psychologists and Code Of Conduct.* Washington D. C.: APA, 1995.

Assagioli, Roberto. *Psychosynthesis.* New York: Penguin Books, 1991.

Blacker, Star. *Official Training Manual of Body Mind Integrative Therapy.* Santa Fe: Somatic Therapy Institute, 1993.

Bokar, Rinpoche. *Death and the Art of Dying in Tibetan Buddhism.* San Francisco: Clear Point Press, 1993.

Shinoda Bolen, Jean M.D. *The Tao of Psychology: Synchronicity and the Self,* San Francisco: Harper & Row, 1993.

Campbell, Joseph., ed. *The Portable Jung.* New York: Penguin Books, 1976.

Chodron, Thubten. *What Color Is Your Mind.* Ithaca: Snow Lion Publications, 1993.

Cleary, Thomas., ed. *Vitality Energy Spirit: A Taoist Sourcebook*, Boston: Shambhala Publications, 1991.

Daniels, Marcus. "Advanced States of Healing." *Quality Times* (September/October 1993): 10, 11, 22.

Dossey, Larry M.D. *Space Time and Medicine*. Boston: Shambhala Publications, 1982.

────── *Beyond Illness*. Boulder: New Science Library, 1984.

────── "To holists in medicine: A challenge." *Revision 7* (1) (spring 1984): 83–86.

────── *Recovering The Soul: A Scientific and Spiritual Search*. New York: Bantam Books, 1989.

────── "Era III Medicine: The New Frontier." *Revision,* 14 (3) (winter 1992): 128–139.

Fisher, Joe. *The Case for Reincarnation*. New York: Bantam Books, 1985.

Gallegos, Eligio Stephen. *Animals of the Four Windows: Integrating Thinking, Sensing, Feeling, and Imagery*. Santa Fe: Moon Bear Press, 1992.

Goleman, Daniel. *Healing Emotions: Conversations with the Dalai Lama on Mindfulness, Emotions, and Health*. Boston: Shambhala Publications, 1997.

Ferrucci, Piero. *What We May Be*. Los Angeles: J. P. Tarcher, 1982.

Lama Anagarika Govinda. *Way of White Clouds.* Berkeley: Shambhala Publishing, 1970.

Grof, Stanislav. *Beyond the Brain.* Albany: State University of New York Press, 1985.

Grof, Stanislav with Hal Bennett. *The Holotrophic Mind: The Three Levels of Human Consciousness and How They Shape Our Lives.* New York: Harper Collins, 1993.

Halifax, Joan. *The Fruitful Darkness: Reconnecting with the Body of the Earth.* San Francisco: Harper Collins, 1993.

Hunt, Valerie. 2nd International Psychology of Consciousness, Energy Medicine and Dynamic Change Conference Tape" NICABM recordings, 1998.

Johanson, Greg and Ron Kurtz. *Grace Unfolding: Psychotherapy in the Spirit of the Tao Te Ching.* New York: Bell Tower, 1991.

Joy, Brugh B. MD. *Joy's Way a Map for the Transformational Journey: An Introduction to the Potentials for Healing with Body Energies.* Los Angeles: J. P. Tarcher, 1979.

King, Serge Kahili. *Kahuna Healing: Philosophy and Practice.* Malibu, Huna International, 1979.

────── *Kahuna Healing: Holistic Health and Healing Practices of Polynesia.* Wheaton: The Theosophical Publishing House, 1983.

────── *Mastering The Hidden Self: A Guide to The Huna Way.* Wheaton: The Theosophical Publishing House, 1985.

Kornfield, Jack. *A Path With Heart: A Guide Through The Perils and Promises of Spiritual Life.* New York: Bantam Books, 1993.

Lao Tsu. *Tao Te Ching.* New York: Random House, 1972.

Levine, Peter. *Waking The Tiger: Healing Trauma,* Berkeley: North Atlantic Books, 1997.

Levine, Stephen. *Healing Into Life and Death.* New York: Doubleday, 1987.

Levine, Stephen and Ondrea. *Embracing The Beloved: Relationship as a Path of Awakening.* New York: Doubleday, 1995.

Lowenthal, Martin & Lars Short. *Opening The Heart of Compassion: Transform Suffering Through Buddhist Psychology and Practice.* Rutland: Charles E. Tuttle, 1993.

Mackenzie, Vicki. *Reborn In The West: The Reincarnation Masters.* London: Blooms bury, 1995.

———*The Boy Lama.* Boston: Wisdom Publications, 1989.

Mindell, Arnie. *Working with the Dreaming Body.* London: Arkana, 1989.

Deng, Ming-Dao. *365 Tao Daily Mediations.* San Francisco: Harper Collins, 1992.

Mookerjee, Ajit. *Kundalini: The Arousal of Inner Energy.* Merrimac: Destiny Books, 1983.

Moss, Richard M.D. *The I That Is We: Awakening to Higher Energies*

Through Unconditional Love. Berkeley: Celestial Arts, 1981.

Motz, Julie. *Hands of Life.* New York: Bantam, 1998.

Pattee, Rowena. *Moving with Change: A Woman's Re-Integration of the I Ching.* London: Arkana, 1986.

Pearsall, Paul. *The Heart's Code: Tapping the Wisdom and Power of Our Heart Energy.* New York: Broadway, 1998.

Pert, Candace. *Molecules of Emotion: Why You Feel The Way You Do.* New York: Scribner, 1997.

——— "The Wisdom of the Receptors: Neuropeptides, The Emotions and Bodymind." *Advances* 3 (3) (summer 1986): 8–16.

Progoff, Ira. *Depth Psychology and Modern Man.* (2nd ed.). New York: Mc Graw Hill, 1973.

Rothberg, Daniel. "How Straight is the Spiritual Path. [Conversations with Buddhist Teachers Jack Kornfield and Michele Mc Donald-Smith]" *Revision* 19 (1) (summer 1996): 25–39.

Sabini, Meredith. "Beyond Spirituality Belief in Ancestry Reincarnation" *Noetic Sciences Review* 55 (March-May 2001): 17-21.

Satprem. *The Mind of the Cells.* Paris: Institut de Recherches Evolutives, 1992.

Schwarz, Jack. *Voluntary Controls* New York: E.P. Dutton, 1978.

Sogyal Rinpoche. *The Tibetan Book of Living and Dying.* New York: Harper Collins, 1992.

Bishop Sprong, John Shelby, ed. *Proceeding from the Symposium on Consciousness and Survival: An Interdisciplinary Inquiry into the Possibility of Life Beyond Biological Death.* Sausalito: Institute of Noetic Sciences, 1987.

Stevenson, Ian M D. *Twenty Cases Suggestive of Reincarnation.* (2nd ed.). Charlottesville: University Press of Virginia, 1974.

Swami Rama, Rudolph Ballentine and Swami Ajaya. *Yoga and Psychotherapy: The Evolution of Consciousness.* (7th ed.). Honesdale: Himalayan International Institute of Yoga Science and Philosophy, 1993.

Terr, Lenore M. D. *Unchained Memories: True Stories of Traumatic Memories Lost and Found.* New York: Basic Books, 1994.

Chögyam Trungpa Rinpoche. *Journey Without Goal: The Tantric Wisdom of the Buddha.* Boston: Shambhala Publications, 1981.

Von Dürckheim, Karlfried G. *Hara: The Vital Centre of Man.* London: Mandala Books, 1962.

Wade, Jennie. *Changes of Mind: A Holonomic Theory of the Evolution of Consciousness.* New York: State University of New York Press, 1996.

Wallace, B. Alan. *Tibetan Buddhism from the Ground Up: A Practical Approach to Modern Life.* Boston: Wisdom Publications, 1993.

Welwood, John., ed. *Awakening the Heart: East/West Approaches to Psychotherapy and the Healing Relationship.* Boston: Shambhala Publications, 1983.

Wong, Eva., trans. *Seven Taoist Masters: A Folk Tale from China.* Boston: Shambhala Publishing, 1990.

Wright, Peggy Ann. "A Psychobiological Approach to Shamanic Altered States of Consciousness." *Revision* 16 (4), (spring 1994.): 164–172.

———. "The Interconnectivity of Mind, Brain, and Behavior in Altered States of Consciousness: Focus on Shamanism." *Alternative Therapies* 1 (3), (July 1995): 50–56.

Lama Zopa Rinpoche. *Practicing the Good Heart.* Boston: Wisdom Publications, 1996.

Zweig, Connie and Jeremiah Abrams., ed. *Meeting the Shadow: The Hidden Power of the Dark Side of Human Nature.* New York: G. P. Putnam's Sons, 1991.

RESOURCES

Tibetan Yungdrung Bon Institute
Lama Khemsar Rinpoche
www.yungdrungbon.com

Tassajara Zen Mountain Center
Carmel Valley, CA (831) 659-2229
www.sfzc.org

Nyingma Institute
Berkeley, CA (510) 843-6812
www.nyingmainstitute.com

Pema Osel Ling
Watsonville, CA (831) 761-6266
www.vajrayana.org

Spirit Rock Meditation Center
Woodacre, CA (415) 488-0164
www.spiritrock.org

Insight Meditation Society
Barre, MA (978) 355-4646
www.dharma.org

Institute of Noetic Sciences
Petaluma CA (707) 775-3500
www.noetic.org

Transforming Embodiment Institute
Tiburon, CA (415) 435-8015
www.healingorigins.com

Esalen Institute
Big Sur, CA (831) 667-3005
www.esalen.org

Aloha International
Volcano, HI (808) 985-8880
www.huna.org

Qigong Association of America
Corvallis OR (541) 752-6599
www.qi.org

International Society for the Study
of Subtle Energies and Energy Medicine
Golden, CO (303) 278-2228
www.nekesc.org/~issseem

Institute of Classical Homeopathy
San Francisco, CA (415) 551-1020
www.classicalhomeopathy.org

Institute of Traditional Medicine
Portland OR. (503) 233-4907
www.itmonline.org

PERMISSIONS & CREDITS

Interior Photo: Mountain Ridges in Mists/ Huang Shan/ Anhui Province: by Art Wolfe © permission granted for use. www.artwolfe.com.

Credit Line: From Embracing the Beloved by Stephen and Ondrea Levine, copyright © 1995 by Stephen and Ondrea Levine. Used by permission of Doubleday, a division of Random House, Inc.

Credit Line: From A Path with Heart by Jack Kornfield, copyright © 1993 by Jack Kornfield. Used by permission of Bantam Books, a division of Random House Inc.

Credit Line: From Recovering the Soul by Larry Dossey, MD., copyright © 1989 by Larry Dossey, MD. Used by permission of Bantam Books, a division of Random House Inc.

Credit Line: From A Heart's Code by Paul Pearsall copyright ©1998 by Paul Pearsall. Used by permission of Broadway, a division of Random House Inc.

Credit Line: 525 words (used in text and opening quotes) from The Holotropic Mind by Stanislav Grof copyright © 1992 by Stanislav Grof and Hal Zina Bennett. Reprinted by permission of Harper Collins Publishers.

Credit Line: 459 words (used in text and opening quotes) from the Tibetan Book of Living and Dying by Sogyal Rinpoche and edited by Patrick Gaffney and Andrew Harvey copyright © 1993 Rigpa Fellowship Reprinted by Permission of Harper Collins Publishers.

Form of Acknowledgment: Reprinted with permission of Scribner, an imprint of Simon and Schuster Adult Publishing Group, from Molecules of Emotion by Candace B. Pert Copyright © 1997 by Candace Pert Foreward Copyright © By Deepak Chopra, MA. All rights.

Credit Line: From What We May Be by Piero Ferrucci Copyright © 1982 J.P. Tarcher. Reprinted by Permission by Penguin Group USA Inc.

Credit Line: © Vicki Mackenzie, 1988, 1996. Excerpted from Reincarnation: The Boy Lama with permission of Wisdom Publications, 199 Elm St., Somerville MA .02144 www.wisdompubs.org.

Credit Line: Extract from Reborn in the West: The Reincarnation Masters by Vicki Mackenzie copyright © 1995 by Vicki Mackenzie. Reproduced with the permission of Bloomsbury Publishing.

Credit Line: From Waking the Tiger: Healing Trauma by Peter Levine Copyright © 1997 by Peter Levine. Reprinted by Permission of North Atlantic Books.

Credit Line: Reprinted by permission of Sll/Sterling Lord Literistic, Inc. From Psychosynthesis Copyright © 1965 by Roberto Assagioli.

CREDITS

Drawings/Illustrations: Meagan Shapiro & Dale Nutley

Cover & Interior Design: H. Elizabeth Burke

Author's Photo: Marilyn Rivas-Tate

ABOUT THE TYPE

The text body of this book was set in Palantino, designed by the German typographer Herman Zaph. It was named after the Renaissance calligrapher Giovanbattista Palantino. Zaph designed it between 1948-1952, and it was his first typeface to be introduced to America. It is a face of unusual elegance.[317]

INDEX

A

acceleration 249, 250
acceptance 16, 33, 56, 69, 120, 122, 126, 153, 222, 223, 254, 259, 260, 290, 302, 305
Achterberg, Jeanne 130, 132, 181, 185
ah-ha 257, 258, 268, 316
Alia 12, 185, 213
Amelia 214, 252, 253, 254, 264 269
ancestral memories 189
ancient beliefs 246
ancient histories 56, 80,133, 236
ancient lifetimes 124
anger 65, 69, 73, 96, 98, 99, 120, 124, 127, 134, 143, 153, 168, 170, 171, 208, 210, 213, 237, 238, 249, 259, 260, 261, 262, 269, 278
Assagioli, Roberto 139, 218, 220
attraction 85, 232
aumakua 22, 114, 115, 140, 141, 142, 145, 146, 220, 230, 242, 262, 303, 304
aura 22, 55, 102, 155, 180, 191, 265, 267, 307
avoidance 232
awareness 20, 48, 52, 58, 59, 70, 71, 72, 83, 84, 97, 98, 101, 109, 110, 111, 112, 113, 123, 124, 126, 127, 140, 141, 144, 146, 147, 154, 160, 180, 183, 184, 190, 198, 201, 211, 212, 213, 214, 222, 227, 228, 229, 231, 233, 240, 249, 250, 251, 252, 264, 274, 290, 302, 307, 309

B

bardo 85, 99, 100, 101, 284, 285, 286
beliefs 11, 13, 14, 51, 57, 58, 59, 63, 68, 74, 95, 103, 120, 122, 131, 136, 140, 142, 144, 145, 147, 148, 152 153, 154, 157, 162, 179, 180, 181, 182, 183, 184, 185, 189, 190, 191, 193, 194, 195, 196, 197, 198, 199, 200, 201, 206, 207, 208, 212, 216, 217, 218, 219, 220, 221, 223, 232, 233, 235, 238, 239, 243, 246, 247, 258, 263, 264, 265,266, 267, 268, 269, 286, 291, 298, 299, 301, 305, 310, 316
belief systems 16, 123, 133, 150, 154, 194, 195, 196, 197, 198, 201, 216, 217, 218, 229, 246, 250, 316
body consciousness 133, 148, 165, 181, 190, 196, 238
body knowing 48
body of experience 66, 82, 103, 179, 189, 190, 195, 198, 200, 240, 309, 314
body wisdom 39, 199, 236
Bokar Rinpoche 99
boundaries 27, 80, 120, 140, 152, 169, 228, 232, 233, 234, 242, 273, 290, 297, 298, 307, 308, 309
Buddhist 16, 31, 32, 41, 42, 60, 83, 95, 96, 97, 98, 99, 100, 105, 128, 133, 136, 149, 221, 285, 286

C

causal relationships 15
cause-effect relationships 15, 212, 232, 241, 243, 267, 312, 315
cellular memories 36, 44
chakras 16, 18, 25, 26, 31, 41, 55, 66, 72, 98, 102, 111, 148, 149, 150, 151, 152, 153, 154, 155, 157, 180, 183, 191, 200, 206, 208, 221, 262, 264, 265, 291, 292, 306, 315
chakra energy 155
channel 16, 26, 30, 31, 32, 82, 132, 135, 136, 274, 278, 280
channeled 107, 221
channeling 32, 107
consciousness 12, 13, 15, 16, 25, 26, 27, 40, 41, 42, 43, 44, 45, 47, 48, 58, 60, 74, 79, 80, 81, 82, 83, 85, 86, 87, 90, 92, 93, 96, 98, 100, 101, 102, 103, 104, 110, 112, 114, 124, 125, 131, 132, 133, 135, 139, 140, 141, 145, 149, 176, 182, 184, 188, 189, 190, 191, 193, 194, 196, 197, 200, 206, 207, 209, 210, 212, 227, 228, 231, 232, 235, 246, 249, 250, 252, 254, 258, 260, 263, 264, 265, 269, 274, 278, 292, 298

creativity 153, 266
current life triggers 15, 206

D

Dalai Lama, His Holiness 47, 86, 88, 149, 176
decoding 264, 266
Depth Psychology 218
detachment 53, 162, 182, 223, 248, 249, 251, 265, 302, 308, 309
disease 14, 36, 100, 123, 130, 150, 153, 200
distrust 147, 208, 247
DNA 13, 42, 97, 98, 99
Dossey, Larry 80, 81, 82, 83, 84
duality 86, 128, 130, 232

E

effortless effort 106, 228
embodied memory 189, 190
embodiment 60, 100, 125, 155
empowerment 53, 56, 60, 88, 216, 220, 262
emptiness 30, 109, 110, 166, 168, 228
energy 14, 15, 16, 17, 18, 20, 21, 22, 26, 30, 31, 32, 35, 36, 37, 39, 41, 42, 43, 44, 47, 48, 50, 51, 52, 53, 54, 55, 56, 57, 58, 60, 65, 67, 80, 81, 92, 99, 100, 102, 105, 106, 107, 108, 109, 110, 111, 112, 113, 114, 120, 124, 125, 127, 129, 130, 131, 132, 134, 135, 136, 140, 143, 144, 146, 147, 148, 149, 150, 152, 153, 154, 155, 157, 160, 163, 164, 170, 177, 180, 183, 186, 188, 189, 191, 197, 198, 199, 200, 206, 209, 215, 221, 228, 229, 230, 231, 232, 233, 234, 236, 242, 252, 256, 262, 266, 267, 274, 278, 280, 281, 289, 290, 291, 292, 293, 298, 302, 303, 304, 306, 307, 308, 312, 315
energy body 26, 31, 55, 179, 186, 262, 267
energy centers 16, 39, 41, 48, 120, 150, 152, 154, 157, 215
energy field 127, 177, 180, 234

energy patterns 81, 200, 266, 315
energy system 102, 157, 221, 292, 315
epiphanies 268, 269
equanimity 16, 18, 90, 102, 120, 222, 232, 233, 248, 291, 302, 307
essential Self 198, 199

F

false memory 188
flipping 249, 250, 315
forgiveness 123, 147, 214, 222

G

Gallegos, Stephen 121, 132
genetic memory 189
Grof, Stanislav 12, 13, 121, 194, 290
grounding 20, 21, 22, 67, 72, 155, 163, 209, 307

H

habits 123, 142, 143, 144, 145, 187, 194, 196, 212, 223
Hawai'i 59, 127, 128, 141, 142, 148, 179, 193, 220
healing 12, 13, 14, 15, 16, 17, 18, 25, 32, 36, 37, 48, 58, 59, 61, 64, 66, 68, 75, 119, 120, 121, 122, 123, 124, 125, 126, 127, 128, 129, 130, 131, 132, 133, 141, 146, 147, 148, 150, 161, 167, 181, 182, 185, 186, 187, 189, 191, 195, 198, 199, 200, 203, 207, 212, 214, 215, 216, 218, 219, 220, 221, 222, 228, 230, 233, 234, 241, 242, 247, 249, 250, 254, 255, 260, 262, 263, 266, 267, 268, 269, 270, 273, 280, 285, 297, 298, 299, 302, 308, 316
healing origins 63, 208,
healing process 122, 125, 131, 229, 230, 248, 259, 303, 308
higher Self 145, 199, 304
humor 31, 32, 123
Huna 15, 139, 140, 142, 143, 144, 146, 147, 148, 194, 200, 220, 251
Hunt, Valerie 17, 48, 51, 177, 218

Index

I

illness 14, 26, 32, 64, 121, 122, 123, 127, 142, 146, 150, 197, 199, 237, 258, 278, 286
imagery and memory 15, 184
imprints 13, 41, 42, 43, 98, 100, 102, 120, 265, 266, 268, 278
injuries 187, 306
inner child 251
integration phase 242, 243, 267, 269, 314
intuition 14, 15, 17, 18, 28, 108, 130, 141, 142, 145, 154, 181, 183, 186, 199, 215, 216, 227, 228, 229, 231, 232, 233, 234, 236, 240, 241, 250, 262, 265, 290, 311, 312
intuitive 15, 16, 17, 85, 107, 120, 140, 154, 157, 181, 183, 184, 205, 206, 216, 217, 219, 220, 223, 227, 229, 231, 232, 233, 234, 236, 238, 239, 241, 264, 301, 307, 308, 309, 310, 311, 316

J

Jennifer 292
Jessie 91, 92, 93
Jordan 185, 208, 209, 210, 211, 213, 241, 242, 246, 247, 248, 249, 250, 251, 259, 260, 268, 291, 310, 313, 314
Joy, Brugh 157
June 237, 238, 281, 283

K

kahuna, kahunas 86, 145, 199, 200, 220, 221
kahuna healing 146
kanaloa 142, 146
karma 58, 85, 86, 96, 98, 100, 286
King, Serge Kahili 141, 144
Kornfield, Jack 182, 199
ku 142, 143, 144, 145, 146, 148, 195, 196, 304
kundalini 26, 111

L

Lama Yeshe 88, 89, 90, 91
Lama Zopa Rinpoche 90
layers 51, 81, 91, 132, 136, 200, 201, 218, 236, 240, 246, 249, 258, 270, 314
Levine, Peter 49, 50, 51, 52, 179, 186, 187
Levine, Stephen 27, 121, 124
Levine, Stephen and Ondrea 127, 289
lono 142, 143, 144, 145, 146, 304
love 29, 31, 35, 45, 124, 125, 126, 127, 128, 131, 134, 147, 152, 153, 162, 163, 165, 170, 197, 208, 211, 223, 246, 256, 259, 260, 269, 274, 275, 276, 277, 278, 281, 282, 287, 290, 304, 305
loving-kindness 261, 302
Lynn 11, 12, 64, 66, 73, 74, 247, 269

M

Mackenzie, Vicki 88, 90, 91, 97
Madison 207
mana 144, 146, 147, 148, 199
Marika 26, 31, 32, 132, 134
meditation 16, 17, 20, 22, 25, 27, 30, 31, 66, 83, 90, 106, 107, 120, 128, 140, 149, 158, 198, 212, 221, 222, 223, 251, 267, 286, 291, 306, 308, 316
merging 112, 183, 228, 252, 312
merging minds 81
mind-body 14, 135, 176, 182, 274
Mindell, Arnie and Amy 293
Mindell, Arnold 121
mindfulness 18, 125, 270
Motz, Julie 37, 51

N

neuropeptides 35, 36, 37, 38, 39, 40, 41, 42, 43, 81, 177, 178, 189
non-judgment 222, 232, 291, 302 305, 307
nonlocal 43, 44, 45, 80, 81, 82, 83, 85, 103, 104, 303
nonlocality 81, 82, 83, 85
not-knowing 232

O

one percent shaman 251
organic process 220
original trauma 56, 57, 60
origins 12, 13, 14, 15, 60, 64, 123, 136, 171, 176, 184, 185, 188, 190, 191, 200, 206, 207, 212, 213, 214, 216, 217, 223, 236, 240, 241, 246, 247, 257, 258, 260, 266, 267, 268, 269, 270, 298, 310, 311, 313
other lifetimes 48, 56, 58, 59, 102, 103, 133, 183, 185, 187, 188, 190, 194, 212, 214, 215, 240, 242,
other life memories 14, 102, 187, 257

P

pain 14, 27, 52, 55, 59, 82, 110, 120, 122, 123, 124, 125, 126, 127, 136, 142, 143, 144, 148, 152, 184, 185, 190, 191, 196, 200, 210, 213, 235, 238, 239, 242, 248, 249, 256, 258, 259, 262, 265, 266, 267, 276, 278, 279, 286, 287, 297, 298, 302, 306, 313
parallel time 274, 277
past life 11, 13, 87, 103, 162, 164, 168, 184, 185, 188, 268, 273, 274, 311
past life events 15, 207
past life experiences 48, 73, 163, 184, 185, 190, 195, 245
past life memories 11, 48, 64, 103, 162, 187, 190, 256, 310
past lives 12, 13, 14, 32, 48, 87, 134, 184, 185, 187, 207, 210, 212, 219, 259, 267, 268, 274, 291, 315
Pearsall, Paul 35, 36, 45, 80, 85, 157, 176, 177, 189
Pert, Candace 35, 36, 37, 38, 39, 41, 42, 43, 44, 50, 176, 177, 179 189, 200
prenatal 195, 207, 257
presence 21, 45, 69, 88, 113, 120, 140, 147, 155, 232, 248, 252, 286, 301, 315
process 12, 14, 15, 16, 32, 33, 41, 51, 52, 58, 63, 82, 85, 92, 98, 100, 101, 102, 119, 120, 121, 122, 125, 126, 130, 131, 132, 144, 145, 169, 170, 171, 182, 183, 188, 190, 196, 198, 199, 201, 206, 209, 212, 215, 218, 220, 229, 230, 233, 236, 238, 239, 240, 241, 242, 243, 245, 246, 247, 248, 250, 254, 258, 259, 260, 261, 264, 267, 270, 291, 292, 293, 298, 302, 303, 304, 305, 306, 307, 308, 311, 312, 313, 315, 316
Progoff, Ira 217, 218, 219
psychic 14, 16, 26, 27, 81, 110, 111, 136, 142, 206, 215, 234, 306, 308
psycho-spiritual 215, 236
psychosomatic symptoms 14, 263, 338
Psychosynthesis 182, 218, 219, 220

Q

questioning 47, 236, 313
questioning phase 239
questioning process 236, 239, 313
questions 14, 32, 119, 122, 123, 126, 128, 143, 161, 184, 186, 206, 229, 230, 231, 236, 239, 240, 242, 243, 247, 291, 301, 302, 307, 310, 311, 312, 314

R

rapport 163, 205, 261, 289, 290, 291, 306, 308, 311, 315,
re-experiencing 15, 187, 212, 252, 267
rebirth 14, 16, 45, 85, 86, 87, 91, 95, 96, 97, 98, 99, 100, 103, 191, 268
reincarnation 14, 16, 45, 86, 87, 88, 89, 90, 91, 95, 96, 103, 185, 268
relationships 14, 26, 50, 57, 73, 74, 91, 100, 130, 131, 133, 134, 153, 162, 163, 168, 181, 187, 199, 208, 211, 212, 223, 229, 238, 239, 241, 242, 266, 268, 269, 290, 309, 310, 312, 313, 314, 315, 316
release 12, 13, 14, 15, 41, 51, 54, 56, 57, 59, 60, 64, 92, 102, 122, 123, 124, 133, 135 142, 147, 162, 170, 198, 200, 206, 208, 209, 211, 212, 213, 214, 215, 221, 236, 238, 246, 248, 249, 250, 251, 252, 255, 261, 263, 264, 265, 266, 269, 279, 298, 307, 309, 316
reliving 245, 251, 264, 265

remembering 44, 59, 66, 74, 102, 148, 162, 164, 165, 166, 171, 176, 184, 186, 187, 188, 190, 206, 208, 212, 241, 242, 243, 245, 246, 247, 252, 255, 259, 261, 264, 268, 269, 302, 312, 313, 314, 315, 316
repetitive patterns 123, 196, 197, 207, 216, 235, 260
repressed memories 102, 103, 188
resentment 99, 134, 208, 260
resolution 104, 121, 247
reweaving 267
roots 14, 58, 61, 126, 133, 134, 148, 162, 184, 221, 246, 248, 297

S

Sara 12, 64, 161, 162, 163, 164, 165, 166, 167, 168, 169, 170, 171 187, 188, 214, 250, 254, 255, 256, 257, 266, 269, 306
Satprem 111
Schwarz, Jack 157
shaman, shamans 59, 86, 110, 111, 128, 179, 184, 193, 194 305, 306, 311
Sogyal Rinpoche 83, 84, 139, 140, 141, 199, 220
somatic 37, 112, 213, 216, 221
Source 16, 32, 82, 106, 107, 109, 110, 111, 112, 113, 134, 141, 142, 148, 209, 210, 228, 239, 262, 292, 301, 302, 303, 304, 305, 306, 307
spaciousness 82, 109, 112, 120, 160, 209, 220, 221, 222, 228, 232, 252, 302, 305
spiritual 14, 16, 36, 42, 44, 48, 58, 60, 81, 86, 88, 90, 95, 104, 105, 109, 110, 115, 122, 125, 131, 133, 134, 135, 136, 139, 140, 141, 142, 154, 178, 183, 215, 219, 220, 221, 236, 290, 298
spiritual agreements 133, 134
spiritual awakening 110
spiritual being 139, 142, 220,
spiritual challenges 58, 60
spiritual contracts 133, 135, 136, 155
spiritual crisis 290
spiritual energy 105, 183
spiritual experience 109
spiritual insights 125
spiritual journey 298
spiritual practices 90, 141, 221
spiritual questions 134
spiritual Self 139, 141, 199, 230, 236, 266, 302, 303, 304, 306, 316
spiritual traditions 42, 44, 95, 221,
Stevenson, Ian 60, 86, 87, 91, 96
stillness 16, 17, 30, 31, 108, 109, 110, 111, 112, 128, 205, 209, 228, 231, 237, 302
strong emotions 50, 54, 102, 103, 143, 195, 196, 207
survival of consciousness 14, 15, 43, 85, 86, 103
Susan 258
symptoms 12, 13, 14, 20, 50, 56, 57, 58, 59, 60, 64, 65, 66, 71, 72, 74, 75, 82, 101, 102, 119, 120, 121, 122, 123, 131, 134, 143, 149, 150, 152, 181, 182, 184, 185, 186, 187, 188, 190, 193, 194, 195, 199, 200, 206, 207, 208, 212, 213, 214, 215, 217, 220, 221, 229, 235, 239, 243, 246, 258, 264, 268, 269, 279, 290, 310, 316
systemic memory 14, 36, 43, 189

T

Tao 105, 106, 107, 109, 110
Taoist, Taoist's 16, 30, 31, 32, 105, 107, 221, 228
TE 14, 214, 219, 221
Thurman, Robert 96, 97, 98, 100, 101
time-shifting 214, 249, 250
transformation 13, 111, 113, 123, 126, 130, 135, 182, 198, 246, 266, 359
Transforming Embodiment 13, 14, 15, 16, 26, 33, 48, 58, 63, 75, 82, 102, 103, 122, 124, 125, 150, 181, 183, 190, 195, 199, 205, 207, 208, 212, 213, 215, 216, 217, 218, 219, 220, 221, 227, 231, 235, 260, 261, 297, 298, 299, 301, 303, 305, 312

transpersonal experiences 13, 110, 221, 297, 298
transpersonal psychology 13, 104, 221
trauma 12, 49, 50, 51, 52, 54, 55, 56, 57, 58, 59, 60, 61, 63, 81, 102, 136, 152, 162, 171, 181, 182, 186, 187, 189, 190, 191, 213, 216, 251, 262, 263, 304, 316
traumatic events 15, 48, 52, 56, 59, 60, 103, 190, 206, 235, 241, 245, 246, 260, 274, 302, 313
Tso Wong 30
tulku, tulkus 16, 86, 87, 88, 89, 91

U

Universal Mind 82, 84, 85 110, 252

V

Void 30, 31, 32, 105, 109

W

Wallace, B. Alan 101, 102, 128
wisdom self 15, 18, 123, 125, 139, 140, 154, 186, 233, 265
wise inner Self 139, 183
wu wei 228

Author's Note

[1] Stanislav Grof with Hal Bennett, The Holotrophic Mind: The Three Levels of Human Consciousness And How They Shape Our Lives (New York: Harper Collins, 1993), 127.

[2] Ibid., 130–131.

[3] Stanislav Grof Beyond the Brain (Albany: State University of New York Press, 1985), 357.

[4] Healing and spiritual practices of ancient Hawai'i.

[5] Tulku: a reincarnated realized spiritual master in the Tibetan tradition.

Prelude

[6] Larry Dossey MD. *Recovering the Soul: A Scientific And Spiritual Search* (New York: Bantam Books, 1989), 23.

[7] "In many cultures a shaman may be called to his or her work through an illness, either physical or psychological in nature." (Wright 1994, 166). In *Fruitful Darkness*, Dr. and Roshi Joan Halifax outlines what cultural historian, Arnold Van Gennep describes as the journey of initiation. This journey has three phases: severance, which is a time of preparation and seclusion; threshold, which is a fallow chaos, where the limits of the self are recognized and boundaries are tested and broken; and finally return, when one emerges in a new way with a new body and life and returns to society.

[8] This experience forced me to connect in other ways than just the physical. And to this day my mother and I have an uncanny relationship which, she calls "spooky".

[9] It was during this time that I understood from the core of my being that we are eternal, that our consciousness does not die but is reborn, and that we often reincarnate with those we have loved or known in our past lives.

[10] "...images come to them [his subjects] quite involuntarily and without effort or expectation of remembering the past on their part." (Stevenson 1992, 351).

[11] To sit refers to a quiet deeply yin and reflective meditative practice.

[12] Tso Wong is a natural meditation from the Ch'an school and is said to be the older brother of Zen Buddhism.

[13] "I know without knowing, see without seeing, I have no ears, no eyes, no mind, no thought, no cognition. Thus having nothing, then reaching absence of even nothingness, after that the mind cannot be disturbed by anything. Being imperturbable is called sitting forgetting." (Cleary 1991, 85).

[14] A member of the monastery, who would become my husband.

[15] "Throughout the ages, people have received information from suprahuman entities and spirit guides. Sometimes the recipients keep the information for their own use; at other times they act as mediators, sharing the communications with others. In recent times, such shared communication has been referred to as channeling (Grof 1993, 152).

[16] Her energy is one of an ancient priestess, shamaness, and spiritual warrior.

[17] Source is defined as the beginning point from which everything emerged out of. The energy of Source is a deep compassionate penetrating energy that is vibrantly moving and at once still. This energy is full of unimaginable wisdom about the nature of personal reality, energy, relationships past lives health, and spirit. It has taught others and me for two decades.

[18] Holding space means that my husband would sit in meditation with me and help ground the energy that flowed in and around me.

[19] This firing process includes my kundalini awakening, being a channel and the

clearing and processing that is demanded of me by the channel itself.

Chapter One

[20] Paul Pearsall, *The Heart's Code: Tapping The Wisdom and Power of Our Heart Energy* (New York: Broadway, 1998), 4.
[21] Ibid., 224.
[22] Ibid., 225.
[23] Ibid., 117.
[24] His (Pearsall's) theories include: "little brain in the heart theory", neuropeptide theory, magnetic field theory, electrophysiological theory, unprepared spirit theory, surprised heart theory, morphic resonance theory, reincarnation theory, hospital grapevine theory, psychometry theory, acorn theory, the "manifestation of nonlocal consciousness, and "lowered recall threshold" theory. (1998).
[25] Julie Motz, *Hands of Life* (New York: Bantam, 1998), 291.
[26] Ibid., 64.
[27] Neuropeptides are small chains of amino acids.
[28] Candace Pert, *Molecules of Emotion: Why You Feel the Way You Do* (New York: Scribner, 1997), 127.
[29] Receptors are the sensing molecules within our body and organism.
[30] Candace Pert, *Molecules of Emotion: Why You Feel the Way You Do* (New York: Scribner, 1997), 72.
[31] Ibid., 187.
[32] Ibid., 143.
[33] Ibid., 147.
[34] Candace Pert, "The Wisdom of the Receptors: Neuropeptides, the Emotions and Bodymind" *Advances*, Institute for the advancement of health vol 3; 3 (1986, Summer): 16.
[35] Ibid., 16.
[36] Candace Pert, *Molecules of Emotion: Why You Feel the Way You Do* (New York: Scribner, 1997), 106.
[37] Paul Pearsall, *The Heart's Code: Tapping The Wisdom and Power of Our Heart Energy* (New York: Broadway, 1998), 225.
[38] Ibid., 79.
[39] Ibid., 43.
[40] Ibid.
[41] Ibid., 76.
[42] Ibid., 76.
[43] Ibid., 76.
[44] Ibid., 77.
[45] Ibid.
[46] Ibid.

Chapter Two

[47] Peter Levine, *Waking the Tiger: Healing Trauma* (Berkeley North Atlantic Books, 1998), 186.
[48] Ibid., 197.
[49] Candace Pert, *Molecules of Emotion: Why You Feel the Way You Do* (New York: Scribner, 1997), 290.
[50] Julie Motz, *Hands of Life* (New York: Bantam, 1998), 30.
[51] Peter Levine, *Waking the Tiger: Healing Trauma* (Berkeley North Atlantic Books, 1998), 137.
[52] In the Hawai'ian view the ku would search for situations from its memory bank

to discover how to react. These memories could include anything that the ku has ever witnessed, seen or experienced and as always, the ku would have the assistance of the aumakua.

[53] Shaking or trembling moves us out of immobility.

[54] Peter Levine, *Waking the Tiger: Healing Trauma* (Berkeley North Atlantic Books, 1998), 159.

[55] The thymus thump is one way to restart the energy body after a shock. It is a simple technique wherein you tap your sternum or breastbone three times in succession.

[56] Peter Levine, *Waking the Tiger: Healing Trauma* (Berkeley North Atlantic Books, 1998), 173.

[57] Ibid., 146.

[58] Ibid., 181.

[59] Candace Pert, *Molecules of Emotion: Why You Feel the Way You Do* (New York: Scribner, 1997), 141.

[60] Peter Levine, *Waking the Tiger: Healing Trauma* (Berkeley North Atlantic Books, 1998), 34.

[61] Ibid., 193.

[62] Ibid., 142.

Interlude

[63] Peter Levine, *Waking the Tiger: Healing Trauma* (Berkeley North Atlantic Books, 1998), 186.

[64] While this felt right in practice, Lynn's heart and mind were deeply unsettled by putting this technique into use. Later in our work together, Lynn's feelings made sense to her. She saw how her present day emotions related to the memories of her life in South America and how they had triggered her heart's erratic behavior.

[65] Grounding, centering, connecting, and protection are four preliminary practices I use. Grounding helps stabilize the inner environment and gives us a foundation to rest on when doing inner work. It also creates a sense of connectedness and stability.

[66] The sum of the individual's inner experience is what I call the body of experience. The body of experience encompasses what occurs in the mind, body, psyche and the subtle energy fields of the body. Memories, experiences, emotions, feelings and their underlying belief systems from this life and other lifetimes would be included in the body of experience. The body of experience naturally includes the spiritual Self, and the innate inner wisdom or a sense of knowing that lies within the being.

[67] "Going in" refers to a shift of attention that leads us into our inner experience. It is a merging with your inner world and inward reality. This can be accomplished by focusing on your breath and allowing the mind to settle and become quiet.

Chapter Three

[68] *Creative Meditation and Multi-Dimensional Consciousness* cited by Larry Dossey MD., *Recovering The Soul: A Scientific and Spiritual Search* (New York: Bantam Books, 1989), 150.

[69] Institute of Noetic Sciences, Matter of Mind Conference Brochure, (1999).

[70] Jennie Wade, *Changes of Mind: A Holonomic Theory of the Evolution of Consciousness* (New York: State University of New York Press, 1996), 23.

[71] Larry Dossey MD. *Recovering the Soul: A Scientific And Spiritual Search* (New York: Bantam Books, 1989), 7.

[72] Paul Pearsall, *The Heart's Code: Tapping The Wisdom and Power of Our Heart Energy* (New York: Broadway, 1998), 215.

[73] Henry Margenau is Professor Emeritus of Physics and Natural Philosophy, Yale University, with a distinguished career in molecular and nuclear physics.
[74] Larry Dossey MD. *Recovering the Soul: A Scientific And Spiritual Search* (New York: Bantam Books, 1989), 165.
[75] Ibid., 66.
[76] Ibid., 67.
[77] Ibid., 180.
[78] Ibid., 262.
[79] Sogyal Rinpoche, P. Gaffney and A. Harvey eds. *The Tibetan Book Of Living And Dying* (New York: Harper Collins, 1992), 46.
[80] Ibid.
[81] Ibid., 47.
[82] Ibid., 47.
[83] Ibid., 47.
[84] Ibid., 48.
[85] Kahuna literally means the one that holds the secret. Kahunas are powerful practitioners of Huna.
[86] I have noticed that what a person believed in this life about death and the afterlife affects one's perceptions and experience of death.
[87] Dr. Robert Thurman is quoted as follows in *Reborn in the West*: "The word tulku in Tibetan is a translation of the Sanskirt work Nirmanakaya, which means the emanation body of a Buddha." (Mackenzie 1995, 89).
[88] In the movie *Kundun*, by Martin Scorsese, such tests as used by monks to confirm the identity of tulkus or reincarnated masters, were depicted.
[89] Vicki Mackenzie, *The Boy Lama* (Boston: Wisdom Publications, 1989), 152.
[90] Ibid., 117.
[91] Ibid., 117.
[92] Ibid., 117.
[93] Ibid., 120.
[94] Ibid., 144.
[95] Ibid., 145.
[96] Ibid., 177.
[97] Ibid., 176.
[98] *Scanning* is a technique used in meditation that I have adapted. When scanning, your attention moves from right to left down your body, all the while you are discerning, tensions temperature changes, colors and the conditions and energies within your body.

Chapter Four
[99] Stanislav Grof with Hal Bennett, *The Holotropic Mind: The Three Levels of Human Consciousness and How They Shape Our Lives* (New York: Harper Collins, 1993), 133.
[100] "...it is difficult to overlook the fact that for thousands of years religious writings from a great many societies have discussed past lives, reincarnation, and karma and have described the impact of these on our present lives." (Grof 1993, 126).
[101] Ian Stevenson, MD. *Twenty Cases Suggestive of Reincarnation* Charlottesville: University Press of Virginia, 1992), 129.
[102] Vicki Mackenzie, *Reborn In The West: The Reincarnation Masters* (London: Bloomsbury, 1995), 88-89.
[103] Ibid., 92.
[104] Ibid., 93.
[105] Lama Zopa Rinpoche, *Practicing the Good Heart* (Boston: Wisdom Publications, 1996), 21.

[106] Ian Stevenson, MD. *Twenty Cases Suggestive of Reincarnation* (Charlottesville: University Press of Virginia, 1992), 129.
[107] Vicki Mackenzie, *Reborn In The West: The Reincarnation Masters* (London: Bloomsbury, 1995), 93-94.
[108] Bokar Rinpoche, *Death and the Art of Dying in Tibetan Buddhism* (F. Jacquemart, and C. Buchet, trans. (San Francisco: Clear Point Press, 1993). 102.
[109] Vicki Mackenzie, *Reborn In The West: The Reincarnation Masters* (London: Bloomsbury, 1995), 95-96.
[110] Bokar Rinpoche, *Death and the Art of Dying in Tibetan Buddhism* (F. Jacquemart, and C. Buchet, trans. (San Francisco: Clear Point Press, 1993). 103.
[111] "Karma is seen as "action-and its result." (Chodron 1993, 167).
[112] Thubten Chodron, *What Color is Your Mind* (Ithaca: Snow Lion Publications, 1993), 42.
[113] Ibid., 42.
[114] B. Allen Wallace, *Tibetan Buddhism from the Ground Up: A Practical Approach to Modern Life* (Boston: Wisdom Publications, 1993), 27-28.
[115] Ibid., 28.
[116] Ibid., 18.
[117] Marcus Daniels, "Advanced States of Healing" *Quality Times*, 10, 11, 22, (September/October 1993): 22.
[118] Thubten Chodron, *What Color is Your Mind* (Ithaca: Snow Lion Publications, 1993), 183.
[119] Stanislav Grof calls systems of belief COEX systems.
[120] Ian Stevenson, MD. *Twenty Cases Suggestive of Reincarnation* Charlottesville: University Press of Virginia, 1992), 329.
[121] Ibid., 379.
[122] Duane Elgin, Our Living Universe, Exploring the Frontier of Consciousness, *Noetic Sciences Review* 54 (Dec-Feb 2001): 11.

Chapter Five
[123] Thomas Cleary, ed. *Vitality Energy Spirit: A Taoist Sourcebook* Translated by Thomas Cleary (Boston: Shambhala Publications, 1991), 233.
[124] Eva Wong, trans. *Seven Taoist Masters: A Folk Tale from China* (Boston: Shambhala Publishing, 1990), 39.
[125] "Tao: The universal law, the force of all life, the way of nature." (Kornfield, 1993, 350).
[126] Joan Halifax, *The Fruitful Darkness: Reconnecting With The Body Of The Earth* (San Francisco: Harper Collins, 1993), 159.
[127] Martin Lowenthal and Lars Short, *Opening The Heart Of Compassion: Transform Suffering Through Buddhist Psychology And Practice* (Rutland: Charles E. Tuttle, 1993), 14.
[128] Lao Tsu. *Tao Te Ching* trans. G. Feng, and J. English, (New York: Random House, 1972), # 25.
[129] "A psychic landscape of emptiness it is a place where we are gestated, and from which we are born into the greater womb of creation." (Halifax 1993, 27).
[130] "The Chinese ideograph for *hsien* and Japanese *sen* is made up of two parts, one meaning person, the other meaning mountain. In Taoism and Ch'an Buddhism, the hsien was a spiritual practitioner who used the mountain as a birthgate to awakening" (Halifax 1993, 164).
[131] Deng Ming-Dao, *365 Tao Daily Mediations* (San Francisco: Harper Collins, 1992), 222.
[132] Stanislav Grof with Hal Bennett, *The Holotrophic Mind: The Three Levels Of*

Human Consciousness And How They Shape Our Lives (New York: Harper Collins, 1993), 170.

[133] Stanislav Grof with Hal Bennett, *The Holotrophic Mind: The Three Levels Of Human Consciousness And How They Shape Our Lives* (New York: Harper Collins, 1993), 164.

[134] Assagioli says "...the experience of the spiritual Self is a sense of freedom, of expansion, of communication with other Selves and with reality, and there is the sense of Universality. It feels itself at the same time individual and universal." (1971, 87).

[135] Richard Moss, MD *The I That Is We: Awakening To Higher Energies Through Unconditional Love* (Berkeley: Celestial Arts, 1981), 2.

[136] Ibid., 1.

[137] "And that vibration feels like a fire. In fact, it is a vibration whose intensity is that of a higher fire. Several times the body has even felt it as the equivalent of a fever." (Mother, cited by Satprem 1992, 89).

[138] Brugh Joy, MD. *Joy's Way A Map for the Transformational Journey: An Introduction to the Potentials for Healing with Body Energies* (Los Angeles: J. P. Tarcher, 1979), p. 196.

[139] Stanislav Grof with Hal Bennett, *The Holotrophic Mind: The Three Levels Of Human Consciousness And How They Shape Our Lives* (New York: Harper Collins, 1993), 146.

[140] Satprem. *The Mind Of The Cells* (Paris: Institut de Recherches Evolutives, 1992), 88.

[141] Ibid., 88.

Chapter Six

[142] Stephen and Ondrea Levine, *Embracing The Beloved: Relationship as a Path of Awakening* (New York: Doubleday, 1995), 4.

[143] See *Zen Mind, Beginner's Mind: Informal Talks on Zen Meditation and Practice* by Shunryu Suzuki Roshi, (New York, John Weatherhill Inc, 1984).

[144] Jack Kornfield, *A Path With Heart: A Guide Through The Perils And Promises Of Spiritual Life* (New York: Bantam Books, 1993), 46.

[145] "Effective therapeutic work must follow the process into the area involved and should not be limited to conceptual considerations" (Grof 1985, 340).

[146] John Welwood, ed. *Awakening The Heart: East/West Approaches To Psychotherapy And The Healing Relationship* (Boston: Shambhala Publications, 1983) 51.

[147] Ibid., 88.

[148] "One implication of what you were saying is that it would be a mark of wisdom for a person or a teacher really to honor exactly what was unfolding at a given moment." (Rothberg, 1996, 36).

[149] This is similar to what is done in *vipassana* meditation.

[150] John Welwood, ed. *Awakening The Heart: East/West Approaches To Psychotherapy And The Healing Relationship* (Boston: Shambhala Publications, 1983) x.

[151] "The client is ultimately the authority as far as his or her own inner experience is concerned." (Grof 1985, 363).

[152] Laughter and deep breathing trigger endorphins, the pleasure chemicals in the brain. In Norman Cousin's book *Anatomy of an Illness* he discusses how he used laughter to bring about a total remission of a life-threatening disease (Pert 1997).

[153] Jack Kornfield, *A Path With Heart: A Guide Through The Perils And Promises Of Spiritual Life* (New York: Bantam Books, 1993), 43.

[154] Stephen Levine, *Healing Into Life And Death* (New York: Doubleday, 1987), 6.

[155] Daniel Rothberg, "How Straight is the Spiritual Path. [Conversations with Buddhist Teachers Jack Kornfield and Michele Mc Donald-Smith]" *Revision*, 19 (1)

(1996, Summer): 37.

[156] Chögyam Trungpa, Rinpoche *Shambhala: The Sacred Path of the Warrior* (Boston: Shambhala Publications, 1984), 36.

[157] Stephen and Ondrea Levine, *Embracing The Beloved: Relationship As A Path Of Awakening* (New York: Doubleday, 1995), 28.

[158] Ibid., 234-235.

[159] 1970 quote, seen on flyer in Santa Fe NM.

[160] B. Allen Wallace, *Tibetan Buddhism from the Ground Up: A Practical Approach to Modern Life* (Boston: Wisdom Publications, 1993), 147.

[161] Ibid., 186.

[162] Conversation with Chonyi Richard Allen, February, 1996.

[163] "As a western woman, whatever I have learned about the nature of self, both the local and the extended self, has been by going inward and down into the fruitful darkness, the darkness of culture, the darkness of psyche, the darkness of nature." (Halifax 1993, 4).

[164] Jeanne Achterberg, *Woman as Healer: A Panoramic Survey of the Healing Activities of Woman From Prehistoric Times to The Present* (Boston: Shambhala Publishing, 1990), 194.

[165] Duane Elgin, "Our Living Universe, (Exploring the Frontier of Consciousness" *Noetic Sciences Review*, 54 (Dec-Feb 2001):10.

[166] Stephen and Ondrea Levine, *Embracing The Beloved: Relationship As A Path Of Awakening* (New York: Doubleday, 1995), 71.

[167] Ibid., 75.

[168] By blending what is offered by both systems a more balanced healing system will emerge, she believes.

[169] Candace Pert, *Molecules of Emotion: Why You Feel the Way You Do* (New York: Scribner, 1997), 186.

Chapter Seven

[170] Sogyal Rinpoche, P. Gaffney and A. Harvey eds. *The Tibetan Book of Living and Dying* (New York: Harper Collins, 1992), 120.

[171] Ibid., 120.

[172] Ibid., 120.

[173] Ibid., 20.

[174] Serge Kahili King, *Mastering The Hidden Self: A Guide to the Huna Way* (Wheaton: The Theosophical Publishing House, 1985), 19.

[175] Serge Kahili King, *Kahuna Healing: Philosophy and Practice* (Malibu, Huna International, 1979), 44.

[176] Ibid., 43.

[177] Ibid., 43.

[178] "Feelings and emotions are considered by the kahunas to be energetic responses to the stimulation of belief patterns, and as such are meant to inform lono of what beliefs are in operation." (King 1979, 43).

[179] Psychosynthesis recognizes the spiritual Self, and believes this spiritual aspect is as fundamental as the instinctive energies that Freud described.

[180] Serge Kahili King, *Kahuna Healing: Philosophy and Practice* (Malibu, Huna International, 1979), 41.

[181] Ibid., 42.

[182] Serge King, January 26,1996, personal communication.

[183] Serge Kahili King, *Kahuna Healing: Philosophy and Practice* (Malibu, Huna International, 1979), 19.

[184] "Aka is the essence of matter and it acts like a mirror to reflect patterns of

thought. The word itself means luminous, transparent, shadow, reflection, mirror, or essence. Aka acts as a vessel for mana and the more mana it contains the denser it appears. Aka has four aspects, solids, liquids, gases, and plasma." (King, 1979, 31–32).

[185] Serge Kahili King, *Kahuna Healing: Philosophy and Practice* (Malibu, Huna International, 1979), 67.

[186] Ibid., 48.

[187] Huna training, 1988.

[188] Paul Pearsall, *The Heart's Code: Tapping The Wisdom and Power of Our Heart Energy* (New York: Broadway, 1998), 223.

[189] Daniel Goleman, *Healing Emotions: Conversations with the Dalai Lama on Mindfulness, Emotions and Health* (Boston: Shambhala Publications, 1997), 234-235.

[190] "It [chakras] provides the student with a structured inner space." (Swami Rama, et al 1993, 217).

[191] Jack Schwarz, *Voluntary Controls* (New York: E.P. Dutton, 1978), 89.

[192] The subtle body operates in tandem with the physical body and is composed of vital energy that includes the chakras, and nadis.

[193] "Within each one of these dynamic centers can be seen, in condensed form, the relationship between certain aspects of the physical world, the energy system, the mind, and higher consciousness." (Swami Rama, et al 1993, 221).

[194] Swami Rama, et al, *Yoga and Psychotherapy: The Evolution of Consciousness* (7th ed.). (Honesdale: Himalayan International Institute of Yoga Science and Philosophy, 1993), 225.

[195] Karlfried Grag Von Dürckheim, *Hara: The Vital Centre of Man* trans. S. M. von Kospoth, and E. R. Healey, (London: Mandala Books, 1962), 21.

[196] The inability to maintain one's own identity and to become entangled in the energy, and emotions of others, often in a co-dependent way.

Interlude

[197] As channeled by Elizabeth Burke.

[198] She attended a year-long chakra, intuition, and meditation training, a six-week course in Transforming Embodiment, and a set of classes I have presented on Hawai'ian shamanism.

Chapter Eight

[199] Paul Pearsall, *The Heart's Code: Tapping The Wisdom and Power of Our Heart Energy* (New York: Broadway, 1998), 225.

[200] Candace Pert, *Molecules of Emotion: Why You Feel the Way You Do* (New York: Scribner, 1997), p. 185.

[201] Paul Pearsall, *The Heart's Code: Tapping The Wisdom and Power of Our Heart Energy* (New York: Broadway, 1998), 225.

[202] Ibid., 67.

[203] Candace Pert, *Molecules of Emotion: Why You Feel the Way You Do* (New York: Scribner, 1997), 187.

[204] Ibid., 188.

[205] *Riverside Webster's II Dictionary* (New York: Berkeley Books, 1996) 430.

[206] Paul Pearsall, *The Heart's Code: Tapping The Wisdom and Power of Our Heart Energy* (New York: Broadway, 1998), 115–116.

[207] Ibid., 115.

[208] Ibid., 116.

[209] Candace Pert, *Molecules of Emotion: Why You Feel the Way You Do* (New York:

Scribner, 1997), 306.
[210] Jeanne Achterberg, *Imagery and Healing: Shamanism and Modern Medicine* (Boston: Shambhala Publishing, 1985), 96.
[211] Ibid., 88.
[212] Lenore Terr, MD. *Unchained Memories: True Stories of Traumatic Memories Lost and Found* (New York: Basic Books, 1994), 241.
[213] Daniel Rothberg, "How Straight is the Spiritual Path. [Conversations with Buddhist Teachers, Jack Kornfield, and Michele Mc Donald-Smith]" *Revision*, 19 (1), 1996, Summer): 35.
[214] Ian Stevenson, MD. *Twenty Cases Suggestive of Reincarnation* Charlottesville: University Press of Virginia, 1992), 352.
[215] Ibid., 253.
[216] Stevenson also says "...in a small number of cases, the images are projected so that the subject sees his previous self as another person external to himself who he watches, somewhat like instances of seeing one's own body or double." (1992, 352).
[217] Irving Oyle is an osteopathic physician and former medical director of Headlands Healing Service as noted in Jeanne Achterberg's, *Imagery and Healing: Shamanism and Modern Medicine* (Boston: Shambhala Publishing, 1985).
[218] Jeanne Achterberg, *Imagery and Healing: Shamanism and Modern Medicine* (Boston: Shambhala Publishing, 1985), 98.
[219] "It is of the utmost importance to understand that, even though this experience was imagined, because of the presence of the felt sense, the experience was in every way real for Marcius as the original one, that is, mentally, physiologically and spiritually." (Levine 1997, 118).
[220] Peter Levine, *Waking the Tiger: Healing Trauma*, (Berkeley North Atlantic Books, 1998), 202. (Emphasis in the original).
[221] Ian Stevenson, MD. *Twenty Cases Suggestive of Reincarnation* Charlottesville: University Press of Virginia, 1992), 384.
[222] A cue is a quick, strong, perceptual stimulus, or a swift, strong perception.
[223] These memories may be a form of state dependent memory that transcended time because her body was remembering her ancient past.
[224] The exercises in the introduction can help stabilize your mind and are recommended before direct work with symptoms relationship or emotional issues.
[225] Ian Stevenson, MD. *Twenty Cases Suggestive of Reincarnation* Charlottesville: University Press of Virginia, 1992), 350.
[226] Ibid., 351.
[227] Ibid., 351.

Chapter Nine
[228] Serge King, *Kahuna Healing: Holistic Health and Healing Practices of Polynesia* (Wheaton: The Theosophical Publishing House, 1983), 47.
[229] "To the kahuna it is important to note that an emotion is characterized by a movement of energy that occurs in the body along with a thought. This is what makes it an emotion. Emotions arise when beliefs are stimulated." (King 1979, 47).
[230] Huna means "the secret "in Hawai'ian and the huna teachings are centuries-old, spiritual, and healing practices that have been secret until recently.
[231] Serge Kahili King, *Kahuna Healing: Philosophy and Practice* (Malibu, Huna International, 1979) 21–22.
[232] *Kuana* means unsteady or insecure.
[233] "...COEX systems affect every area of our emotional lives. They can influence the

way we perceive ourselves, other people, and the world around us. They are the dynamic forces behind our emotional and psychosomatic symptoms setting the stage for the difficulties we have relating to ourselves and other people. There is a constant interplay between the COEX systems of our inner world and events in the external world...our perceptions can function like complex scripts through which we recreate core themes of our own COEX systems in the external world." (Grof 1993, 25-26).

[234] Ibid., 24-25.

[235] The body of experience is the sum of all experience, either known or unknown, that we have ever perceived. The body of experience is the imprint that we work from to function in our daily lives. It is this aspect of our consciousness that we contact, heal, and transform when needed in TE.

[236] Joan Halifax, *The Fruitful Darkness: Reconnecting With The Body Of The Earth* (San Francisco: Harper Collins, 1993), 93.

[237] Muscle testing is done by two people. One person, who is being tested, holds their arm out while the second person lightly presses down on the outstretched arm.

[238] Your arm will remain firm or strong with the positive thought and weaken with the negative thought.

[239] "...witnessing results in an alert and aware state of consciousness it is vastly different from ordinary consciousness in which our awareness is oriented outward; narrowly focused and intent on accomplishing some goal, fast, automatic, and habitual; and structured by a context of time and space." (Johanson and Kurtz 1991, 13).

[240] The energy fields of the body include the chakras aura and energy channels or meridians.

[241] Written communication from Peggy Ann Wright, 1/30/96.

[242] Daniel Rothberg, "How Straight is the Spiritual Path. [Conversations with Buddhist Teachers Jack Kornfield and Michele Mc Donald-Smith]" *Revision*, 19 (1) (1996, Summer): 35.

[243] Serge Kahili King, *Kahuna Healing: Philosophy and Practice* (Malibu, Huna International, 1979, 48.

[244] Stress is also a reaction to environmental conditions, which includes our thoughts and emotions.

[245] "Imagery is the thought process that invokes and uses the senses: vision, audition, smell, taste, the senses of movement, position and touch." (Achterberg 1985, 3).

Chapter Ten

[246] Jeanne Achterberg, *Imagery and Healing: Shamanism and Modern Medicine* (Boston: Shambhala Publishing, 1985), 3.

[247] Stephen and Ondrea Levine, *Embracing The Beloved: Relationship as a Path of Awakening* (New York: Doubleday, 1995), 107.

[248] Thubten Chodron, *What Color is Your Mind* (Ithaca: Snow Lion Publications, 1993), 33.

[249] Joining the client occurs when one maintains a detached awareness while also being empathically connected to the client. By merging in this way one achieves the ability to follow the client at an intuitive level. This detached awareness allows the practitioner to hold the "space" or create a healing environment, while also acting as a guide.

[250] Peter Gay, ed. *The Freud Reader* New York: W. W. Norton, 1989.), 98.

[251] "Freud's starting point was Breuer's cathartic method, which consisted in

Endnotes

[251 cont.] recalling to the consciousness of the patient the forgotten trauma or impressions which had produced the symptoms and releasing the strong emotions associated with them." (Assagioli 1971, 12).

[252] "In developing psychoanalysis, Freud repudiated the idea of traumatic origins and developed a theory based on the repression of innate drives." (Gay 1989, 12).

[253] Ira Progoff, *Depth Psychology and Modern Man* (2nd ed.) (New York: Mc Graw Hill, 1973), 189.

[254] Ibid., 190.

[255] Morton Hunt, *The Story of Psychology* (New York: Doubleday, 1993), 578.

[256] Ira Progoff, *Depth Psychology and Modern Man* (2nd ed.) (New York: Mc Graw Hill, 1973), 8.

[257] Ibid., 246.

[258] Ibid., 246.

[259] Ibid., 247.

[260] Piero Ferrucci, *What We May Be* (Los Angeles: J. P. Tarcher. 1982), 22.

[261] Ira Progoff, *Depth Psychology and Modern Man* (2nd ed.) (New York: Mc Graw Hill, 1973), 7.

[262] Piero Ferrucci, *What We May Be* (Los Angeles: J. P. Tarcher. 1982), 130–131.

[263] In TE wholeness is believed in. With wholeness the process takes on a more creative, open and circular form. Movement in all directions is allowed and encouraged. The process ebbs and flows, and the individual is given the power to move in whatever way is necessary to create a greater sense of wholeness and growth. Ferrucci (1982) notes that when growth is balanced and healthy, it proceeds in all directions. This is precisely what can occur in TE. I believe that this belief in wholeness may also allow for and open individuals to "other life" experiences, because all time becomes a part of this wholeness. Time and space become more fluid when viewed as a part of an inherent wholeness.

[264] The idea that psychological process is an organic process also can be found throughout the work of Dr. Arnold Mindell, the founder of Process Oriented Psychology and Dreambody work.

[265] Chapter Twelve in *What We May Be* (Ferrucci 1982) lists a wide variety of superconscious experiences that have been reported to Ferrucci.

[266] Piero Ferrucci, *What We May Be* (Los Angeles: J. P. Tarcher. 1982), 22.

[267] Serge Kahili King, *Kahuna Healing: Philosophy and Practice* (Malibu, Huna International, 1979), 55.

[268] "Meditation then, provides a basic practice for awakening the heart—which includes both developing warmth and compassion toward all our fears, insecurities and emotional entanglements, as well as discovering our basic openness and goodness underneath them." (Welwood 1983, xiii).

[269] Contemplative reflection can be any activity that allows the mind to gently settle and relax, so the flow of thoughts falls away into the background. When this occurs the mind expands and the referent of the Self begins to dissolve.

[270] John Welwood, ed. *Awakening The Heart: East/West Approaches To Psychotherapy And The Healing Relationship* (Boston: Shambhala Publications, 1983), 48.

Chapter Eleven

[271] Swami Rama, et al, *Yoga and Psychotherapy: The Evolution of Consciousness* (7th ed.) (Honesdale: Himalayan International Institute of Yoga Science and Philosophy, 1993), 265.

[272] Unknown source, from Alexandra Kennedy, 1981.

[273] There are many names for this aspect of wisdom. I use innate inner wisdom interchangeably with spiritual Self, wisdom Self, aumakua and spirit.

[274] "Intuition unquestionably comes from the highest source of knowledge. It dawns bit by bit with the growth of consciousness." (Swami Rama, et al 1993, 265).

[275] We can never know how something will transpire, if we use only our rational minds and emotions in making decisions. Sally had asked the channel for advice, but upon hearing it she felt she could not do what was asked, it just didn't feel right. Four years later after considerable suffering she told me that events in her past had made it impossible for her to follow the earlier advice of the channel. She said she understood now that her perception had been limited by her past experience. She noted that the broader view the channel offered would have saved her much grief. In working with the intuition it is vital to stay nonattached and open.

Chapter Twelve

[276] Tarthang Tulku *Teaching from the Heart* (Berkeley, Dharma Publishing 1998), 53.

[277] "Through imagining and envisioning our inner difficulties, we are able to rework the wounds and struggles, the conflicts of the past. As we hold them in our consciousness and feel them in our body we can finally allow ourselves to feel the full effect of our energies. In doing so, our consciousness opens. Instead of being quite so identified with just one part of the picture, we may see other perspectives." (Kornfield 1993, 115).

[278] Jeanne Achterberg, *Imagery and Healing: Shamanism and Modern Medicine* (Boston: Shambhala Publishing, 1985) 8.

[279] Readings are different from process work and are generally more directive than process work. This session with June began as a reading and took on aspects of the process work as we continued. A reading is a place where the client asks questions about a specific problem they are experiencing. I then address these questions as a channel and psychic. The information in a reading can illuminate blocks, energetic patterns or reveal the origins of a problem. In this case the information I gave June provided her with a starting point, so she might find her own imagery and experience. The information in the reading evoked strong emotions in June. These emotions needed to be worked with, so techniques of the process work were incorporated. I could have tried to have June find her own material, but this would have disregarded her question and her sense of overwhelming emotions that the experience with her tenant had evoked.

[280] Daniel Rothberg, "How Straight is the Spiritual Path. [Conversations with Buddhist Teachers Jack Kornfield and Michele Mc Donald-Smith]" *Revision*, 19 (1), (1996, Summer): 34.

Chapter Thirteen

[281] Stanislav Grof with Hal Bennett, *The Holotrophic Mind: The Three Levels of Human Consciousness and How They Shape Our Lives* (New York: Harper Collins, 1993), 133.

[282] "Valuable personal changes can occur, especially with highly charged negative images. ...The secret is always to have the courage to face the negative image and the patience to stay with it. Very often a transformation happens if we face it long enough and let the corresponding feeling freely emerge." (Ferrucci, 1982, 41).

[283] Swami Rama, et al, *Yoga and Psychotherapy: The Evolution of Consciousness* (7th ed.). (Honesdale: Himalayan International Institute of Yoga Science and Philosophy, 1993), 190.

[284] Ibid., 187.

[285] Marcus Daniels, "Advanced States of Healing" *Quality Times*, 10, 11, 22, (September/October 1993) 11.

[286] Mindell Seminars, Jan. 1994.
[287] "Frolic" seemed an unusual word to use, especially as Sara had referred to sex as "making love" earlier, so I felt Sara was deeply in the remembering process.
[288] "The shadow most closely approaches what Freud understood as 'the repressed.'" (Zweig and Abrams 1991, 4).
[289] Connie Zweig and Jeremiah Abrams, ed. *Meeting The Shadow: The Hidden Power Of The Dark Side Of Human Nature* (New York: G. P. Putnam's Sons, 1991), 4.
[290] John Welwood, ed *Awakening The Heart: East/West Approaches To Psychotherapy And The Healing Relationship* (Boston: Shambhala Publications, 1983) 51.
[291] Morton Hunt, *The Story of Psychology* (New York: Doubleday, 1993), 200.
[292] Joseph Crane, April 1996, personal communication.
[293] Connie Zweig and Jeremiah Abrams, ed. *Meeting The Shadow: The Hidden Power Of The Dark Side Of Human Nature* (New York: G. P. Putnam's Sons, 1991), 6.
[294] She was visiting Santa Fe and lived out of state.
[295] Sandra Ingerman works within the Native American tradition and practices Soul Retrieval and she has written a book of the same title.

Chapter Fourteen
[296] Stanislav Grof *Beyond the Brain* (Albany: State University of New York Press, 1985), 360.
[297] Piero Ferrucci, *What We May Be* (Los Angeles: J. P. Tarcher. 1982), 22.

Interlude
[298] Robert Thurman, cited by Vicki Mackenzie, *Reborn in the West: The Reincarnation Masters* (London: Bloomsbury, 1995), 90 & 95.
[299] It is the same emotional feeling that allows these memories to surface and be remembered.
[300] Later I would learn that when Koa and I had been twin sisters in another lifetime I had died of a snake-bite wound and left him (as my twin sister) behind.

Chapter Fifteen
[301] "The five precepts of nonharming are: refraining from killing, stealing, false speech, sexual misconduct, intoxicants that cause heedlessness or loss of awareness." (Kornfield 1993, 341-342).
[302] Jack Kornfield, *A Path With Heart: A Guide Through The Perils and Promises of Spiritual Life* (New York: Bantam Books, 1993), 343.
[303] Dr. Brian Luke Seaward is quoted in *Molecules of Emotion* and says "All healers—shamans the wisdom keepers—tell you they're tapping into a higher source of energy they call love and that they are sharing this love with whomever they're healing.'" (Pert, 304).
[304] Spiritual emergent states would include shamanic crisis, awakening of the kundalini episodes of unitive consciousness, psychological renewal through a return to the center, crisis of psychic opening, past life experiences, communication with spirit guides or channeling, near death experiences, experiences with close encounters and with UFO's and possession states. (Grof 1989).
[305] Stanislav Grof, *Beyond the Brain* (Albany: State University of New York Press, 1985), 362.

Chapter Sixteen
[306] Jack Kornfield, A *Path with Heart: A Guide Through The Perils and Promises of Spiritual Life* (New York: Bantam Books, 1993), 47.

Addendum

[307] John Welwood, ed. *Awakening the Heart: East/West Approaches to Psychotherapy and the Healing Relationship* (Boston: Shambhala Publications, 1983), xi.

[308] As told by Baker Roshi, 1988.

[309] Injuries can be a body's way of getting our attention, so we can resolve old wounds, and emotional pain.

[310] Transforming Embodiment maintains the standards and ethics as set forth by the American Psychological Association (1995) Any future practitioners of TE should also uphold these standards. The general principles of the APA are also observed. These include: concerning competence, integrity, professional and scientific responsibility, respect for people's rights and dignity, concern for others' welfare and social responsibility are also adhered to. Ethical standards as set forth in the general standards, sections three through six and section eight of the code, pertaining to private practice regarding the following professional standards, boundaries of competence, maintaining expertise, respecting others, sexual and other harassments, human differences, avoiding harm, personal problems and conflicts, misuse of psychological influences and work, exploitative relationships, consultations and referrals, third party requests for service, fees and financial arrangements, advertising and other published statements, and therapy, teaching, training, research and publishing guidelines. Confidentiality and the preservation of good boundaries are the only ways that trust can be established and sustained in therapy. Sessions have to be a safe and confidential environment where clients can express and experience themselves. It is my firm belief that the therapist should not abuse the privileged relationship with clients in any way. The Insight Meditation organization has created a code of ethics for their teachers that addresses ethics problems. These guidelines can be found at the end of *A Path with Heart* (Kornfield 1993), 340–344.

[311] Singing the space means that I use sound and vibration to wash away any residual energy from a space.

[312] Many years ago this aspect of a voice speaking inside my mind took me into trance states where information was received without my conscious awareness. This phenomenon is known as channeling. The works of Jane Roberts documents this phenomenon extensively. Researchers such as Charles Tart have also been exploring this phenomenon or aspect of consciousness.

[313] "The one essential ingredient that most graduate schools neglect to train is the therapist's ability to draw on his intuition in responding to the client." (Welwood 1983), ix.

Glossary

[314] I Jack Kornfield, *A Path with Heart: A Guide Through The Perils and Promises of Spiritual Life* (New York: Bantam Books, 1993), 51.

[315] Attributed to Shinzen Young from Dharma Talk 1a, Sounds True catalog, date unknown.

[316] Ibid.

About the Type

[317] Jimmy Buffett, *A Pirate Looks at Fifty* (New York: Random House, 1998), 460

ABOUT THE AUTHOR

Twenty-four years ago Elizabeth Burke survived a three year-long kundalini awakening. She emerged from this intense experience with a deep understanding of energy, embodiment and spirit. This awakening gave her a profound understanding of transpersonal experiences and a deeply personal grasp of how to heal the mind, body, and spirit. She maintains a private practice in CA and hopes to build a retreat and teaching center in Northern NM.

CONTACT INFORMATION

TO ORDER THIS BOOK
http://www.healingorigins.com/store/page3.html
OR FOR MORE INFORMATION
about trainings and personal sessions
Visit:
www.healingorigins.com
www.elizabethburkema.com
www.memoryinourbones.com

Aloha and Mahalo,
Elizabeth Burke

EarthSong Foundation Press